AA004282

SENSORCOMM 2019

The Thirteenth International Conference on Sensor Technologies and Applications

October 27 - 31, 2019

Nice, France

SENSORCOMM 2019 Editors

Jaime Lloret Mauri, Polytechnic University of Valencia, Spain
Manuela Vieira, ISEL-CTS/UNINOVA, Portugal
Amirali Soroush, CSIRO, Australia

Printed from e-media with permission by:

Curran Associates, Inc.
57 Morehouse Lane
Red Hook, NY 12571

proceedings.com

Some format issues inherent in the e-media version may also appear in this print version.

Copyright© (2019) by International Academy, Research, and Industry Association (IARIA)
Please refer to the Copyright Information page.

Printed with permission by Curran Associates, Inc. (2020)

International Academy, Research, and Industry Association (IARIA)
412 Derby Way
Wilmington, DE 19810

Phone: (408) 893-6407
Fax: (408) 527-6351

petre@iaria.org

Additional copies of this publication are available from:

Curran Associates, Inc.
57 Morehouse Lane
Red Hook, NY 12571 USA
Phone: 845-758-0400
Fax: 845-758-2633
Email: curran@proceedings.com
Web: www.proceedings.com

Table of Contents

SENSORCOMM 2019

Forward

The Thirteenth International Conference on Sensor Technologies and Applications (SENSORCOMM 2019), held between October 27, 2019 and October 31, 2019 in Nice, France, was a multi-track event covering related topics on theory and practice on wired and wireless sensors and sensor networks.

Sensors and sensor networks have become a highly active research area because of their potential of providing diverse services to broad range of applications, not only on science and engineering, but equally importantly on issues related to critical infrastructure protection and security, health care, the environment, energy, food safety, and the potential impact on the quality of all areas of life.

Sensor networks and sensor-based systems support many applications today on the ground. Underwater operations and applications are quite limited by comparison. Most applications refer to remotely controlled submersibles and wide-area data collection systems at a coarse granularity.

In wireless sensor and micro-sensor networks energy consumption is a key factor for the sensor lifetime and accuracy of information. Protocols and mechanisms have been proposed for energy optimization considering various communication factors and types of applications. Conserving energy and optimizing energy consumption are challenges in wireless sensor networks, requiring energy-adaptive protocols, self-organization, and balanced forwarding mechanisms.

We take here the opportunity to warmly thank all the members of the SENSORCOMM 2019 technical program committee, as well as all the reviewers. The creation of such a high quality conference program would not have been possible without their involvement. We also kindly thank all the authors who dedicated much of their time and effort to contribute to SENSORCOMM 2019. We truly believe that, thanks to all these efforts, the final conference program consisted of top quality contributions.

We also thank the members of the SENSORCOMM 2019 organizing committee for their help in handling the logistics and for their work that made this professional meeting a success.

We hope that SENSORCOMM 2019 was a successful international forum for the exchange of ideas and results between academia and industry and to promote further progress in the area of sensor technologies and applications. We also hope that Nice, France provided a pleasant environment during the conference and everyone saved some time to enjoy the charm of the city.

SENSORCOMM 2019 Chairs

SENSORCOMM Steering Committee
Sergey Yurish, IFSA, Spain
Brendan O'Flynn, Tyndall National Institute | University College Cork, Ireland
Jaime Lloret Mauri, Polytechnic University of Valencia, Spain
Elad Schiller, Chalmers University of Technology, Sweden
Jiannan Zhai, Florida Atlantic University, USA
Stefano Mariani, Politecnico di Milano, Italy
Manuela Vieira, ISEL-CTS/UNINOVA, Portugal
Tadashi Okoshi, Keio University, Japan
Jerker Delsing, Lulea University of Technology, Sweden

SENSORCOMM Industry/Research Advisory Committee

Shaohan Hu, IBM Research, USA

SENSORCOMM 2019
Committee

SENSORCOMM Steering Committee

Sergey Yurish, IFSA, Spain
Brendan O'Flynn, Tyndall National Institute | University College Cork, Ireland
Jaime Lloret Mauri, Polytechnic University of Valencia, Spain
Elad Schiller, Chalmers University of Technology, Sweden
Jiannan Zhai, Florida Atlantic University, USA
Stefano Mariani, Politecnico di Milano, Italy
Manuela Vieira, ISEL-CTS/UNINOVA, Portugal
Tadashi Okoshi, Keio University, Japan
Jerker Delsing, Lulea University of Technology, Sweden

SENSORCOMM Industry/Research Advisory Committee

Shaohan Hu, IBM Research, USA

SENSORCOMM 2019 Technical Program Committee

Majid Bayani Abbasy, National University of Costa Rica, Costa Rica
Rajat Aggarwal, DreamVu Inc., USA
Amin Al-Habaibeh, Nottingham Trent University, UK
Jesús B. Alonso Hernández, Institute for Technological Development and Innovation in Communications (IDeTIC) | University of Las Palmas de Gran Canaria (ULPGC), Spain
Maykel Alonso Arce, CEIT and Tecnun (University of Navarra), Spain
Mário Alves, Politécnico do Porto (ISEP/IPP), Portugal
Kaz Arimoto, Okayama Prefectural University, Japan
Andy Augousti, Kingston University, UK
Paolo Bellavista, University of Bologna, Italy
Souheila Bouam, University of Batna 2, Algeria
An Braeken, Vrije Universiteit Brussel, Belgium
Erik Buchmann, Hochschule für Telekommunikation Leipzig, Germany
Maria-Dolores Cano, Universidad Politécnica de Cartagena, Spain
Juan-Vicente Capella-Hernández, Universitat Politècnica de València, Spain
Vítor Carvalho, IPCA-EST-2Ai | Portugal & Algoritmi Research Centre, UM, Portugal
Luca Caviglione, National Research Council of Italy (CNR), Italy
Amitava Chatterjee, Jadavpur University, India
Edmon Chehura, Cranfield University, UK
Omar Cheikhrouhou, Taif University, Saudi Arabia
Bill Chen, University of Macau, Macau
Dixiang Chen, National University of Defense Technology, China
Sungrae Cho, Chung-Ang University, South Korea
Mario Cifrek, University of Zagreb, Croatia
Victor Cionca, Cork Institute of Technology, Ireland
Federico Corò, Gran Sasso Science Institute (GSSI), L'Aquila, Italy

Gautam K. Das, Indian Institute of Technology Guwahati, India
Francesco G. Della Corte, Università degli Studi Mediterranea, Italy
Jerker Delsing, Lulea University of Technology, Sweden
Baban P. Dhonge, Indira Gandhi Center for Atomic Research, Kalpakkam, India
Alexandar Djordjevich, City University of Hong Kong, Hong Kong
Dulce Domingos, University of Lisbon, Portugal
Alexis Duque, Rtone, Lyon, France
El-Sayed M. El-Alfy, King Fahd University of Petroleum and Minerals, Saudi Arabia
Imad Ez-zazi, University of Abdelmalek Essaadi, Morocco
Biyi Fang, Michigan State University, USA
Zoltan Fekete, Pazmany Peter Catholic University (PPKE), Hungary
Paulo Felisberto, LARSys | University of Algarve, Portugal
Stefan Fischer, University of Lübeck, Germany
Antoine Gallais, Inria LNE / Université de Strasbourg, France
Yann Garcia, Université catholique de Louvain, Belgium
Matthieu Gautier, IRISA | University of Rennes 1, France
Paulo Gil, University of Coimbra, Portugal
Chris Gniady, University of Arizona, USA
Arda Gumusalan, George Mason University, USA
Malka N. Halgamuge, University of Melbourne, Australia
Jason O. Hallstrom, Florida Atlantic University, USA
David Hasenfratz, Sensirion AG, Staefa, Switzerland
Mehrdad Hessar, Paul G. Allen School - University of Washington, USA
María del Carmen Horrillo Güemes, Instituto de Tecnologías Físicas y de la Información (ITEFI) | Consejo Superior de Investigaciones Científicas (CSIC), Spain
Shaohan Hu, IBM Research, USA
Chao Huang, University of Notre Dame, USA
Yanqiu Huang, University of Bremen, Germany
Tarikul Islam, Jamia Millia Islamia (University), India
Shin-ichi Ito, Tokushima University, Japan
Miao Jin, University of Louisiana at Lafayette, USA
Shuanggen Jin, Shanghai Astronomical Observatory | Chinese Academy of Sciences, China
Anand Joshi, G.H.Patel College of Engineering & Technology, India
Abdelmajid Khelil, Landshut University, Germany
Young-Jin Kim, Ajou University, Republic of Korea
Grigoris Kaltsas, Technological Educational Institute (T.E.I) of Athens, Greece
Yuriy P. Kondratenko, Petro Mohyla Black Sea State University, Ukraine
Boris Kovalerchuk, Central Washington University, USA
Sisil Kumarawadu, University of Moratuwa, Sri Lanka
Andrew Kusiak, University of Iowa, USA
Seongsoo Lee, Soongsil University, Korea
Cherkaoui Leghris, Hassan II University, Casablanca, Morocco
Chiu-Kuo Liang, Chung Hua University, Hsinchu, Taiwan
Tiong Hoo Lim, Universiti Teknologi Brunei, Brunei
Thomas Lindh, School of Technology and Health - KTH, Sweden
Jingbin Liu, Finnish Geospatial Research Institute, Finland / Wuhan University, China
David Lizcano, Madrid Open University (UDIMA), Spain
Jaime Lloret Mauri, Polytechnic University of Valencia, Spain

Benny Lo, The Hamlyn Centre for Robotic Surgery | Imperial College London, UK
Beatriz López, University of Girona, Spain
Flaminia Luccio, University Ca' Foscari of Venice, Italy
Boushra Maala, Tishreen University, Syria
Elsa María Macías López, University of Las Palmas de Gran Canaria, Spain
Paulo Jorge Maia dos Santos, Instituto Superior de Engenharia | Universidade do Algarve, Portugal
Abdallah Makhoul, University of Bourgogne Franche-Comté, France
Piero Malcovati, University of Pavia, Italy
Stefano Mariani, Politecnico di Milano, Italy
José-Fernán Martínez-Ortega, Universidad Politécnica de Madrid, Spain / Mälardalen University, Sweden
Francisco Martins, University of Lisbon, Portugal
Carlo Massaroni, Università Campus Bio-Medico di Roma, Italy
Nader Mbarek, LIB laboratory | University of Burgundy, France
Natarajan Meghanathan, Jackson State University, USA
Lei Mei,California Research Center - Agilent Technologies, USA
Carosena Meola, University of Naples Federico II, Italy
Fabien Mieyeville, University Claude Bernard Lyon 1 | Polytech Lyon, France
Lyudmila Mihaylova, University of Sheffield, UK
Umair N. Mughal, UiT The Arctic University of Norway - Campus Narvik, Norway
Dmitry Namiot, Lomonosov Moscow State University, Russia
Jagriti Narang, School of chemical and life sciences - Jamia Hamdard, India
Androula G. Nassiopoulou, Institute of Nanoscience and Nanotechnology (INN), Athens, Greece
Mir Mohammad Navidi, West Virginia University, USA
Thabile Ndlovu, University of Swaziland, Kwaluseni, Swaziland
Kamen N. Nedev, University of Sofia, Bulgaria
Michael Niedermayer, Beuth University of Applied Sciences - Berlin, Germany
Shahriar Nirjon, UNC Chapel Hill, USA
Yuuki Nishiyama, University of Oulu, Finland
Claro Noda, Mid Sweden University, Sweden
Brendan O'Flynn, Tyndall National Institute | University College Cork, Ireland
Tadashi Okoshi, Keio University, Japan
Vytautas Ostasevicius, Kaunas University of Technology, Lithuania
Carlos Enrique Palau Salvador, Universidad Politecnica de Valencia, Spain
Henryk Palus, Silesian University of Technology, Poland
Sung-Joon Park, Gangneung-Wonju National University, South Korea
Lorena Parra, Universitat Politècnica de València, Spain
Luigi Patrono, University of Salento, Italy
Nuno Pereira, School of Engineering of the Polytechnic of Porto, Portugal
Rafael Pérez del Real, Tenured Scientist at Institute of Materials Science of Madrid, Spain
Francisco Pérez-Ocón, University of Granada, Spain
Samuela Persia, Fondazione Ugo Bordoni, Italy
Dirk Pesch, University College Cork, Ireland
Ivan Pires, University of Beira Interior, Covilhã / Altran Portugal, Lisboa, Portugal
Rajeev Piyare, Bruno Kessler Foundation, Trento, Italy
Nuno Pombo, University of Beira Interior, Portugal
Patrick Pons, LAAS-CNRS, France
James Pope, University of Bristol, UK
Yuankai Qi, Harbin Institute of Technology, China

Ginu Rajan, University of Wollongong, Australia
Susan Rea, Cork Institute of Technology, Ireland
Yenumula B. Reddy, Grambling State University, USA
Càndid Reig, University of Valencia, Spain
Girish Revadigar, Huawei International Pte Ltd, Singapore
Christos Riziotis, National Hellenic Research Foundation (NHRF), Athens, Greece
Jorge Rodolfo Beingolea Garay, Polytechnic School of the University of Sao Paulo, Brazil
Juha Röning, University of Oulu, Finland
Lorenzo Rubio-Arjona, Universitat Politècnica de València, Spain
Ulrich Rückert, Bielefeld University, Germany
Sain Saginbekov, Nazarbayev University, Nur-Sultan (Astana), Kazakhstan
Prasan Kumar Sahoo, Chang Gung University / Chang Gung Memorial Hospital, Taiwan
Addisson Salazar, Universitat Politècnica de València, Spain
Emiliano Schena, Università Campus Bio-Medico di Roma, Italy
Elad Schiller, Chalmers University of Technology, Sweden
Christian Schindelhauer, University of Freiburg, Germany
Savio Sciancalepore, Hamad Bin Khalifa University (HBKU), Qatar
Rudi Seitz, University of New Hampshire, USA
Vijay K. Shah, University of Kentucky, USA
Sheng Shen, University of Illinois at Urbana-Champaign, USA
Kuei-Ping Shih, Tamkang University, Taiwan
Amir Shirkhodaie, Tennessee State University, USA
LihChyun Shu, National Cheng Kung University, Taiwan
Patrick Siarry, Université de Paris 12, France
Marius Silaghi, Florida Institute of Technology, USA
Andrzej Skowron, University of Warsaw, Poland
Biljana Risteska Stojkoska, University Ss Cyril and Methodius Skopje, Macedonia
Mu-Chun Su, National Central University, Taiwan
Alvaro Suárez Sarmiento, University of Las Palmas de Gran Canaria, Spain
Hamadoun Tall, Clermont Auvergne University, France
Xuyuan Tao, ENSAIT, France
Pedro Renato Tavares Pinho, ISEL - Instituto Superior de Engenharia de Lisboa | Instituto de Telecomunicações (IT-AV), Aveiro, Portugal
Rui Teng, Advanced Telecommunications Research Institute International, Japan
Sivan Toledo, Blavatnik School of Computer Science | Tel-Aviv University, Israel
Goce Trajcevski, Iowa State University, USA
Carlos Travieso González, University of Las Palmas de Gran Canaria, Spain
Janez Trontelj, University of Ljubljana, Slovenia
Ugo Vaccaro, University of Salerno, Italy
Fabrice Valois, INSA Lyon, France
Manuela Vieira, ISEL-CTS/UNINOVA, Portugal
Klaus Volbert, Technical University of Applied Sciences, Germany
Hiroo Wakaumi, Tokyo Metropolitan College of Industrial Technology, Japan
You-Chiun Wang, National Sun Yat-sen University, Taiwan
Julian Webber, Osaka University, Japan
Chih-Yu Wen, National Chung Hsing University, Taiwan
Hui Wu, The University of New South Wales, Australia
Zongwei Xu, Tianjin University, China

Murat Kaya Yapici, Sabanci University, Istanbul, Turkey
Wanli Yu, University of Bremen, Germany
Chau Yuen, Singapore University of Technology and Design (SUTD), Singapore
Sergey Y. Yurish, International Frequency Sensor Association (IFSA), Spain
Marco Zennaro, International Centre for Theoretical Physics (ICTP), Italy
Jiannan Zhai, Florida Atlantic University, USA
Xiaohong Zhou, Tsinghua University, China
Zhe Zhou, Huzhou University, China
Cherif Zizoua, Research Centre for Scientific and Technical Information, Algiers, Algeria
Chengzhi Zong, Microsoft, USA

Copyright Information

For your reference, this is the text governing the copyright release for material published by IARIA.

The copyright release is a transfer of publication rights, which allows IARIA and its partners to drive the dissemination of the published material. This allows IARIA to give articles increased visibility via distribution, inclusion in libraries, and arrangements for submission to indexes.

I, the undersigned, declare that the article is original, and that I represent the authors of this article in the copyright release matters. If this work has been done as work-for-hire, I have obtained all necessary clearances to execute a copyright release. I hereby irrevocably transfer exclusive copyright for this material to IARIA. I give IARIA permission or reproduce the work in any media format such as, but not limited to, print, digital, or electronic. I give IARIA permission to distribute the materials without restriction to any institutions or individuals. I give IARIA permission to submit the work for inclusion in article repositories as IARIA sees fit.

I, the undersigned, declare that to the best of my knowledge, the article is does not contain libelous or otherwise unlawful contents or invading the right of privacy or infringing on a proprietary right.

Following the copyright release, any circulated version of the article must bear the copyright notice and any header and footer information that IARIA applies to the published article.

IARIA grants royalty-free permission to the authors to disseminate the work, under the above provisions, for any academic, commercial, or industrial use. IARIA grants royalty-free permission to any individuals or institutions to make the article available electronically, online, or in print.

IARIA acknowledges that rights to any algorithm, process, procedure, apparatus, or articles of manufacture remain with the authors and their employers.

I, the undersigned, understand that IARIA will not be liable, in contract, tort (including, without limitation, negligence), pre-contract or other representations (other than fraudulent misrepresentations) or otherwise in connection with the publication of my work.

Exception to the above is made for work-for-hire performed while employed by the government. In that case, copyright to the material remains with the said government. The rightful owners (authors and government entity) grant unlimited and unrestricted permission to IARIA, IARIA's contractors, and IARIA's partners to further distribute the work.

Rapid Fabrication Approach of Graphene Sensor for Biological Application

Idris Musa and John Hedley
School of Engineering, Newcastle University,
Newcastle Upon Tyne, UK
Email: i.musa@newcastle.ac.uk, john.hedley@newcastle.ac.uk

Abstract- **In this work, we show that sensitive sensing platforms can be derived from the laser irradiation of a non-conducting and flexible material using a laser machine, which can then be used to implement the sensing element of a biosensor to detect and determine the concentration of the target analyte. The aim is to investigate and develop new ways of producing an inexpensive Graphene sensor, implemented as a Radio Frequency (RF) filter for biological application. A Graphene-like material can be produced by the laser irradiation (Laserscribe) of Kapton tape in the form of a filter. The fabrication of this designed filter geometry was achieved by using a laser machine to irradiate the Kapton tape on the chosen substrate (Flame Retardant 4 (FR-4)), by applying the earlier obtained parameters for the fabrication. Several power ratings were used for their fabrication and their conductivity was found to range from 171 x10^{-6} S/mm to 279 x10^{-6} S/mm. The ANSYS (Analysis of System) simulation indicates good results, and options to enhance the material property are also being reviewed. Tests are currently on the way to using a Vector Network Analyser (VNA) to verifying their viability of being employed as the sensing element of a biosensor, thereby leading to their potential application in biological sensing.**

Keywords-Laserscribe; Graphene; Biosensor; Radio Frequency filter; Kapton tape.

I. INTRODUCTION

There is a need in the medical diagnostics for accurate, fast and inexpensive devices, which can be routinely used. In this context, biosensors are considered to provide a viable solution to the problems posed by the contemporary healthcare industry. This is because these sensing devices offer considerable advantages such as: specificity, small size, faster response than laboratory test and cost. These cost-effective, practical, portable, and robust diagnostic devices have received significant interest since there is an important need for bio-devices that can rapidly and precisely analyse biological samples. Diverse ranges of chemicals, biochemical and biological analytes have been detected using sensors made form carbon materials. The electron transfer rate and the performance of these devices are significantly affected by the structure of the carbon material itself. This is due mainly to the electronic states density, and the edge plane site obtainable on the carbon material surface [1][2]. There has been previous work on Laserscribe Graphene Oxide (LSG) like in [1], where Graphene Oxide (GO) film was used to produce LSG electrode, using lightscribe Digital Versatile Disc (DVD) label writing technology, which allows for direct laser writing of the DVD on the GO. Tian et al. fabricated a flexible strain sensor using a light scribed DVD burner to reduce GO film, they achieved a flexible Graphene strain sensor with a low Gauge Factor (GF) for high a deformation application, and a high GF for a low strain sensing application [3].

The shortage of Graphene growth and patterning techniques has become a serious issue affecting its deployment in several specialised applications [3]. Graphene, through synthesis and engineering design, can possess 3-dimensional (3D) structures and porosity, earning them wide range of applications like: composite filter, disposable electronics, energy storage devices and flexible electronics [4]-[6]. In spite of these merits, the current synthesis method of porous Graphene requires high temperature processing of multi-stepped chemical synthesis routes, thereby limiting their widespread commercial applications [4]. Therefore, straightforward synthesis of Graphene based materials in a scalable manner is still an important technological goal in achieving commercialised applications for Graphene material especially in the field of biochemical and biological applications [4]. Glassy carbon has been produced from insulating Polyimide (PI) through pulse ultraviolet laser treatment [4][7], and microsupercapacitor was produced from commercial polymer film using CO_2 infrared laser [4].

However, the technique of laser scribing for the fabrication of an RF low pass filter microstrip transmission line has hitherto not been demonstrated. In this work, we show the production of a microstrip filter made of a Graphene-like material from a non-conducting film by laser reduction technique, which has indicated a vista in the biological sensing application of LSG. Maher et al. used a standard light scribe DVD optical drive to do direct laser reduction of graphite Oxide film to Graphene [8]. Their mechanical strength, electrical conductivity and specific surface area indicated good results, which was then used directly as electrochemical capacitor electrodes, where devices made from these electrodes indicates high energy density values in different electrolytes, while maintaining good electrochemical attributes under high mechanical stress, making them a good contender for high power flexible electronics [8]. All these previous works have shown the viability of an LSG material in biological and electrochemical applications, hence, the need to develop cheaper and easily fabricated means of deriving a suitable sensing platform from LSG material. Since the material for implementing a sensing platform is determined, the next is to look at the shape this sensing platform should take.

There is an increase in demand for microwave systems to meet the emerging telecommunication challenges with respect to cost, size and performance [9]. This work describes the design of a microstrip filter for biological application. Microstrip is an electrical transmission line which can be fabricated using a Printed Circuit Board (PCB) technology, employed to carry microwave frequency signal [9]. It comprises a conducting strip separated form a ground plane by a dielectric substrate and it much cheaper than the traditional waveguide technology [9]. This microstrip will be designed in the form of a filter. Since filters are crucial components in microwave communication systems and RF circuits, they are used to either combine or separate the selected frequencies in the band, to fulfil the required specification [10].

Microstrip line is a good technique for filter design due to its benefits of low cost, light weight, compact size, planar structure and its ease of integration with other component on a single board [11]. By extension microwave filters can be divided in to two different types; the lumped element, consisting of capacitors and inductors and the distributed element which used lengths and widths of transmission lines to create their inductance or capacitance value [11][12], resulting in an Inductor Capacitor (LC) ladder type stepped impedance Low Pass (LP) microstrip Filter if a LPF was the design intension [13]. The structure of this work is as follows. Section II deals with the microstrip mathematical design, while Section III deals with the experimental techniques. In Section IV, the results were illustrated, and the Section V handles the discussion and conclusion.

II. DESIGN METHODS

A. *Microstrip Transmission Line Design*

Several different equations have been developed for use in determining the characteristic impedance for microstrip design. Probably the most convenient are the following which are stated to be accurate to within about 1% [13]. A simple but accurate equation for microstrip characteristic Impedance is shown below with Figure 1 being the microstrip arrangement [14]:

$$Z0 = \frac{60}{\sqrt{\varepsilon eff}}\left\{log\left(8\frac{h}{w}+\frac{w}{4h}\right)\right\} \quad (1)$$

where the effective dielectric constant is given by (2) as:

$$\varepsilon eff = \frac{\varepsilon r+1}{2}+\frac{\varepsilon r-1}{2}\left\{\left(1+12\frac{h}{2w}\right)^{-1/2}+0.04\left(1-\frac{w}{h}\right)^{2}\right\} \quad (2)$$

while (3) and (4) are for when $w/h \geq 1$

$$Z0 = \frac{120\pi}{\sqrt{\varepsilon eff}\left\{\frac{w}{h}+1.393+0.667log\left(\frac{w}{h}+1.444\right)\right\}} \quad (3)$$

where:

$$\varepsilon eff = \frac{\varepsilon r+1}{2}+\frac{\varepsilon r-1}{2}\left\{\left(1+12\frac{h}{2w}\right)^{-1/2}\right\} \quad (4)$$

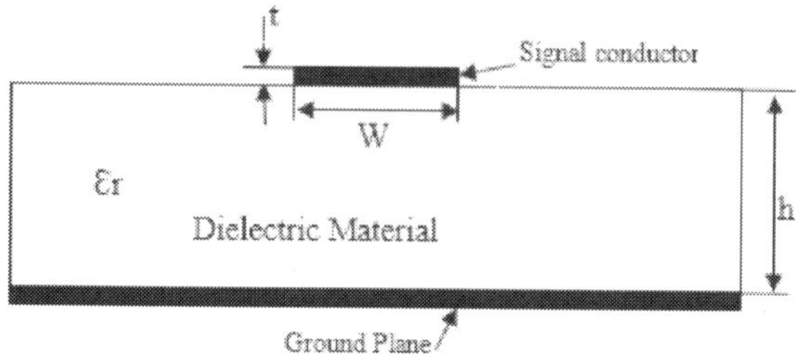

Figure 1. Microstrip Transmission line arrangement

For the purpose of this work, the design was based on the second sets of conditions where $w/h \geq 1$, hence equations (3) and (4) had to be employed.

B. *Microstrip Transmission Line Design for A Single Strip Case*

From equations (3) and (4), the width of the proposed microstrip line was then calculated since for a wide microstrip (i.e. width=W), nearly all of the electric field lines will be focused between the metal planes, similar to the case of a parallel plate capacitor. On the other hand, for narrow W the electric field lines will be about equally divided between the air and the board dielectric [13].

To get the effective dielectric constant, (4) would have been used, however, there are two unknowns, as a result, the formula that gives an approximate value of the characteristics impedance was then used, which is given as shown in (5) below [12][15].

$$Z0 = \frac{87}{\sqrt{\varepsilon r+1.41}}\left\{log\left(\frac{7.48h}{w-1.25T}\right)\right\} \quad (5)$$

From which:

$$w = \frac{7.48h}{e^{\left(Z0\frac{\sqrt{\varepsilon r+1.41}}{87}\right)}}+(1.25t) \quad (6)$$

For the purpose of this work, an FR-4 dielectric material was employed, with a dielectric constant ranging from 4 to 4.47 [12][16]. From the pre-test samples, the thickness T was found to be 4.8532 mil. The Material used for this work was, an FR-4 board of dielectric thickness of 10mil. The characteristic impedance of choice for the material is 50Ω. From the information above, the following was deduced:

T=4.8532mil

H=10mil

Z0=50 Ω εr=4.4

By putting all these parameters in equation (6) above the width of the material can be calculated as shown below:

$$w = \frac{7.48\times 10}{e^{50\left(\frac{\sqrt{4.4+1.41}}{87}\right)}}+(1.25\times 4.8532)$$

w=24.7852mil≈25mil

w=0.635mm

This value is close to the value measured using a Mitutoyo stylus surface roughness measuring tester (Surftest SJ-410) where the thickness value was measured to be 0.4835mm.

C. Microstrip Transmission Line Design for A Multiple Strip Case

For this case, the strip was made up of several single strips (for this work, several single strips were used), as such to calculate the width of this strip, it would have been the addition of the width of the individual single strips and the resultant sum becomes the width of this strip (i.e. a multiple strip). However, this is not so because during the production of this material it was observed that the machine always makes overlapping tracks on the Kapton tape which means the width of the material produce would not be brought about as expected. As a result, the width of this material was not calculated but was measured using the Surftest SJ-410, from this measurement the width was obtained as 1.75875 mm which is equivalent to70 mil. In a bid to obtain the accurate results for each of the slope of the results measured from the resistance of the materials along its length, an analytical method of determining the slope of the straight line was used. To achieve this, the method of least squares was employed.

III. EXPERIMENTAL TECHNIQUE

The mathematical design of the microstrip was done in the previous section where the calculation (Mathematical formulation) of the width and expected thickness was made. The implementation of this design was achieved using the laser scribe technique for making GO. This technique of GO production is one of the do-it-yourself methods of producing Graphene. This technique has exposed one to a new way of making a Graphene Oxide or rather a Graphene Oxide-like material. To achieve this task several experiments were conducted, and the materials that were initially used were; Kapton tape, silver paint, plywood (substrate), digital multimeter and laser machine (Laserscript HPC laser) with laser spot size of 0.2 mm and a vertical scanning position. There are two basic categories of material, from which eight samples of these materials with varying parameters were produced. The two categories of samples were; the Multiple-Strip (MS) line and the Single Strip (SS) line. The two main parameters that were varied are the speed at which the laser engraves on the Kapton tape and the thickness of the width of the strip line.

The MS line sample has four set of samples, where each sample is made up of five materials with varying laser power settings ranging from 26% to 34% in increment of 2% (this was determine base on test carried out on the pre-test samples to ascertain the power settings that would produce a material with the best property). This fabrication principles also applies to the single strip-line, it has the same fabrication principles and the same parameters as its multiple-strip counterpart but differ by the number of strip line on it (in its own case it is just a single strip line). For the multiple strip, the two main parameters which were the speed at which the laser engraves on the Kapton tape and the width of the microstrip, these were chosen and set. These parameters changes from sample to sample to produce the four sets of samples for each category of sample. The same principles apply to the single strip samples. For both the MS line and the SS line the samples main parameters are shown in Table I below.

TABLE I. SETTINGS USED TO PRODUCE THE MICROSTRIP

parameter	Sample 1	Sample 2	Sample 3	Sample 4
Speed (mm/s)	300	300	400	400
Width (μm)	300	350	300	350
% power	26, 28, 30, 32, 34.	26, 28, 30, 32, 34.	26, 28, 30, 32, 34.	26, 28, 30, 32, 34.

These sets of settings were employed for both the multiple strip line and the single strip line, which resulted in samples amounting to eight in total. To achieve the design of these samples several steps were followed; Firstly, after the mathematical design, some Kapton tapes were then laid (taped) unto the surface of FR-4 material. After which, the settings for the category of interest was done on the system (computer). Then, the settings for the material of interest was also done on the system before transferring these settings to a flash drive, and on to the laser machine. The sample obtained from the first step above was then introduced into the working area of the laser machine to begin the irradiation process. The same procedure was repeated from the first step to the fourth step for all the two categories to produce the entire forty materials. From these samples produced, several tests were carried out on them using a digital multimeter to obtain necessary resistance values from the resulting materials (Graphene Oxide-like). The reason for carrying out this test is to determine the resistivity of the resultant material to ascertain the viability of its being employed as a material that has the required property for use as the sensing element of the proposed biosensing platform. The two categories of samples (the multiple strip and the single strip) were tested to explore which material from any of the two sets of materials (twenty different materials for the multiple strip and twenty for the single strip) is viable and results were taken.

The results of these tests carried out were recorded. From these results, several plots were also done, and with further manipulations it led to the determination of the material parameters that is optimum and suitable for the design of the material of interest. In order to determine the suitable resistivity of the materials produced, the areas of each material needed to be determined, and to achieve this task, the thickness and the width of the individual materials were measured using the Mitutoyo stylus surface roughness measuring tester (Surftest SJ-410), with this device the measurement were done to the nearest micron. This technique was used to fabricate a 5th order LPF microstrip LSG on a PCB substrate for use in the intended application. Figure 2 below gives the steps by step process of fabricating the LSG microstrip LPF, while Figure 3 shows the fabrication machine and the filter during fabrication.

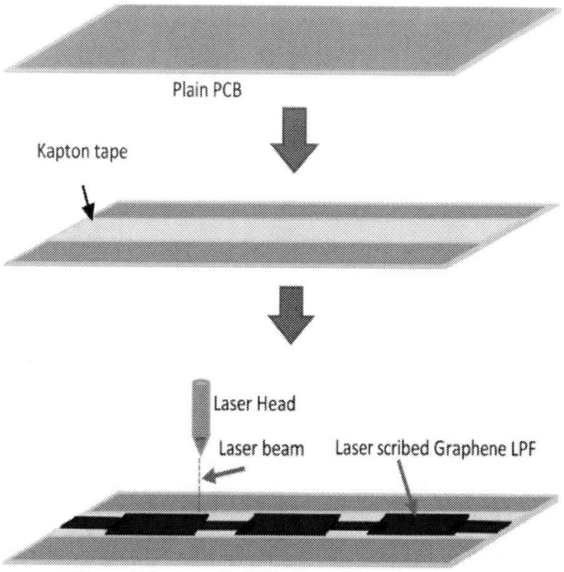

Figure 2. Laser scribed Graphene fabrication process

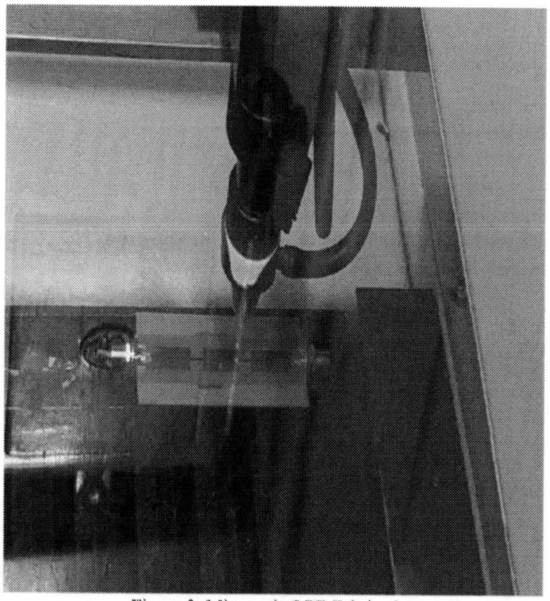

Figure 3. Microstrip LPF Fabrication

IV. SAMPLE RESULTS

The results of the test carried out for the different parameters of the different materials developed, were recorded as measured. From the results obtained it was observed that certain resistance values do not increase linearly with increase in length (i.e. they are irregular). As such, these give an idea of which material, from this set of samples that might possess the needed property for the intended usage. From these results, plots were made to determine the slope which is the resistance per unit length of the produced material. A typical slope for these results is as shown in Figure 4 below. The same procedure was followed to obtain results of the single strip line, using the same equipment as used for the multiple strip line above, results were obtained and recorded as shown below. From these results, plots were also made to determine the slope which is the resistance per unit length of the produced material. A slope typical to these results is as shown in Figure 5 below.

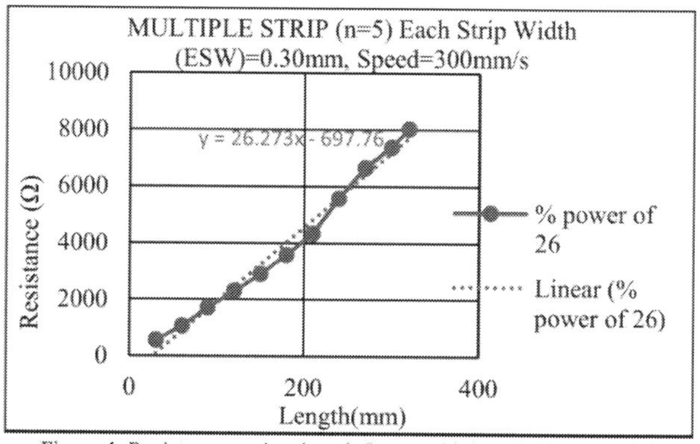

Figure 4. Resistance against length for a multiple strip line material.

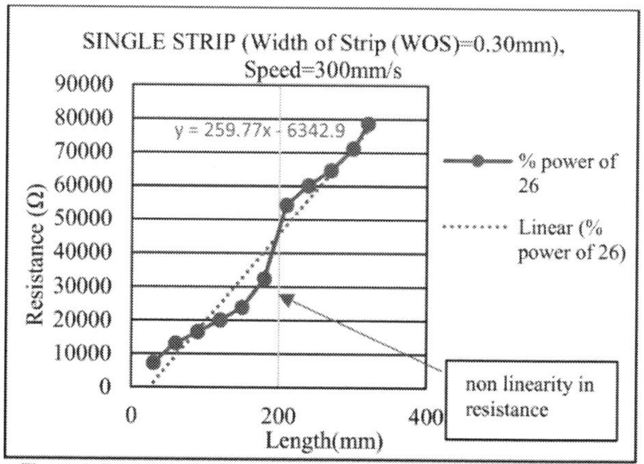

Figure 5. Resistance against length for a typical single strip line material.

From the above results, the resistance per unit length was plotted against the percentage power in both categories for all the strips. The results are as shown in Figures 6a and 6b. From these plots, it has become obvious that there is more discontinuity associated with the SS materials. These materials and the percentage powers at which these discontinuities occurred become evident from the plots. From the plot it can be observe that certain points were enlarged, this highlights the materials with observed abnormalities and the corresponding percentage powers at which they were fabricated. These plots have also helped in narrowing down the material with the needed property from either category. As can be seen from the results shown below in Figure 6a and 6b, it can be observed that the resistance per unit length (on the vertical axis) for the single strip material is about ten times that of the Multiple-Strip (MS) material. More so, the number of defective materials as indicated with bold black dots are more prevalent in the single strip materials than its multiple strip counterpart. This is an indication that the multiple strip material has shown promising characteristics to make it a viable option for its design scheme to be implemented for the designing of the microstrip transmission line, which will in turn serve as the sensing element of the biological sensor whose efficacy is dependent on the resistivity of the material.

In a bid to determine the most suitable fabrication scheme for this method of producing this laser scribed Graphene Oxide material, further processing of the results was done which resulted in the plots of Figure 6c and 6d below. These results show typical plot for both categories, from which useful data about the material and the method of making the material can be obtained. ANSYS simulation was done using the conductivity value derived from the test results and the results indicated that the fabricated filter's response was similar to the theoretical lowpass filter as shown in Figure 7.

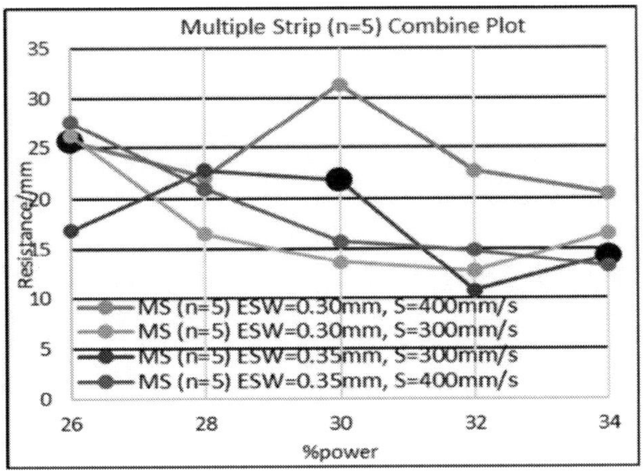

Figure 6a. Resistance/ mm of multiple strip category with black dots indicating defective material

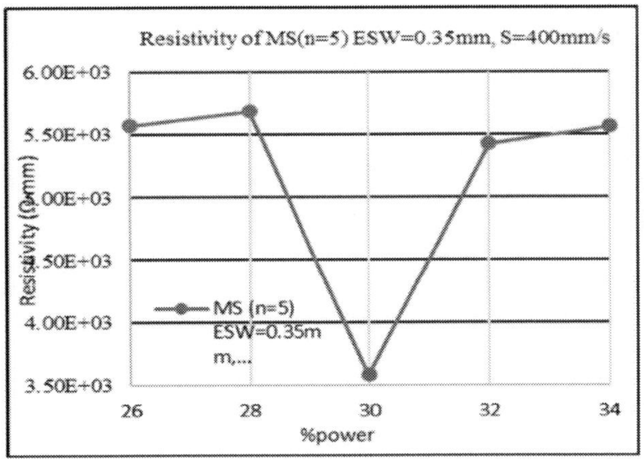

Figure 6c. Resistivity of the multiple strip category with estimated strip width (ESW) of 0.35mm.

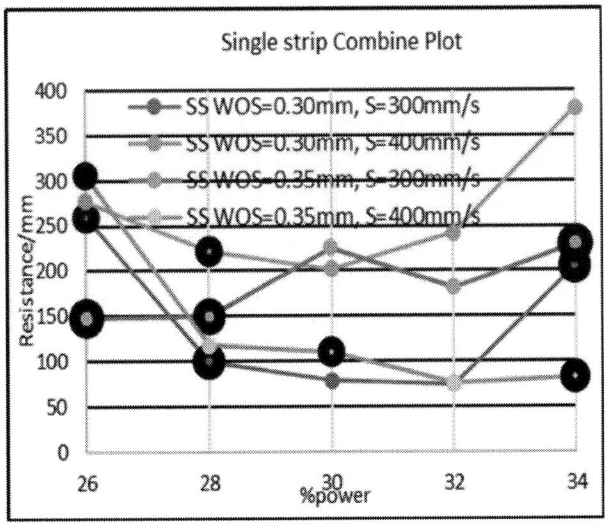

Figure 6b. Resistance/mm of single strip category with black dots indicating defective material

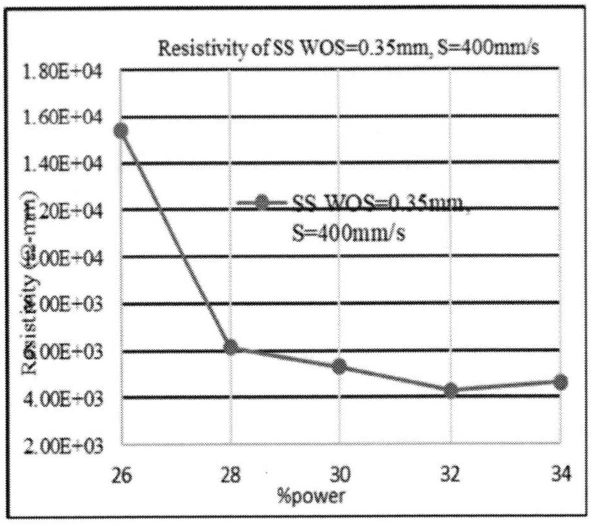

Figure 6d. Resistivity of the single strip category with width of strip (WOS) of 0.35mm

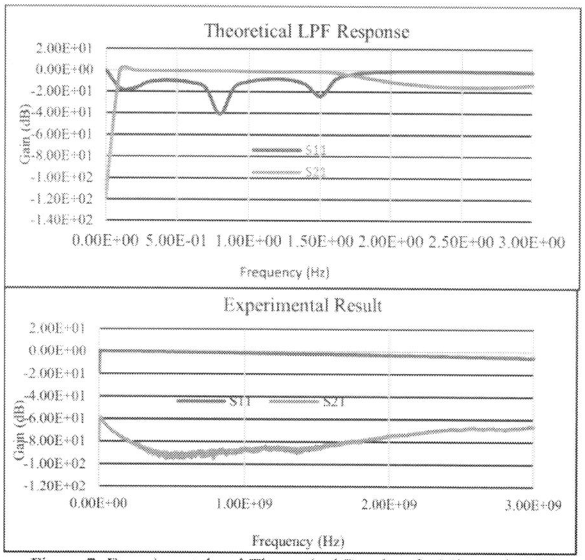

Figure 7. Experimental and Theoretical Results of a Microstrip LPF

Haven produced the 5th order LPF using the MS line technique. VNA was used to measure its S-parameters, to determine suitability for the intended application. From the observed results shown in Figure 7, there is a difference between the expected and the experimental/simulation response of a microstrip LPF, thereby indicating that more fine-tuning of the fabrication parameters is necessary.

V. CONCLUSION AND FUTURE WORK

The aim of this work was to develop new ways of producing a Graphene sensor, starting with cheap rapid prototyping of implementing an inexpensive and flexible electronic material that is easily reproduceable, with high conductivity, and can be deployed for use as a sensor for biological application. The results indicated that the multiple strip line material has a promising conductivity value ranging from 171 $x10^{-6}$ S/mm to 279 $x10^{-6}$ S/mm, signalling its viability for the proposed application. From these results, it can be concluded that this LSG can also be a fine application in various sensing platforms where light weight and flexible conductor is desired. The results of the microstrip LPF implementation indicated the need to fine tune fabrication parameters so as to improve the filter response. The future work includes fine tuning the fabrication parameters and the use as biological sensor. Then, testing the device with a mouse IgG needs to be done, to show its applicability as a biological sensor before moving on to more sensitive analytes like Prostate-specific antigen (PSA). To achieve that, in this work, both a Chebyshev type 5th and 7th order low pass and bandpass filters are to be implemented as the sensing surface using the insertion loss method.

ACKNOWLEDGMENT

This work was sponsored by Petroleum Technology Development Fund (PTDF). We also thank Frank Atkinson for his support.

REFERENCES

[1] K. Griffiths, C. Dale, J. Hedley, M.D. Kowal, R.B. Kaner and N. Keegan, Laser-scribed Graphene presents an opportunity to print a new generation of disposable electrochemical sensors. Nanoscale, 2014. 6(22): pp. 13613-22.

[2] R. L. McCreery and M.T. McDermott, Comment on electrochemical kinetics at ordered graphite electrodes. Anal Chem, 2012. 84(5): pp. 2602-5.F

[3] H. Tian et al., Scalable fabrication of high-performance and flexible Graphene strain sensors. Nanoscale, 2014. 6(2): pp. 699-705.

[4] J. Lin et al., Laser-induced porous Graphene films from commercial polymers. Nat Commun, 2014. 5: pp. 5714.

[5] X. Wang et al., Three-dimensional strutted Graphene grown by substrate-free sugar blowing for high-power-density supercapacitors. Nat Commun, 2013. 4: pp. 2905.

[6] Z. Chen et al., Three-dimensional flexible and conductive interconnected Graphene networks grown by chemical vapour deposition. Nat Mater, 2011. 10(6): pp. 424-8.

[7] M. Schumann, R. Sauerbrey, and M.C. Smayling, Permanent increase of the electrical conductivity of polymers induced by ultraviolet laser radiation. Applied Physics Letters, 1991. 58(4): pp. 428-430.

[8] M. El-Kady et al., Laser Scribing of High-Performance and Flexible Graphene-Based Electrochemical Capacitors. Science (New York, N.Y.), 2012. 335: pp. 1326-30.

[9] K. Rajasekaran, J. Jayalakshmi, and J. Thangaiyan, Design and Analysis of Stepped Impedance Microstrip Low Pass Filter Using ADS Simulation Tool for Wireless Applications. 2013. 3: pp. 1-5.

[10] N. B. Mohd Hashim, M. Shahrazel Razalli., S. Z. Ibrahim and F. Farid, Compact Ultra Wideband Stepped Impedance Low Pass Filter Utilizing Open Circuit Stub Resonator. ARPN Journal of Engineering and Applied Sciences, 2015. 10: pp. 9120-9126.

[11] I. Mansour, H. Elhennawy, and A.S. Tag El-dein, Design of Stepped Impedance Microstrip Low Pass Filter with DGS. International Journal of Engineering Research and Development, 2014. 10(7): pp. 58-67.

[12] V.M. Anerao, Implementation of Stepped Impedance Microstrip Low Pass Filter. International Journal of Emerging Trends in Electrical and Electronics (IJETEE) 2013. 2(2): pp. 89-92.

[13] N. Garvansh, A Kumar, Design and Synthesis of Stepped Impedance Microstrip Line Low Pass Filter. International Journal of Scientific Research Engineering & Technology, 2014: pp. 48-50.

[14] I. Rosu, Microstrip Stripline and CPW Design, http://www.qsl.net/va3iul.

[15] S.H. Hall, G.W. Hall, and J.A. McCall, High Speed Digital System Design A Handbook of Interconnect Theory and Design Practices. 2000.

[16] C. Wang, Determining Dielectric Constant and Loss-Tangent in FR-4, UMR EMCLaboratory Technical Report TR-00-1-041, March, 2000.

Adaptive Optical Sensors

Ivan Krejci, Karel Dvorak
Department of Technical Studies
College of polytechnics Jihlava, VSPJ
Jihlava, Czech Republic
e-mail: krejci19@vspj.cz, dvorak96@vspj.cz

Abstract—**The sensors containing microcontrollers, digitizers and some standard communication line(s), offering digital output expressed in corresponding units of measured quantities, are usually called intelligent sensors. This contribution offers another view on the sensor intelligence – on the ability to adapt their measuring range to different tested materials' physical properties to get accurate results. The article describes two methods of measurements and control of band material position by means of optical sensors, which adapt their range to the current optical properties of the material used (steel, web or plastic foil).**

Keywords- optical sensors; band material; optical transmitter and receiver; microcontroller.

I. Introduction

The task of band material positioning is very frequent in companies manufacturing band shape materials such as tyre makers, sheet rolling mills, conveyor belts, and textile or plastic film rolls producers. In these cases, the central position or constant width of the soft material bands are required during the technological process. The importance of the accurate measurement of the belt position and its dimension (the width) is crucial, if a good quality of the final product is to be achieved. This measurement must be worked out without any mechanical contact with the measured band material. For this purpose, optical sensors are usually used. The sensors create the measurement part of an automation control system, the goal of which is the position or dimension control of a processed band material. The basic tasks of the band material position control can be explained from the schematic diagrams in Figures 1 and 2.

The case of the band material centre is shown in Figure 1. The position is measured by two optical sensors positioned symmetrically with respect to the longitudinal axis of the technological equipment, e.g., a rolling mill, calendar, etc. If the signals from both sensors are identical (their difference is equal to zero), then the band is situated in the centre of the machine. Achieving this position is the goal of the control task.

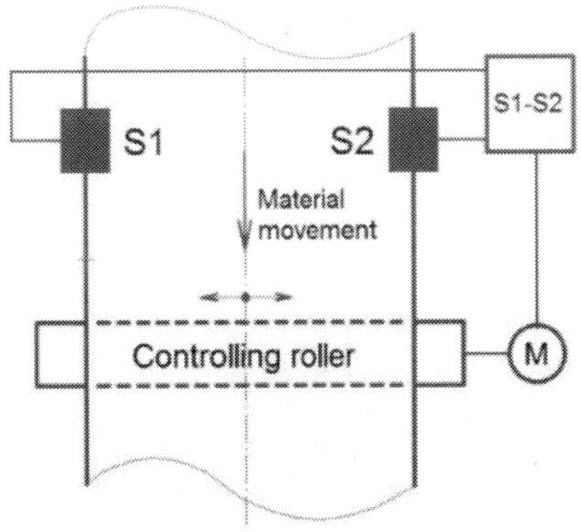

Figure 1. The basic principle of the belt material automatic centering. S1, S2 – optical sensors, S1-S2 electronic unit, M – actuating mechanism.

The band transversal position can be changed by a roll, which can be moved in the direction orthogonal to the band movement. If the centered material does not transmit any light, then, in many cases, only a single sensor is used to determine the central material position. In such configuration, the optical centre of the sensor determines the required position of the material edge.

Similar to this task is the setting of the processed band width, the principle of which is shown in Figure 2. If a soft material (plastic foil, textile, cord, etc.) is processed, its width is changing with the pulling force causing the band movement.

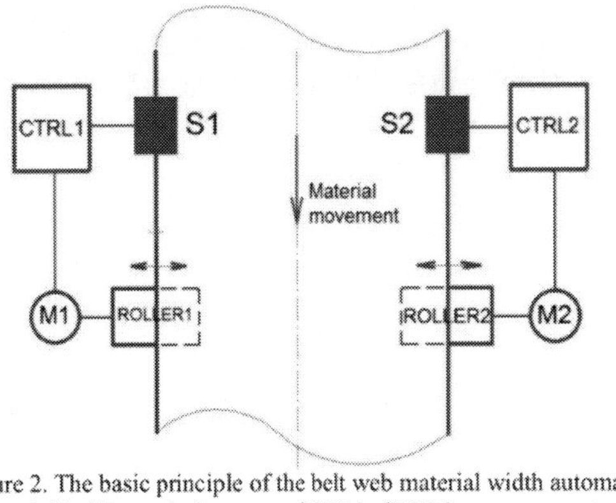

Figure 2. The basic principle of the belt web material width automatic control. S1, S2 – optical sensors, CTRL1, CTRL2, measurement and control units, M1, M2 – actuating mechanisms.

A pair of optical sensors placed symmetrically with respect to the longitudinal axis of the technological equipment again measures the band edge position. Besides, their centers are fixed in distance which is equal to the required width of the band. If both sensors show a half of their measuring range, then the width is set correctly. If one or both sensors give a false position, the band width is adjusted using two independent rolls, which correct individually the material edge position in the required width.

Both methods have some bottlenecks that should be overcome to achieve satisfying results.

The rest of the paper is divided into the following sections. Section II contains the present state overview. Section III describes the new concept of the system solution. Section IV includes the sensors realization and results of the first test. The acknowledgment and conclusions close the article.

II. STATE-OF-THE-ART

A. Mechanical Arrangement

At present, optical sensors consist of an optical transmitter, which involves the light source, usually Light Emitting Diodes (LED) operating in the InfraRed (IR) region of the light spectrum, and an optical receiver, which uses phototransistors operating also in the IR region. The optical elements of both sensor parts are arranged in the shape of a row array, and both arrays are placed against each other [1]. The optical transmitter and receiver are built in a frame that can have either a narrow rectangle or a horse-shoe shape. Usually, the measuring system contains a pair of the sensors, each equipped with one transmitter and one receiver. The centered material is led in the gap between sensors so that its edges will lie in the active range of sensors, in the gap between the transmitter and receiver inside the frame. The principle arrangements of both shapes of sensor frames are shown in Figures 3 and 4.

Figure 3 shows the position of optical sensors in the rectangular frame. The red fields assign the IR flux emitted by the optical transmitters and accepted by the optical receivers. The range of the material width is given by the difference MAX – MIN. This type of frame is usually used if the centered band width is within the range from 1 to 2 m (cords for tires or conveyor belts). The row array of the sensor parts must be wider than this measuring range. The advantages of this sensor arrangement are its simplicity and no need for manipulation if the material width is changed for another type of final product during the process of production. But this performance requires a very careful match of several tens of applied optoelectronic elements for transmitters and receivers to ensure good linearity and symmetry of both sensors [2].

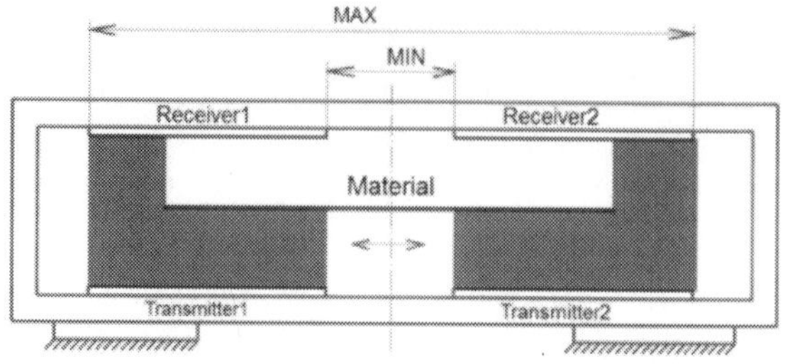

Figure 3. The frame performance of the optical sensor for the automatic centering task.

The sensor shown in Figure 4 takes advantage of two horse-shoe frames placed on carrier 3, equipped with an adjustable mechanism 1,2,5,6, which makes it possible to set the distance of both sensors 5 according to the actual width of the band material 7 [2]. This arrangement requires much fewer matched optoelectronic elements, but its mechanical construction is more complicated (slide way of frames, bidirectional set screw, width scale, etc.). This type of the sensor is often used either if the belt material is extremely wide (more than 2 m) or not flexible (steel plates).

The principal problems of this sensor type are the match of optoelectronic components for the IR radiation generating and sensing, and undulated edges of non-flexible materials. The only solution of these problems is the precise match of components with the same characteristics on one side, and the subjective decision of a rolling-mill worker about which plate edge could be the reference one, if the centering process determines only one edge position.

The sensors for the material width measurement are very similar to the horse-shoe shaped sensors; the only difference is that the frames are fixed so that their centres will be positioned at the measured distance. In this case, only one width can be measured and, thus, these sensors are built in special purpose machines. The problem of the measurement is that the material, a web, is more or less transparent. This material property causes errors in measurement, especially if the transparency (the material optical density) varies from place to place.

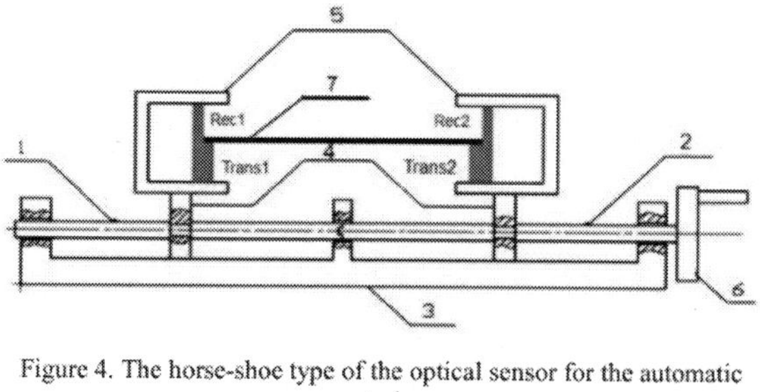

Figure 4. The horse-shoe type of the optical sensor for the automatic centering.

B. Electrical Equipment

The electronic units of the sensors serve to supply the optical receivers and to process the received signal proportional to the luminous flux passing through the material in the operating space of the sensor. To prevent unwanted influence of outer sources of the IR radiation, the LEDs of receivers are supplied with a constant current source which operates in the switching mode so that the luminous flux is modulated. The signals from the receivers are demodulated, amplified and subtracted using a differential amplifier. All present systems we have met in various factories take advantage of the analogue principle. The sensors are calibrated in two points, at the zero luminous flux and the maximum luminous flux, when no object is placed in the working place of the calibrated sensor. In both cases, the LEDs are fully excited from their current source.

In systems with the horse-shoe frame, which use only one sensor selected by the operator, the reference position is determined by the active sensor centre. The electronic equipment must be able to handle both sensors individually, because the reference sensor is selected during the material processing.

The sensors measuring the band material width are used to control the leading rolls position. Each of the sensors controls its own roll so each sensor has its own electronic control unit taking advantage of a similar signal processing as in the previous task.

C. Band Position Control Problems

It is no problem to control the width of band materials that are not transparent, but if the material is more or less transparent (plastic foils) or diaphanous (textile, tyre cord) the measurement becomes very problematic. For instance, if the receiver measures 50% of the full scale luminous flux, the material edge is in the centre of the sensor in case of an opaque material. But this is not true if some light passes through the material. Then, the material must cover more than 50% of the sensor active space to get the same signal. Thus, the sensor offers a false result of the width measurement. The error depends on the material transparency. To avoid this problem, it is necessary to calibrate the sensor whenever the material transparency changes. This is very problematic because it requires a production interruption, but in case of the inhomogeneous material (tyre cord) such calibration does not bring sufficient improvement. Certain suppression of this effect can be achieved, if the sensor frame is turned a bit so that the light beam is not orthogonal to the material surface (Figure 5) and the gaps between material threads are smaller. Again, the problem is reduced, not eliminated. Besides, the sensor can be damaged because of the material longitudinal swing if the angle between the light beam and the material surface is acute.

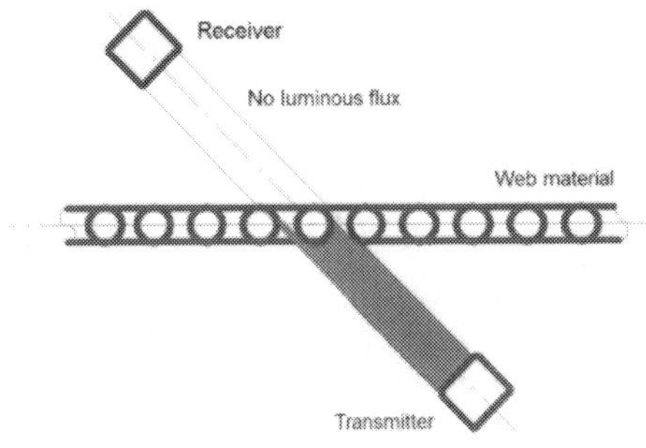

Figure 5. Turning of the sensor drops off the material transparency error.

III. NEW CONCEPTION

Our effort was turned to the width control and automatic reference edge selection tasks as a reaction to the requirements of industrial companies. To address the above mentioned problems requires a new strategy of the sensor and electronic equipment conception. If the system has to change its properties automatically, or has to make any decision, if the process conditions are changing, it is necessary to use the digital principles of the control. The following paragraphs show the solutions of two tasks, measurements of the width of materials the transparency of which varies in time and the automatic reference steel sheet edge selection during its procession in the rolling mill.

A. Band Width Measurement

The basic goal of this task is the measurement of the processed material transparency, its evaluation and the system recalibration based on the measurement results. It was necessary to develop an original type of the optical sensor capable of the continual material transparency measurement and then to calculate the material width.

The sensor mechanical concept comes out of the horse-shoe shape, but it consists of three sections (Figure 6), equipped with three optical transmitters (Tr1 – Tr3) and receivers. These are placed in the working space so that the first section is fully covered by the band material, the second one, the measuring part of the sensor, is partially covered by the tested material, and the third section is clear of the material. All the three transmitters are connected in series and take advantage of the pulse current, the peak value of which is 10 mA. The signals from the first receiver (REC1) and the third one (REC3) provide the zero and full scale points of the material coverage. The central, measuring part of the sensor is provided by the signal of the second section receiver REC2, which lies between the boundaries defined by the signals REC1and REC3. Then, the degree of the measuring sensor coverage D can be calculated:

$$D = (REC2 - REC1) / (REC3 - REC1) \qquad (1)$$

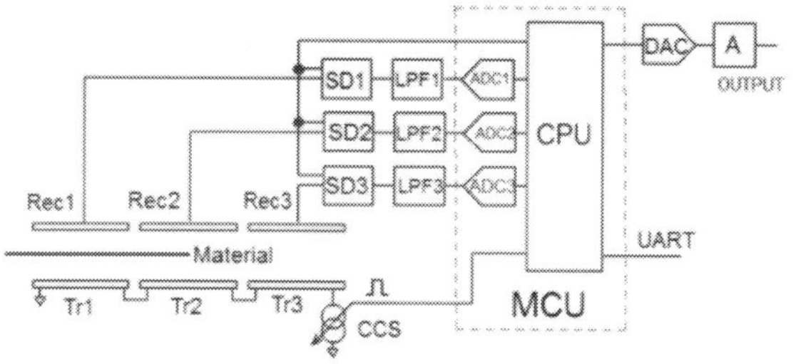

Figure 6. The basic block diagram of the three - section sensor for the width measurement.

If all three sections provide the same signals after the calibration of signal traces, and if the centre of the second section determines the correct material width, then the goal of the control task is to reach the value of 0.5.

According to Figure 2, there are two identical sensors located on both material edges (S1 and S2). The distance between the measuring section centers is equal to the required material width.

The signal trace function is controlled by a built in MicroController Unit, MCU, (Texas Instruments MSP430AFE253) [3], which ensures excitation pulses for optical transmitters (Tr1, Tr2 and Tr3) supplied with the Constant Current Source (CCS), and switching pulses for Synchronous Detectors (SD1, SD2 and SD3) processing the received signals from all three sensor sections. These signals are then led to the Low-Pass Filters (LPF1, LPF2 and LPF3) that reject high frequency modulation products presented in the detected signals. The signals are then digitized in three independent 16-bit Analogue-to-Digital Converters (ADC1, ADC2 and ADC3). The digitized signals are calculated in compliance with (1). If the value of D is different from 0.5, a non-zero error signal is generated. This digital signal is converted to the analogue form using a 12-bit Digital-to-Analogue Converter DAC, Analog Devices AD 5320 [4]. This analogue signal is amplified in amplifier A and used for the control of the position roller that adjusts the material width.

The MCU measures and controls the material optical density in 100 ms intervals, and so continuously adapts the measuring range to the actual optical transparency of the processed band material. This arrangement completely eliminates the material transparency error. For the purposes of the basic signal trace calibration, the MCU serial Universal Asynchronous Receiver Transmitter (UART) is used for communication with the host PC. The block diagram of the sensor and its signal trace are shown in Figure 6. The electronic unit is supplied from the mains electricity, 230 V, 50 Hz.

B. *Steel Plate Centering*

This task is solved during the roll-milling process, when the processed band is led to the centre of the rolling-mill machine. The plate is then rolled up to a spool, the centre of which is also localized in the centre of the rolling-mill machine and it is necessary to put the turns of the plate onto each other with minimum position fluctuation. The sensing mechanism consists of two horse-shoe optical sensors, the positions of which are controlled by a bidirectional screw (if the screw turns clock-wise, the horse-shoes distance diminishes, if the screw is turned in opposite direction, the distance rises). The active width of each sensor is 60 mm. The sensors are fixed so that the distance of their centres is equal to the input material width. For this purpose, the sensors are equipped with a scale, so that the required width of the material can be adjusted before the controlling process starts. During this process, only one sensor is active to measure the band position. The problem of this position control is in undulated edges of the plate because of unequal material tensions. These undulations cause control errors. Therefore, it is suitable to select the less undulated edge as the reference one to reach better results of the control. As mentioned above, the choice is worked out by the worker who is in the control room several meters from the processed material and, thus, his decision is very subjective. To get a more objective choice, the decision was committed to a MCU controlled sensor unit, which learns the material edges fluctuations during the process and after a time period (30 seconds) is able to evaluate the undulations because of that learning. The less undulated side of the plate is determined as the reference one. During the learning period, the control is running on the default or previously optimized reference edge. The undulation errors are, in most cases, within a range of +/- 10 mm. To get the best results, the maximum gain of the control unit is required round the sensor centre. Therefore, the dynamic range of the controller manipulating variable was divided into two ranges (Figure 7). The highest gain of the control loop was within the range of +/- 6 mm from the zero point of the sensor. In this region, one half of the output 12-bit DAC dynamics was used for the control. The other half of the DAC dynamics is intended for the control within the rest of the sensor range – the sensor adapts its sensitivity to the error magnitude. It should be noticed that the material position data from both sensors must be mirrored to get the proper direction of the position correction (it is necessary to resolve the right and left side sensors).

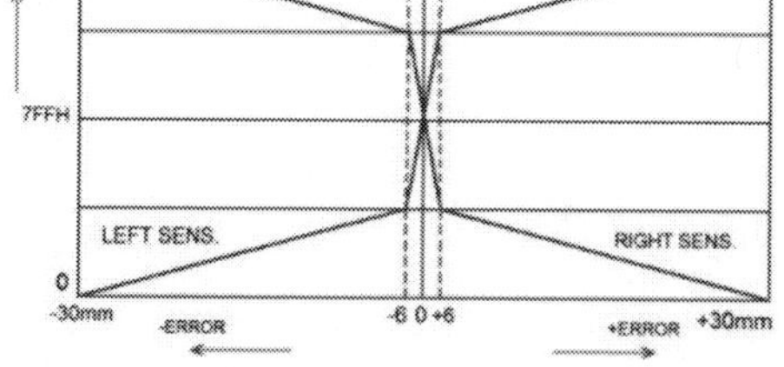

Figure 7. The sensitivity versus error characteristic of the horse-shoe sensors for the steel plate centering during the roll-mill process.

The sensor electronic unit takes advantage of the same electronic circuits and the signal processing as in the case of the width measurement, but only two measuring channels are used. The basic difference is in the firmware of the MCU, because the tasks of the measurement are different.

IV. SENSORS REALIZATION AND RESULTS

Both types of sensors were designed and manufactured as per the mechanical and electrical construction specifications. Figure 8 shows the width sensor arrangement with three measuring sections.

Figure 8. The three sections sensor for the belt width measurement.

The sensor is placed on a welded frame formed by square profiled tubes. To save space, the sensor part which is never covered by the band is placed upright to the remaining two sections. The sensor takes advantage of three sections; the active width of each section is 60 mm. There are glass windows protecting the sensor optoelectronic elements on the active sides of the sensor. They protect the sensor elements against the mechanical stresses and dust.

The Printed Circuit Boards (PCB) of the sensor transmitter and receiver are shown in Figure 9. The PCBs are built in the sensor frame. The figure shows two sections of the sensor. Note the linear arrangement of the optoelectronic elements. The dimensions of the sensor carriers are 200 x 15 mm.

The PCB electronic circuitry is shown in Figure 10. It includes the mains power supply, supply of the optical transmitter and all three signals analogue and digital traces processing the transmitter's signals. This PCB is built in the BOPLA Elegant box, and its dimensions are 130 x 75 mm.

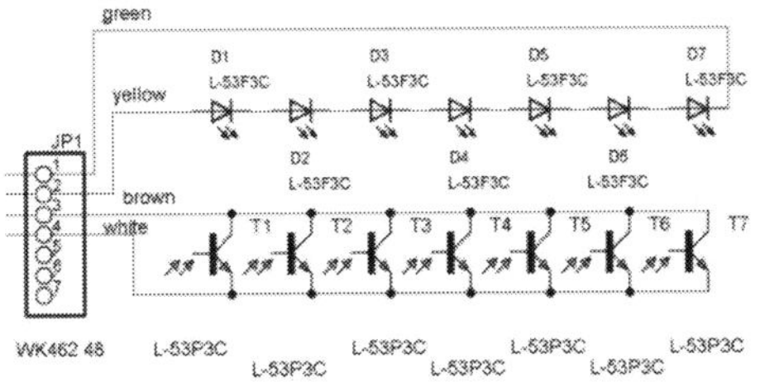

Figure 9. One section schematic diagram of the transmitter (upper) and receiver (lower) optical elements.

Figure 10. The PCB with all controlling and measuring electronics of a three sections sensor.

The sensor for the centering of the steel sheet band is shown in Figure 11. This figure shows its implementation during the tests in the roll-mill. See the adjusting wheel (RK) for setting the sensor centre to the required position.

The firmware for both tasks' solutions was created and the sensor's functionality was tested.

V. CONCLUSIONS

The first function tests in the real industrial environment were successful because the achieved results of the control process were much better compared with previous solutions. The width control error was within the range of +/- 1 mm (at the material width of 2000 mm); the error of the control in the case of centering of the steel plate was +/- 2 mm at the output spool. However, these errors are the errors of the entire control process caused by the propagation delay between the points of measurement and the position actuating, by the hydraulics of the manipulator, etc. These tests showed improved properties of the systems and confirmed expected results. At present, a new test tool has been designed and is being produced. This will let us perform detailed analysis of the system parameters.

Figure 11. The implementation of the horse-shoe sensor in the roll-mil machine.

The sensor parameters (accuracy, resolution, repeatability and stability) will be evaluated in the following weeks because the project dealing with these sensors is not yet finished.

ACKNOWLEDGMENT

The topic of adaptive optical sensors is supported by an internal project granted by the College of Polytechnics Jihlava, Czech Republic. The authors thank the manufacturers Barum-Continental Ltd. and Bilstein AG (Czech Republic) that made it possible to test the sensor functionality in a rough industrial environment.

REFERENCES

[1] Electronic publication: Highly Precise, Non-contact Width Measurement of Webs and Boards. https://www.elovis.com/en/applications/non-contact-widths-heights-diameter-measurement/webs boards-plates/, ELOVIS GmBH, Germany 2019. [retrieved: 9, 2019]

[2] User Manual of the Centering System of bands width 950 - 2200 mm. [In Czech] HAAL, s.r.o., Brno, Czech Republic, 2001.

[3] Electronic publication: 16-bit Ultra-Low-Power Microcontroller, http://www.ti.com/lit/ds/symlink/msp430afe253.pdf, pp. 28, 35, 38, Texas Instruments Incorporated, Dallas, Texas 75265, USA, 2019. [retrieved: 9, 2019].

[4] Electronic publication: 2.7 V to 5.5 V, 140 μA, Rail-to-Rail Output 12-Bit DAC in an SOT-23. https://www.analog.com/media/en/technical-documentation/data-sheets/AD5320.pdf, pp. 1, 11, 12, Analog Devices, USA, 2019 [retrieved: 9, 2019].

Distributed Kalman Filter Investigation and Application to Leak Detection in Water Pipeline Monitoring Using Wireless Sensor Networks with Non-intrusive Sensors

Valery Nkemeni, Fabien Mieyeville, Jacques Verdier
University of Lyon, Université Claude Bernard Lyon 1, Ecole Centrale de Lyon, INSA Lyon, CNRS, Ampère, F-69621, Villeurbanne, France
e-mail: valery.nkemeni@etu.univ-lyon1.fr, fabien.mieyeville@univ-lyon1.fr, jacques.verdier@insa-lyon.fr

Pierre Tsafack
University of Buea, Faculty of Engineering and Technology
P.O Box 63; Buea, Cameroon
e-mail: tsafack.pierre@ubuea.cm

***Abstract*— Wireless Sensor Networks (WSN) have found a wide range of applications in monitoring, with most deployments done in a centralized fashion. This results in high energy consumption and latency, as such centralized schemes are characterized by periodic long-distance transmissions. In this work, we demonstrate the benefits of trading off transmission for computation. We propose a solution where local and distributed computing are used to improve the accuracy of anomaly detection in physical systems without the need for long distance transmissions to some central base station. We practically demonstrate this in detecting leaks on a water pipeline testbed, since water losses via leaks is a major problem in most developing countries, including Cameroon. Unlike other works for leak detection in water pipelines available in literature, we build a low-cost sensor node, which is feasible for deployment in developing countries from cheap off-the-shelf commercial elements. The accuracy of the measured vibrations on the surface of pipes is improved using a distributed Kalman filter, where every node independently computes the optimal state estimate used for leak detection by running a local Kalman filter to obtain an accurate local estimate from local measurements and also fusing it with those of its close neighbors. Results show that the distributed Kalman filter improves the reliability of leak detection.**

Keywords- distributed computing; wireless sensor networks; distributed Kalman filter; water pipeline monitoring; non-intrusive sensors.

I. INTRODUCTION

A WSN consists of a number of distributed nodes with sensing, processing and wireless communications capabilities, deployed over an area of interest to monitor physical or environmental conditions. Application areas of WSNs include geographical monitoring, habitat monitoring, transportation, military systems, business processes, microclimate research, medical care and others [1][2]. They are spatially distributed systems that exploit wireless networking as main inter-node interaction channel and are typically constrained in terms of energy, computing power, memory and communication bandwidth.

A. WSN: Shifting towards a distributed approach

Most WSN monitoring applications in literature are centralized [3][4]. This has led to the underutilization of the processing unit and overutilization of the communication unit of sensor nodes since the primarily role of the sensor nodes is to collect and transmit data periodically to an intelligent central base station where all the processing is done in order to detect anomalous behaviors [2][5][6]. In large scale monitoring applications, most of the sensor nodes are geographically far away from the base station and from power supply and are usually battery-driven. The main drawback of such a centralized approach is that of huge energy consumption as periodic transmission of raw data over long distances to the base station leads to fast depletion of sensor node's battery and shortens the lifespan of a WSN [6]-[8]. This is the reason for the numerous research works involved in the development of low energy consumption protocols specifically for WSNs. Other drawbacks include low reliability, longer response time, high bandwidth cost, low level data safety and privacy [6]-[9] [11].

B. The stakes of Water Supply in Developing Countries

Water represents a primary necessity for everyday life and for an effective accomplishment of many industrial processes. In the most remote and isolated regions, as in the most urbanized ones, water provisioning to domestic premises represents a fundamental living necessity. The lack of water may prevent the development of business activities from handicraft manufacturing to goods transformation and energy production [10]. Thus, making accessible potable water is one of the critical essentials to human survival and economic growth of today's society.

In most civilized societies, water transportation via pipelines to clients seems to be the most economical way [12] and consists of water supply systems comprising of two different parts: (1) Transmission mains, which are pipes responsible for transporting water to tanks and (2) Water Distribution Networks (WDN), which pipes and service connections for distributing water to customers. However, these infrastructures are not completely watertight as even in the most recent and well-built WDN, some level of leakage and occasional pipe bursts occur, leading to water losses [13]. Water pipeline leakages are one of a few challenges to the water utility companies all over the world. Water loss through leakages is recognized as a costly problem worldwide, due to the waste of precious natural resources, as well as from the economic point of view [14]. A recent report published by the World Bank in 2016 indicated that in developing countries, roughly 45 million cubic meters of water are lost daily with an economic value of over US $3 billion per year. The report also stated that saving half of those losses would provide enough water to serve at least 90 million people [15]. In Cameroon, a developing Sub-Saharan African country, the level of non-revenue water is at 4.67% [16][17]. The reason for this high level of non-revenue water is explained by limited and dilapidated infrastructure that creates physical losses through leaks and/or bursts.

Water demand is increasing continuously and rapidly as a result of the growth of the Earth's population, but water resources are facing a problematical and constant decrease caused by global heating and climate change. Unlike other more peculiar phenomena, water scarcity is common to both developing and developed countries [10]. The scarcity of water thus requires that water losses due to leaks be minimized and if possible, completely eradicated. This has led to enormous research over the years in the field, providing a wide range of methods for detecting and locating leaks in water pipelines.

C. *Water Pipeline Monitoring: State of the Art*

WSNs for Water Pipeline Monitoring (WPM) consist of a number of sensor nodes with low-cost sensors that periodically collect leak signals from the pipe. The signals are then processed to detect the presence of a leak on the pipeline. The biggest problem with leak detection in WPM using low-cost sensors is that the leak signals may be noisy and may result in false alarms in the leak detection system. Thus, the issue of reliably identifying a leak signal in the midst of errors from a number of sources (commonly called noise) is a fundamental challenge of any leak detection system [18].

A number of centralized schemes for WPM using WSN have been proposed in literature [19]-[22]. The sensor nodes periodically collect leak signals from the pipe where they are installed and transmit to a central base station (where the leak detection algorithm is found) for further processing in order to detect the presence of a leak on the pipeline. Such centralized schemes are characterized by a large number of long-distance transmissions which depletes the sensor node's energy faster.

The purpose of this research is to demonstrate the benefits of trading off communication for computation in WSNs by exploiting the sensor node's processing unit to implement local processing and distributed computing. The role of local processing is to improve the accuracy of measurements made locally whereas distributed computing is there to improve the performance of anomaly detection and to make the WSN to be autonomous without the need for centralized intelligence.

D. *Organization of the paper*

In this paper, we will present a distributed computing solution for the detection of leaks in water pipelines since water losses due to leaks and/or bursts are a major problem in most developing countries, including Cameroon's WDN. We practically demonstrate our proposed solution on a water pipeline testbed, where we show how distributed computing can be used to minimize the chances of having a false alarm while also maximizing the leak detection sensitivity of the system thereby increasing the performance or reliability of leak detection in WPM. We implement a distributed Kalman filter algorithm [24], on each sensor node as the signal processing approach for filtering the noisy signals collected by the sensors, thus improving the accuracy of leak detection without needing to transmit sensor readings over long distances to a central base station. In our work, distributed computing is implemented using a distributed Kalman filter algorithm and local processing is implemented using a local Kalman filter.

The rest of the paper is organized as follows. Section II reviews some related works in WPM using WSN with non-intrusive sensors. A detailed description of our proposed node architecture and the distributed Kalman filter implemented are presented in Section III. In Section IV, we describe the testbed used to demonstrate our solution, while Section V is involved with the results and discussions and Section VI concludes the paper and highlights the future work.

II. RELATED WORK

In this section, we review some works in literature that are closely related to our study and which made use of WSNs with non-intrusive sensors for leak detection in water pipelines. The survey is based on the node architectures and the leak detection algorithm implemented in each of these studies.

In [19], the authors described PipeNet, a system based on WSNs which aims to detect, localize and quantify bursts and leaks and other anomalies in water transmission pipelines. A laboratory pipe rig was constructed to evaluate and illustrate the detection and localization of leaks using acoustic and vibration data acquired from densely spaced hydrophones and accelerometers installed along the pipeline. The adopted node was based on Intel commercial mote composed of an ARM7 core, a 64KB RAM, a 512 KB Flash, and a Bluetooth radio for communication. Local processing at each node was implemented by using Fast Fourier Transform (FFT) and compression while cross-correlation was implemented at the central server as the leak detection and localization algorithm. Although this work gives a complete solution for WPM, some significant drawbacks could be mentioned. On one hand, the use of Bluetooth radio as the communication technology by this work is not an energy-efficient solution. In addition, several high processing algorithms were employed which affect the power consumption of the nodes by accomplishing complex tasks. Besides, despite the fact that data was collected at a very high sampling rate and high frequency, which makes this solution real-time, it leads to an increase in energy consumption of the node. A final drawback is that of adopting a centralized approach.

In [20], the authors reported on the design and development of a multimodal Underground Wireless Sensor Network (UWSN) for pipeline structural health monitoring. The sensor node consisted of a PIC16LF1827 microcontroller, an eRA400TRS 433 MHz transceiver, two temperature sensors and one Force Sensitive Resistor (FSR) pressure sensor. According to the authors, power consumption of the sensor nodes was minimized to 2.2 µW based on one measurement every 6 h in order to prolong the lifetime of the network. Two drawbacks could be highlighted from this work. One is the inability to perform real time monitoring and the other results from adopting a centralized approach for leak detection.

The authors in [21] proposed a solution called EARNPIPE which is comprised of a Leak detection Predictive Kalman Filter (LPKF) and other methods to detect and locate leaks. The data collected from sensors were filtered, analyzed and compressed locally with the same Kalman Filter (KF) based algorithm. A laboratory testbed was constructed using plumbing components and the nodes consisted of an Arduino Due board whose processing unit is based on ARM cortex M3 microcontroller, FSR sensors used for pressure measuring and Bluetooth for communication. The main drawback of this solution is the high-power consumption of the sensor nodes, resulting from the choice of sensor node components such as using power-hungry components like the Arduino Due and Bluetooth as the processing and communication units, respectively. The centralized approach adopted for leak detection and localization is also another drawback as it leads to increase in response time due to latency in delivering processed information and also uneven distribution of energy consumption among nodes in the network [11].

The authors in [22] presented the development of a water pipeline monitoring system using vibration sensors. The experimental setup consisted of a MPU6050 sensor for measurement of vibration occurring along the pipes, an Arduino Uno and Xbee module for wireless transmission to a centralized decision support system. The results of the experiment indicated that, for a pressure of 58.8 kPa, the data recorded by the sensor could distinguish between the presence of a leak and when there is no leak. The drawback of this solution is the high energy consumption at the node level resulting from the choice of power-hungry sensor node components such as the Arduino Uno.

In [23], the authors presented an end-to-end water leak localization system, which exploits edge processing and enables the use of battery-driven sensor nodes. The proposed system combined a lightweight edge anomaly detection algorithm based on Kalman filter and compression rates and a localization algorithm based on graph theory. It was validated by deploying non-intrusive sensors measuring vibrational data on a lab-based water test rig that had controlled leakage and burst scenarios implemented. The sensor nodes were based on Intel Edison development boards and NEC Tokin ultra-high-sensitivity vibration sensors. According to the authors, the edge anomaly detection and localization elements of the systems produce a timely and accurate localization result and reduce the communication by 99% compared to the traditional periodic communication. One main drawback of this work is that the choice commercial element (Intel Edison board) that constitutes the sensor node, is not a cost-effective solution for deployment in developing countries. In addition, the use of Bluetooth as a means of communication by the nodes is not energy efficient.

Given the drawbacks of the solutions proposed in literature, the geographic context of our deployment which is to be done in Cameroon (a third world developing country), and being aware of the fact that the choice of architecture and technology of the sensor node is crucial in determining its performance and power consumption, we seek a solution that is low-cost, feasible and also energy efficient. This will be achieved by first optimizing the computing capacity and power consumption of the sensor nodes by integrating very low consumption processing, sensing and communication units from off-the-shelf commercial components.

III. MATERIALS AND METHODS

Price often has a direct bearing on the quality of a node's sensors and influences the accuracy of the result that can be obtained from a single node [25]. Thus, using low-cost sensors in WPM to detect leak signals is usually characterized by noisy measurements and may result in false alarms in the leak detection system. To minimize the errors in measurement, we chose a one-dimensional Kalman filter to remove the noise and to improve on the accuracy of the measurement made locally at each node. In order to maximize leak detection while minimizing the number of false alarms, a distributed Kaman filter is proposed. In our proposed solution, each sensor node runs a local Kalman filter to obtain an accurate local estimate from the local measurements, then later fuses it with those of its neighbor to achieve a more accurate global estimate used for leak detection. In this way, our proposed solution is autonomous and does not need any central intelligence. To the best of our knowledge, this is the first work that uses WSNs with non-intrusive sensors and a distributed Kalman filter for leak detection in WPM.

In this section, we present a description of the off-the-shelf commercial components that make up the sensor node hardware alongside with the distributed Kalman filter algorithm used to improve on the reliability of leak detection in WPM.

A. Sensor Node Architecture

The architecture and technology of a sensor node is crucial in determining its cost, performance and power consumption. We develop a low-cost and low-power node by integrating cheap and low-power off-the-shelf commercial components. Our proposed node consists of an ESP32 from Espressif Systems as the processing unit, an nRF24L01+ transceiver module from Nordic as the communication unit and an LSM9DS1 Inertia Measurement Unit (IMU) from STMicroelectronics as the sensing unit.

1) ESP32: It is a low-cost, low-power System on a Chip (SoC) series Wi-Fi and dual-mode Bluetooth microcontroller [26]. Engineered for mobile devices, wearable electronics, and Intenet of Things (IoT) applications, ESP32 offers Ultra-Low Power (ULP) consumption through power saving features including fine resolution clock gating, multiple power modes, and power scaling [8]. The ESP32, when active (with the modem being off and CPU being operational), consumes current in the range of 20 mA ~ 68 mA and 10 μA ~ 150 μA in the ULP state (only the RTC memory and RTC peripherals are powered on and the ULP co-processor is functional). The choice of this module is based on our exploration of different sensor node architectures existing in literature [8][27][28]. Some of the features of the ESP32 include: an Xtensa Dual-Core 32-bit LX6 microprocessor operating up to 240 MHz, 520 kB Static Random Access Memory (SRAM), 12-bit Analog-to-Digital Converter (ADC) with up to 18 channels, a built-in Wi-Fi card supporting IEEE 802.11 b/g/n standards, and Bluetooth version 4.2 and Bluetooth Low Energy (BLE). In addition, the ESP32 chip features 40 physical General Purpose Input Output (GPIO) pads, which can be used as general purpose I/O to connect new sensors, or can be connected to an internal peripheral signal [8]. This can permit the coupling of the nRF24L01+ transceiver module to the ESP32, thus making the sensor node to have a complete coverage of the various communication technologies used in IoT. Adafruit ESP32 feather (Huzzah32) is our chosen ESP32 board.

2) nRF24L01+: This transceiver operates in the 2.400 to 2.4835 GHz band and is suitable for wireless applications requiring very low power consumption. It is compliant with the IEEE802.15.4 physical layer protocol, a technical standard which defines the physical layer of low-rate wireless personal area networks. The module connects to a microcontroller to communicate via the SPI interface. With peak RX/TX currents lower than 14 mA, a sub μA power down mode, advanced power management, and a 1.9 to 3.6 V supply range, the nRF24L01+ provides a true ULP solution enabling months to years of battery life from coin cell or AA/AAA batteries. The nRF24L01+ uses Gaussian Frequency Shift Keying (GFSK) modulation [4], with data rates from 250 Kbps to 2 Mbps. The range can be nearly 100m and 500m with and without an external antenna respectively at maximum power [29][30]. It has longer range than Bluetooth, consumes lower power than Wi-Fi and is a cheaper alternative to Zigbee.

3) LSM9DS1: It is a 9 Degree of Freedom (DOF) IMU which features a 3D digital linear acceleration sensor, a 3D digital angular rate sensor, and a 3D digital magnetic sensor. The LSM9DS1 has a linear acceleration full scale of ±2g/±4g/±8g/±16g, a magnetic field full scale of ±4/±8/±12/±16 gauss and an angular rate of ±245/±500/±2000 dps. It includes an I^2C serial bus and an SPI serial standard interface for interfacing with the microcontroller. It has analog supply voltage ranging from 1.9 V to 3.6 V and the current consumption of the accelerometer in normal mode is 600 uA [31].

B. Configuration of the Node

The nRF24L01+ transceiver module and LSM9DS1 IMU sensor are interfaced with the ESP32 via the SPI and I^2C interfaces, respectively. The sensitivity of the accelerometer in the LSM9DS1 sensor is configured to ±2g since this has the highest sensitivity, which makes it most appropriate for detecting vibrations of smaller magnitude such as those on the surface of water pipe. The accelerometer collects the vibration in 3D, that is in the X, Y and Z direction given by A_x, A_y and A_z, respectively. The magnitude of the vibration on the surface of the pipe was computed by taking the resultant of the acceleration in all three directions.

C. Distributed Kalman Filter Algorithm

Kalman filtering is a technique of filtering information which is known to have some error, uncertainty, or noise. The goal of the filter is to take in this imperfect information, sort out the useful parts of interest, and reduce the uncertainty or noise [32]. There are two types of noise associated with stochastic estimation, process noise and measurement noise. Process noise can be explained as the difference between the real system and the model, while the measurement noise is the noise associated with the sensors and instrumentation. The Kalman filter minimizes the estimated error covariance in a linear stochastic system, has low memory requirements and low complexity [33], and it is capable of handling situations with a lot of noise or high uncertainty in the data. This thus makes it a perfect candidate for improving the accuracy of noisy measured leak signal and detecting leaks in WPM using WSNs, as nodes are constrained in memory, processing power and energy [23][33][34]. Thus, to remove noise from the readings obtained by the IMU sensors and improve on the accuracy of measurement, we propose the use of a one-dimensional Kalman filter.

The Kalman filter is based on two steps, comprising of a prediction followed by a correction in order to determine the states of the filter. This is sometimes called predictor-corrector, or prediction-update [32].

In the first step, the estimated state x, at time k is predicted from the updated state at time k-1. The prediction of the current state and the covariance matrix is given by [32] [33]:

$$\hat{x}_k^- = A\hat{x}_{k-1} + Bu_k \quad (1)$$

$$P_k^- = A.P_{k-1}.A^T + Q_k \quad (2)$$

where $\hat{x}_k^-$ is the predicted state vector at time k, $\hat{x}_{k-1}$ is the previous estimated state vector, P_k^- represents the predicted state error covariance matrix, A and B are matrices defining the system dynamics, u_k is the input vector, P_{k-1} is the previous estimated state error covariance matrix, and Q is the process noise covariance matrix.

The second step is the correction or update step. This step aims to get an improved estimate by incorporating new measurements into the predicted estimate using the Kalman gain (K_k).

$$K_k = \frac{P_k^- H^T}{(HP_k^- H^T + R_k)^{-1}} \quad (3)$$

$$\hat{x}_k = \hat{x}_k^- + K_k(z_k - H\hat{x}_k^-) \quad (4)$$

$$P_k = (I - K_k H)P_k^- \quad (5)$$

where H is a matrix necessary to define the output equation, R is the measurement noise covariance, I is an identity matrix, $\hat{x}_k$ is the estimated or updated state vector, z_k is the measurement at time k and P_k is the updated state error covariance.

In the model equation, A and B are constants since we are dealing with a one-dimensional Kalman filter. H is 1 because it is known that the measurement is composed of the state value and some noise, while A is 1 because it is assumed that the next value will be the same as the previous one. We derived R from the LSM9DS1 datasheet. The linear acceleration typical zero-g level offset accuracy given in the datasheet is ± 90 mg, thus R is 0.09. Q is obtained after some experimentation. From the datasheet, the sensor in a steady state on a horizontal surface will measure 0 g on both the X-axis and Y-axis, whereas the Z-axis will measure 1 g. We did some experiments with different Q values and selected the one that best approximated the acceleration values at zero-g. Q equal to 0.001 best approximated the zero-g acceleration values.

After noise removal, leaks can be detected accurately. To maximize leak detection and minimize the number of false alarms without using any form of centralized scheme, we proposed the use of a distributed Kalman filter.

A number of distributed Kalman filter algorithms have been presented in literature [24][34]-[36]. In our solution, we implemented the distributed Kalman filter algorithm proposed in [24]. The authors in [24] presented a novel event-triggered distributed state estimator based on a consensus Kalman filtering approach, as well as a transmission triggering condition which essentially requires that the local estimate and/or covariance of a given node be sufficiently far away from the ones computed by neighbors before there can be exchange of data between a node and its neighbors. The paper addresses Distributed State Estimation (DSE) over a network in which each node can process local data as well as exchange data with neighbors. In their proposed DSE algorithm, each node runs a local Kalman filter and then, in order to improve its local estimate, fuses the local information with the one received from its in-neighbors [24].

The implemented distributed Kalman algorithm starts by updating a local information pair (local estimate and state error covariance matrix) in the correction step. In the information exchange step, each sensor node determines whether to transmit its information pair to its out-neighbors or not based on the value of its transmission flag. The transmission flag is set when the discrepancy between the current updated local estimate and the last transmitted local estimate is larger than some threshold, which can be varied to achieve a desired behavior in terms of transmission rate and performance. This means that the data currently computed by a node's out-neighbors are no longer consistent with the data locally available at the node. The transmission test is designed so as to ensure that, in the case of no transmission, the data currently computed by the out-neighbors of a node are close to the data locally available at the node, both in terms of mean and covariance. Thus, the idea is to selectively transmit only when the discrepancy is large. In the information fusion step, a node computes a fused information pair from its local information pair and those received from in-neighbors at time step k. For in-neighbors that did not transmit based on their transmission flag not being set, the node computes an approximate local pair for such nodes from the latest local information pair received from them. Finally, in the prediction step, the fused information pair is propagated in time by applying the Kalman filter prediction step to compute the local predicted information pair at time k+1.

The distributed Kalman filter algorithm is implemented on a network of two nodes with addresses given by 00 and 01 (octal representation) with the node 00 being the base node or Personal Area Network (PAN) coordinator. The nodes, having the Adafruit feather ESP32 (Huzzah32) microcontroller as the processing unit, are programmed with the Arduino C programming language using the Arduino 1.8.9 Integrated Development Environment (IDE). It should be noted that Adafruit recommends the programming of the Huzzah32 board using the Arduino IDE. The RF24Network and RF24 libraries by TMRh20 are used to control the nRF24L01+ transceiver interfaced to the Huzzah32 via SPI. The firmware uploaded to the nodes after compiling the distributed Kalman filter algorithm using the Arduino IDE occupied a storage space of 225 KB. Global variables use 15 KB of dynamic memory, leaving 312 KB for local variables. The implementation did not make use of any operating system, but that will be done in future work.

IV. EXPERIMENTAL SETUP

To practically demonstrate our proposed solution, a laboratory testbed, whose configuration is similar to that of a WDN in Cameroon, was built at the Electrical and Electronic Laboratory of the University of Buea, Cameroon. It consists of two plastic water storage tanks of capacity 1000 L (one being a storage tank placed on a tower of height 9 m and the other being a supply tank placed beneath the tower), a U shaped 13m long PVC pipe having an external diameter of 32 mm and an internal diameter of 30 mm, and an electrical pump with 0.7 Hp motor providing a maximum pump capacity of 40 L/min for filling the upper storage tank. Leakage in the pipeline was induced by opening a valve placed some 4 m away from the inlet of water into the system. Figure 1 displays the testbed setup.

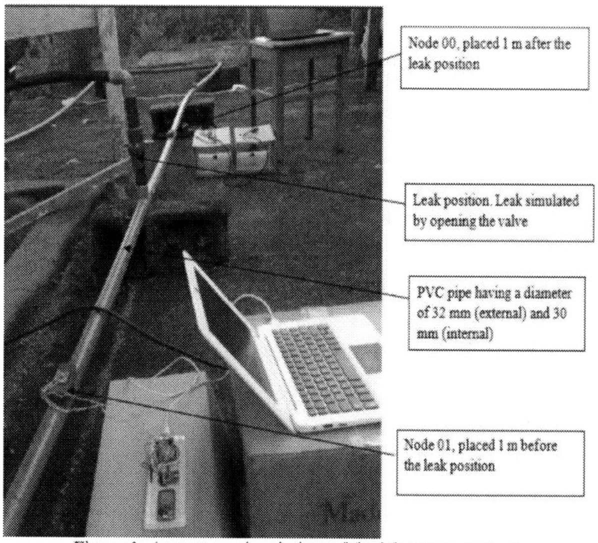

Figure 1. A cross-sectional view of the laboratory testbed.

Our setup consists of two sensor nodes namely Node 00 placed 1 m after the leak position and Node 01 placed 1 m before the leak position, as shown in Figure 1. The mechanical coupling between the pipe and IMU was done by first attaching the IMU firmly to a polyurethane foam to form a single entity. The entity was then glued to the pipe. The role of the IMU sensors is to measure vibrations on the surface of the pipe in the form of acceleration.

V. RESULTS AND DISCUSSION

In this section, we discuss the laboratory deployment results. To measure the performance of our leak detection solution using distributed Kalman filter algorithm, we simulated a leak at a single location along the pipeline, as shown in Figure 1. We used two sensor nodes, one placed 1 m before and the other placed 1 m after the leak position. In this deployment, the leak location is fixed, but we could vary the locations of the sensors to measure the effectiveness of our solution with different sensor positions. We carried out measurements for three scenarios: no Kalman filter implementation, local Kalman filter implementation and distributed Kalman filter implementation. For these experiments, we took traces of data collected from the two sensors, and compared the effectiveness of the approach, that is the effect on leak detection when the sensor nodes implemented distributed computing and the case where they implemented only local computing. In the case of local computing, the nodes run only a local Kalman filter for improving the accuracy of local measurements. In this scenario, each of the sensor node predicts the next state from the previous state and then collects local measurement which is then used to update the predicted state to obtain a more accurate local estimate. There is no exchange of local estimates between nodes in the case of local computing. However, with distributed computing, each of the sensor nodes first obtains its local estimate by performing local computing. In order to achieve a more accurate estimate, the node then shares its local estimate with its neighbor and also fuses its local estimate with the local estimate received from its neighbor. Figure 2 represents the data obtained from Node 00 (sensor after leak position) when the distributed Kalman filter algorithm was implemented on both sensor nodes while Figure 3 represents the results obtained when only a local Kalman filter was implemented on both sensor nodes without distributed computing.

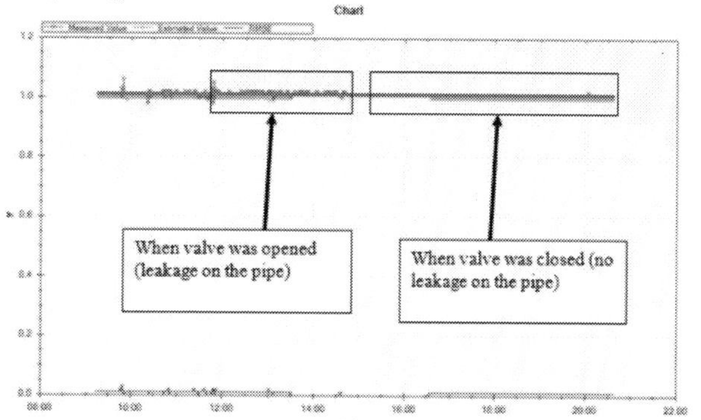

(a)

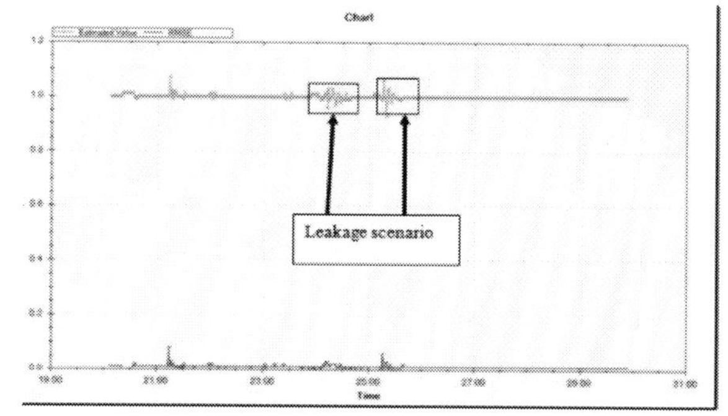

(b)

Figure 2. Estimated acceleration from Node 00 with measured acceleration (a) and without measured acceleration (b) when distributed Kalman filter was implemented

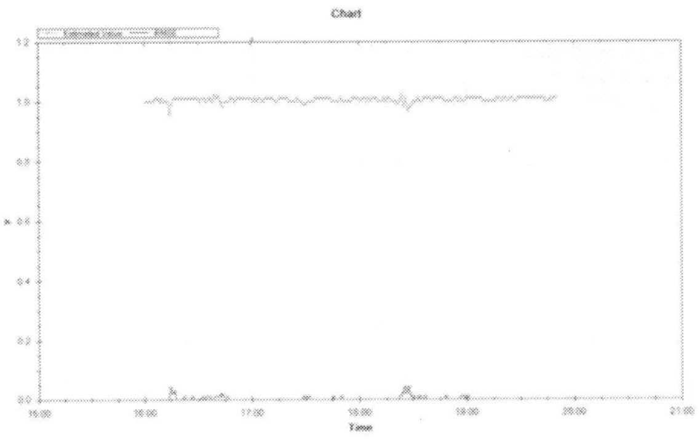

Figure 3. Estimated acceleration from Node 00 when distributed Kalman filter was not implemented

From preliminary results obtained in the field, the estimated acceleration of the pipe when there is no leakage is below 1.01 g while an estimated acceleration greater than 1.01 g corresponds to a leakage on the pipe. This is because when there is a leak, the flow turbulence increases and this is significantly responsible for the vibrations of the pipe walls, since the source of vibration is dissipated energy caused by turbulence.

Comparing the results in Figure 2 (where distributed Kalman filter is used) with those of Figure 3 (where only local Kalman filter is used), reveals that a leakage scenario can be isolated from a non-leakage scenario in the case where distributed Kalman filter is used. This increases the performance or reliability of detecting leaks and minimizes the rate of false alarms. However, it is difficult to distinguish a leakage scenario from a non-leakage scenario when only a local Kalman filter is used. The data displayed in Figure 3 has higher likelihood of producing false alarms since the estimated acceleration computed by the local Kalman filter is still having a lot of uncertainties. As shown in Figure 3, the estimated acceleration is fluctuating rapidly over short time periods. Applying the fixed threshold acceleration of 1.01 g will result in a higher rate of false alarms. This leads to multiple alarms and associated alarm clears as an alarm is declared each time the estimated acceleration fluctuates above the threshold value of 1.01 g and as it fluctuates back below the threshold, the alarm clears.

In our implementation, the Kalman filter performs 10 iterations to compute an optimal local estimate. When there is no leakage, the measured acceleration on the pipe surface is 1.00 g while the estimated acceleration on pipe surface after performing Kalman filtering is 0.99 g.

VI. CONCLUSION AND FUTURE WORK

This paper demonstrates the benefits of trading off long-distance transmission for computation. We propose a solution where local and distributed computing are used to improve the accuracy of anomaly detection without the need for long distance transmission to some central base station. We practically demonstrated this in detecting leaks on a water pipeline testbed.

In terms of sensor node architecture, unlike other works for WPM using WSNs available in literature, we developed a low-cost sensor node, which is feasible for deployment in developing countries, from cheap off-the-shelf commercial elements. The sensor node is composed of an ESP32 microcontroller as the processing unit, an nRF24L01+ transceiver module as the communication unit, and an LSM9DS1 IMU as the sensing unit.

In terms of leak detection algorithm, we use a distributed Kalman filter. Each node independently computes the optimal state estimate used for leak detection by running a local Kalman filter to obtain an accurate local estimate from local measurements and also fusing it with those of its close neighbors. As indicated in the results obtained, this improved on the accuracy of the vibrations measured on the surface of the pipes using the IMU and increased the reliability or performance of leak detection in WPM using WSNs without needing to transmit data over long distances to some central base station.

As future work, we intend to measure and establish an energy profile of the sensor node, where the energy consumption of each of the components that make up the sensor node is taken into consideration. This will enable us to estimate the energy consumption of the sensor node when it is in the idle mode, when it is in computing mode, and when it is transmitting. The end product will be a benchmark that can be used to evaluate the performance and energy consumption of different distributed algorithms. This will provide insights on how different distributed algorithms affect the performance and lifetime of a WSN. In addition, we are currently working on implementing the distributed Kalman filter algorithm as a multithreaded application on the ESP32 using the real-time operating system FreeRTOS [37]. We will investigate the effect of using FreeRTOS on the performance and energy consumption of the sensor node and also analyze the scenarios associated with consumption measures, in order to establish the energy performance of the proposed solution.

REFERENCES

[1] S. R. Jino Ramson and D. J. Moni, "Applications of Wireless Sensor Networks – A Survey" International Conference on Innovations in Electrical, Electronics, Instrumentation and Media Technology (ICEEIMT), Nov. 2017, pp 325-329.

[2] T. Devanaboyina, B. Pillalamarri, and R. M. Garimella, "Distributed Computation in Wireless Sensor Networks: Efficient Network Architectures and Applications in WSNs," International Journal of Wireless Networks and Broadband Technologies, vol. 4, no. 3, pp. 14-19, Jul. 2015.

[3] H. Huang, "Distributed Computing in Wireless Sensor Networks," in Encyclopedia of Mobile Computing and Commerce, pp. 202-206, 2007.

[4] P. Costa, L. Mottola, A. L. Murphy, and G. P. Picco, "TeenyLIME: transiently shared tuple space middleware for wireless sensor networks," In: Proceedings of the international workshop on middleware for sensor networks, ACM, pp. 43-48, 2006.

[5] F. Mieyeville, D. Navarro, and O. Bareille, "Autonomous Wireless Sensor Network for distributed active control," IEEE Vehicle Power and Propulsion Conference (VPPC), pp. 1-6, Dec. 2017.

[6] W. Zhang, B. Chen, H. Song, and L. Yu, "Distributed Fusion Estimation for Sensor Networks with Communication Constraints," 2016, doi: 10.1007/978-981-10-0795-8_1.

[7] D. Datla, X. Chen, T. Tsou, and S. Raghunandan, "Wireless Distributed Computing: A Survey of Research Challenges," Communications Magazine, IEEE, vol. 50, no. 1, pp. 144-152, 2012.

[8] M. A. Quintana-Suárez , D. Sánchez-Rodríguez, I. Alonso-González, and J. B. Alonso-Hernández, "A Low Cost Wireless Acoustic Sensor for Ambient Assisted Living Systems," Applied Sciences, vol. 7, no. 877, pp. 1-15, 2017.

[9] A.C. Sankaranarayanan, R. Chellappa, and R. G. Baraniu, "Distributed Sensing and Processing for Multi-Camera Networks," in Distributed Video Sensor Networks, London, Springer, 2011.

[10] A. R. Iyeswariya, R. M. Shamila, M. JayaLakshmi, K. Maharajan, and V. Sivakumar, "A study on Water Leakage Detection in buried plastic pipes using Wireless Sensor Networks," International Journal of Scientific & Engineering Research, vol. 3, no. 10, Oct. 2012.

[11] E. D. Pascale, I. Macaluso, A. Nag, M. Kelly, and L. Doyle, "The Network as a Computer: a Framework for Distributed Computing over IoT Mesh Networks," IEEE Internet of Things Journal, vol. 5, no. 3, pp. 2107-2119, 2018.

[12] M. Z. Abbas, K. A. Baker, M. Ayaz, and H. Mohamed, "Key Factors Involved in Pipeline Monitoring Techniques Using Robots and WSNs: Comprehensive Survey," Journal of Pipeline Systems Engineering and Practice·, 2018.

[13] L. Ribeiro, J. Sousa, A. S. Marques, and N. E. Simões, "Locating Leaks with TrustRank Algorithm Support," Water, vol. 7, pp. 1378-1401, 2015.

[14] K. B. Adedeji , Y. Hamam, B. T. Abe, A. and M. Abu-Mahfouz, "Towards Achieving a Reliable Leakage Detection and Localization Algorithm for Application in Water Piping Networks: An Overview," IEEE Access, pp. 20272 – 20285, 2017.

[15] C. Bell, "The World Bank and the International Water Association to Establish a Partnership to Reduce Water," World Bank, 2016. [Online]. Available: http://www.worldbank.org/en/news/press-release/2016/09/01/the-world-bank-and-the-international-water-association-to-establish-a-partnership-to-reduce-water-losses. [Accessed 03 September 2019].

[16] African Development Bank Group, "Africa Infrastructure Knowledge Program," 01 January 2016. [Online]. Available: http://www.afdb.org/en/. [Accessed 03 September 2019].

[17] Y. H. Blaise, "Suffering for water, suffering from water: access to drinking-water and associated health risks in Cameroon," J. Health Popul Nutr. Vol. 28, No. 5, pp. 424–435, 2010.

[18] M. Henrie, P. Carpenter, and R. E. Nicholas, Pipeline Leak Detection Handbook, Elsevier, Cambridge, MA 02139, United States, 2016.

[19] I. Stoianov, L. Nachman, S. Madden, T. Tokmouline, and M. Csai, "PIPENET: A Wireless Sensor Network for Pipeline Monitoring," 6th International Symposium on Information Processing in Sensor Networks, Apr. 2007.

[20] A. M. Sadeghioon, N. Metje, D. Chapman, and C. Anthony, "SmartPipes: Smart Wireless Sensor Networks for Leak Detection in Water Pipelines," J. Sens. Actuator Netw. Vol. 3, pp. 64-78, 2014.

[21] F. Karray, A. Garcia-Ortiz, M. W. Jmal, A. M. Obeid, and M. Abid. "EARNPIPE: A Testbed for Smart Water Pipeline Monitoring using Wireless Sensor Network," Computer Science, vol. 96, pp. 285 – 294, 2016.

[22] M. Ismail, R. A. Dziyauddin, and N.A. Ahmad. "Water pipeline monitoring system using vibration sensor", IEEE Conference on Wireless Sensors (ICWiSE), pp. 26-28, Oct. 2014.

[23] S. Kartakis, W. Yu, R. Akhavan, and J. A. McCann, "Adaptive Edge Analytics for Distributed Networked Control of Water Systems," First International Conference on Internet-of-Things Design and Implementation (IoTDI), Apr. 2016.

[24] G. Battistelli, L. Chisci, and D. Selvi, "A distributed Kalman filter with event-triggered communication and guaranteed stability," Automatica, vol. 93, pp. 75–82, 2018.

[25] H. Karl, and A. Willig, Protocols and Architectures Wireless Sensor Networks, John Wiley & Sons, 2005.

[26] Expressif Systems, "ESP32 SoC," [Online]. Available: https://www.espressif.com/en/products/hardware/esp32/overview. [Accessed 03 September 2019].

[27] F. Karray, M. W. Jmal, A. Garcia-Ortiz, M. Abid, and A. M. Obeid "A comprehensive survey on wireless sensor node hardware platforms," Computer Networks, vol. 144, p. 89–110, Oct. 2018.

[28] A. Maier, A. Sharp, and Y. Vagapov. "Comparative Analysis and Practical Implementation of the ESP32 Microcontroller Module for the Internet of Things," Internet Technologies and Applications, pp. 143-148, 2017.

[29] Nordic Semiconductor, —nRF24L01+ Single Chip 2.4GHz Transceiver Product Specification v1.0, September 2008, available at https://www.sparkfun.com/datasheets/Wireless/Nordic/nRF24L01P_Product_Specification_1.0, [Accessed 03 September 2019].

[30] H. Saha, S. Mandal, S. Mitra, S. Banerjee, and U. Saha, "Comparative Performance Analysis between nRF24L01+ and XBEE ZB Module Based Wireless Ad-hoc Networks", I. J. Computer Network and Information Security, vol. 7, pp. 36-44, 2017.

[31] STMicroelectronics, --- LSM9DS1 Datasheet, DocID025715 Rev 2, November 2014, available at https://www.st.com/resource/en/datasheet/DM00103319, [Accessed 03 September 2019].

[32] M. B. Rhudy , R. A. Salguero and K. Holappa, "International Journal of Computer Science & Engineering Survey (IJCSES) , vol. 8, no. 1, 2017.

[33] F. Karray, M. W. Jmal, and M. Abid, "High-performance Wireless Sensor Node Design for Water Pipeline Monitoring," in The Eleventh International Conference on Mobile Ubiquitous Computing, Systems, Services and Technologies, 2017.

[34] Y. He, S. Li, and Y. Zheng, "Distributed State Estimation for Leak Detection in Water Supply Networks"," IEEE/CAA Journal of Automatica Sinica, 2017.

[35] D. Marelli, M. Zamani, M. Fu, and B. Ninness, "Distributed Kalman filter in a network of linear systems," Systems & Control Letters, vol. 116, pp. 71–77, 2018.

[36] Z. Wu, M. Fu, Y. Xu, and R. Lu, "A distributed Kalman filtering algorithm with fast finite-time convergence for sensor networks" Automatica, vol. 95, pp. 63–72, 2018.

[37] O. Hahm, E. Baccelli, H. Petersen, and N. Tsiftes, "Operating Systems for Low-End Devices in the Internet of Things: A Survey," IEEE Internet of Things Journal, vol. 3, no. 1, pp. 720 - 734, 2016.

Simulating a Network:

An Approach for Connecting Multiple SystemC Simulations

Thomas W. Pieber, Fikret Basic, Thomas Ulz, and Christian Steger
Institute for Technical Informatics
Graz University of Technology
Graz, Austria
Email: {thomas.pieber, basic, thomas.ulz, steger}@tugraz.at

Abstract—**Nowadays, sensor networks are widely used. To create new hardware for these networks, simulations are used. These simulations help during the design of the sensor nodes by providing information about internal states, power usage, and expected lifetime. They are useful to design one piece of hardware, however they are cumbersome when multiple of such hardware simulation instances need to interact with each other. This paper explores the possibility of starting multiple instances of a hardware simulation and connecting these via a simulation of the environment they will be used in.**

Keywords–SystemC; Simulation; Parallel; Network.

I. Introduction

The concurrent development of hardware and software enables the accurate simulation of the behavior of a finished sensor node. Rather than focusing solely on the hardware simulation, languages such as SystemC can also calculate the software influences on the system. This is a necessary step towards the complete simulation of a network. To simulate the behavior of a network, multiple such sensor instances need to be simulated simultaneously. These virtual sensor nodes are then connected via a suitable environment simulation.

There are many solutions to the problem of simulating single pieces of hardware. Hardware Description Languages (HDLs) support the simulation of hardware on a low layer of abstraction. The hardware descriptions used in this kind of simulation typically enable the manufacturing of the hardware itself. This means that the description, and thus the simulation, of the device is very accurate. This accuracy comes with the cost of low performance. To simulate more complex systems, a higher layer of abstraction is needed. This increases the simulation speed but decreases the resulting accuracy. A HDL that supports multiple layers of abstraction, such as SystemC [1], can describe the interconnection of hardware components at a high layer of abstraction and, at the same time, keep most of the accuracy for the components themselves [2].

The simulation of a network of computing devices can be challenging. Most of the simulators available are either limited to the sole simulation of the interaction between the network components (e.g., [3]), or can just give rough estimations of the executing time on each component (e.g., [4]).

To be able to simulate a sensor network without sacrificing the accuracy requires the connection of a hardware simulation tool and some tool that performs the interaction between the sensor nodes. Pieber et al. [5][6] described an approach to connect one instance of a SystemC simulation to the Gazebo simulator, a tool that is able to simulate an environment for the sensor. We want to extend this approach by instantiating multiple sensors in the Gazebo simulation and connecting them in this environment.

To test the resulting performance change, a small-scale networked control system has been implemented. This system is then performing some data acquisition, forwarding the data through another network node and finally the data storage at a final sensor node. In contrast to the simulation created by Pieber et al. [5] where one SystemC instance is connected to the Gazebo simulation, this simulation connects multiple instances of SystemC simulations to the Gazebo environment.

The remainder of this paper describes this process. Section II briefly describes the background information and states the related work to this publication. In Section III, the design of our approach is described. The implementation of the necessary parts is described in Section IV. Section V highlights our findings. This publication concludes in Section VI. This section also states our thoughts of what can be done next.

II. Background and Related Work

As concurrent tasks are a vital part of any simulation, mechanisms to cope with this are introduced in every modelling language. There are three main approaches to deal with concurrency in simulations:

1) **Multi-instance-one-simulation** One simulation contains multiple instances of parallel tasks.
2) **One-instance-multi-simulation** One model only contains a single task. These tasks are then run in multiple simulations that communicate with each other.
3) **Multi-instance-multi-simulation** Each simulation contains multiple concurrent tasks. The tasks communicate within a simulation, the simulations communicate within themselves.

A simulation written in SystemC and Gazebo are simulations of the first type. SystemC simulations run its component modules quasi parallel using delta-cycles to reach a stable state. Then, the simulation time is advanced until the next triggered event happens. In the Gazebo simulator, the components are modeled via plugins. These plugins are called sequentially. When all components have been executed, the simulation time is advanced by one time increment and the process restarts.

A more powerful example of a SystemC simulation comprising of multiple instances of modules has been created by

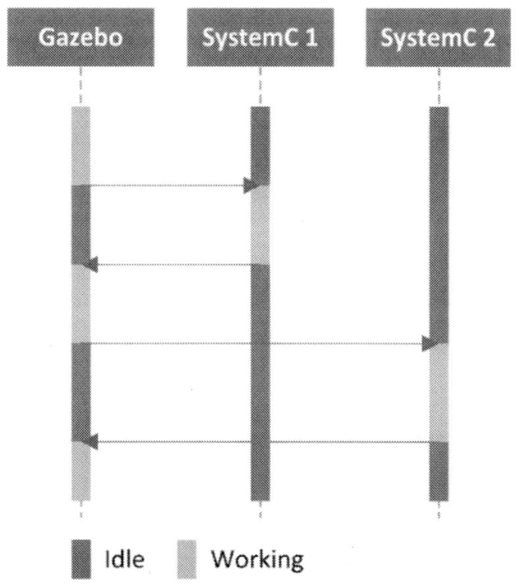

Figure 1. Performance problem using Gazebo and multiple SystemC instances.

Park et al. [7]. In this simulation, a smart house was simulated using SystemC. There, each electrical component has been modeled as a part of the complete simulation. These models are evaluated in parallel.

The combination of these two simulations results in a concurrent simulation of the third type. This is a simulation with multiple instances of different simulations, each containing multiple concurrent modules.

The process Pieber et al. [6] described in their work is intended to simulate one sensor node in an environment. This environment provides the sensor with stimuli that the sensor can work with. Furthermore, a communication channel is provided to communicate with the sensor and get feedback during the simulation time. In this approach, the Gazebo simulation is halted during the execution of one SystemC simulation. This results in a performance issue when using multiple SystemC instances. Figure 1 illustrates this. Here, one SystemC simulation blocks all other simulations. This results in an execution pattern suitable for a single processor core where only one simulation is being executed at a time. In this paper, we try to parallelize the SystemC simulations by introducing a mechanism that starts all SystemC simulation steps in parallel and waits for all to finish.

There are some proposed solutions to parallelize SystemC, such as [8]-[11]. These describe approaches that look for all executable SystemC modules and try to execute them in parallel. This results in a Type 2 concurrent simulation (One-instance-multi-simulation) as each executable model is treated as a single simulation. In these approaches, one large simulation is split into multiple concurrent simulations that are spread over the cores of one computer. In contrast to this, the approach described here uses multiple SystemC simulations and distributes them via a network. This method can spread the simulation on cores of the same machine, but also use additional computational resources of other computers in the network.

Schumacher et al. [9] presented an approach to simulate an Multi-Processor System on Chip (MPSoC). As their solution uses threads to achieve the parallelism, the solution is tied to a single host machine. While the authors claimed a significant performance improvement, it is already argued that this approach is not sufficient for a large sensor network simulation.

The approach of Sinha et al. [11] splits one SystemC simulation into multiple executable processes. In this approach, not only multiple cores or the Central Processing Unit (CPU) of one computer can be utilized, but also the Graphics Processing Unit (GPU).

Chopard et al. [12] propose a method to parallelize the SystemC kernel. In their approach, the researchers achieve a speedup comparable to the number of usable CPU cores.

The article of Jones [13] describes a more optimistic approach of parallelizing SystemC simulations. Jones also addresses the topic of race conditions that can occur when running such simulations in parallel. He also mentions that his technique of accelerating SystemC simulations is not suitable for existing simulations as large portions of code would need to be modified.

The possibility to accelerate SystemC simulations that rely on discrete events is discussed by Dömer et al. [14]. This team of researchers present a scheduler that spreads the runnable simulation nodes on the available CPUs.

Huang et al. [15] presented a SystemC library to handle the distribution of SystemC simulations. This approach is suited to work for multi-core machines as well as for a number of separate hosts. A downside of this approach is the limitation to functional and Transaction Level Modelling (TLM) simulations. Another disadvantage of this approach is the need for every SystemC simulation to handle its own communication with the rest of the simulation. Both of these issues are reflected on in our work by enabling SystemC simulations to be independent of the distribution architecture.

Another approach for simulating multiple computers in a network is used by Simics [3]. This simulator is built such that it can use multiple computers in a network to simulate the interaction of the systems. In this approach, the simulated network nodes are connected via a simulated network. This simulation can be used to simulate a computer network at a high level of abstraction. The integration of analogue signals (measurements of a sensor, or a very low level of abstraction) is not directly possible.

Clement et al. [16] coined the term Internet of Simulation. In their paper, the authors describe the need for heterogeneous simulation systems that can capture the complex nature of Cyber-Physical Systems (CPS). In their terminology, this paper describes a co-simulation for virtual engineering.

This paper is based on the publications of Pieber et al. [5][6]. It improves in the following details:

- **Concurrency:** The original approach uses one Gazebo plugin for each sensor in the environment. Each of these plugins directly creates a SystemC process and communicates with it. This entails that all SystemC processes are located on the same host machine. With the approach presented here, the SystemC instances are started before the main simulation. These simulation instances can be located on different host machines and communicate via a network to the main communication. The plugins in the main simulation communicate to a server plugin that handles the network traffic and connects the SystemC simulations to the intended plugins.

- **Modularity:** As the SystemC simulations are started before the main simulation, multiple different implementations of the same simulation can be connected to the same sensor plugin. This increases the modularity of the simulation as only few changes need to be made in order to exchange the SystemC simulations.

III. Design

To improve the design of Pieber et al. [6] we implemented a server-client structure to spread the simulations to multiple computers. Using this, only a single plugin (the server) connects the SystemC instances. This plugin then blocks the Gazebo simulation until all SystemC tasks are finished. Figure 2 shows the intended execution path. The Gazebo simulator performs the calculations that are necessary for the data transmission. The SystemC simulations receive the data and perform operations on the data. When the simulation steps of all SystemC instances are finished the Gazebo simulator can continue its operation.

In this design, all necessary data from Gazebo is generated during its time step. This information is gathered in the server plugin. The server plugin then forwards the information to the SystemC instances. While the SystemC simulations are performing the simulation step, the Gazebo simulation is halted. During the execution of the SystemC simulation, the generated data is transmitted to the Gazebo simulation. There the server plugin captures the data. When the simulation step is finished, the SystemC simulations are halted and the Gazebo simulation can continue. In this way, no information is lost between the simulations, and all simulations are synchronized at the end of the time steps. As the server starts all SystemC simulations and waits for all to finish, also the SystemC simulations are synchronized.

In this design, the server does not contain simulation relevant operations. It just connects the Gazebo representations of the sensors (sensor plugins) to the SystemC simulations. This server therefore acts as a gateway for the sensor plugins to the SystemC simulations which can be executed anywhere in the network.
The server plugin has three responsibilities:

- **Connecting** the correct SystemC simulation to the intended sensor plugin. This includes the identification of the connected SystemC simulations and the matching to the correct sensor plugin.
- **Passing data** between the sensor plugin and SystemC simulation.
- **Synchronizing** the simulations.

The server plugin runs a thread that listens for incoming connections from remote SystemC simulations. For each

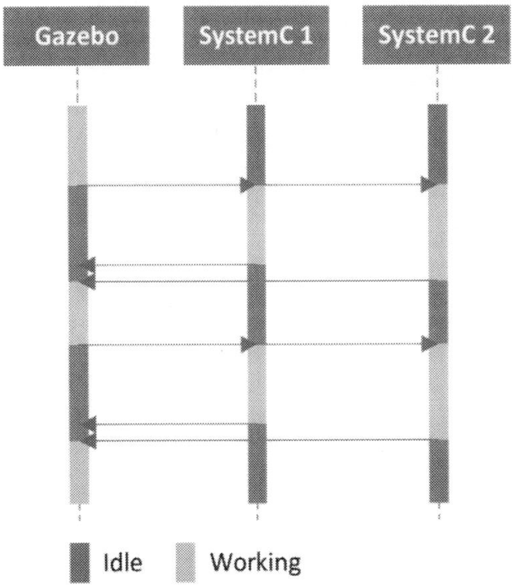

Figure 2. Improved handling scheme for multiple SystemC instances.

connecting simulation, a thread is created that handles the information exchange with the sensor plugin. Additionally, this thread forwards the information to the SystemC simulation and receives the resulting information. Figure 3 shows the top-level structure of the plugin server. The server listens for new SystemC connections and creates a worker thread for each connected simulation. Each worker thread manages the communication between the sensor plugin and the SystemC simulation. To handle the SystemC simulation and the synchronization of the simulations, the thread appends data about simulation states. In addition to all of that, the thread keeps information about the connection to the SystemC simulation. This is information about the Internet Protocol (IP)-address, the port number, the simulation identifier, and the last sent command to which the SystemC simulation has to react.

Each worker thread starts by initializing its own memory. This is followed by the initial checks of the SystemC simulation. These checks are performed by verifying an identifier. If the SystemC simulation can be used for the plugin, an initial configuration for the SystemC simulation is sent. When the initialization is finished, the SystemC simulation needs to respond with its state. For each simulation step, the data for the SystemC simulation is gathered by the sensor plugin. This data includes the change of sensor data, information about incoming messages, and changes of external energy sources (for energy harvesting). This gathered information is then forwarded to the server plugin and the correct worker thread. The worker thread packs the data and adds additional information. This additional information includes changes of simulation states, status information, or commands to the interface on the SystemC side. When the server plugin is being executed, all information is forwarded to the SystemC simulations by the worker threads. Until all worker threads have received the signal that their SystemC simulation has finished its execution, the Gazebo simulation is blocked. During the execution of the SystemC simulation, data that is destined for the Gazebo simulation is sent to the worker thread. This

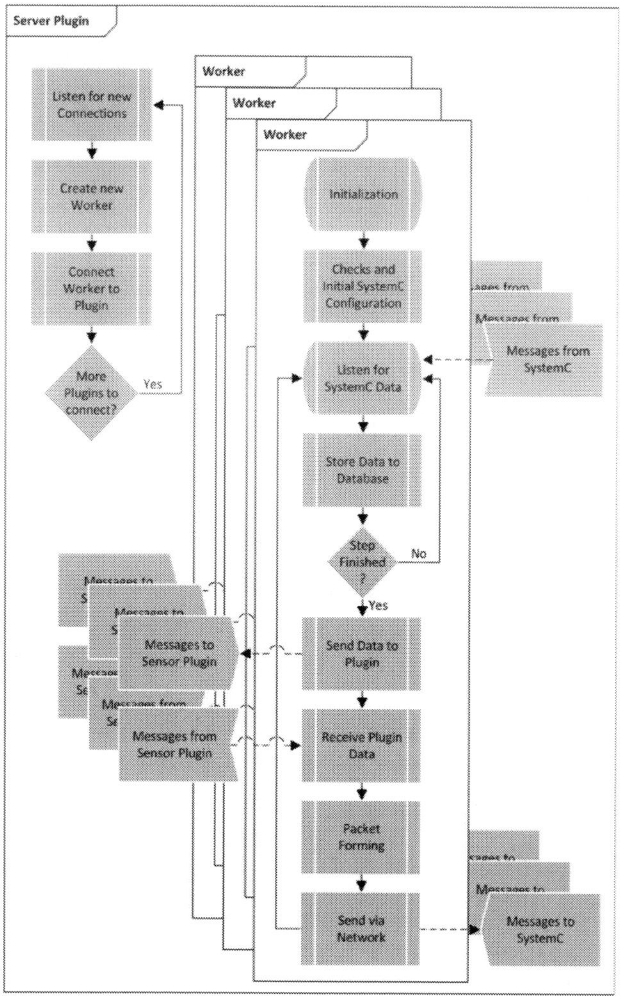

Figure 3. Top-level structure of the server plugin.

information is stored until the simulation proceeds. At the end of the SystemC simulation step, a signal is sent to the Gazebo simulation, informing the worker about the simulation status. If all SystemC simulations have stopped their execution, the Gazebo simulation can proceed. Now the stored data is transferred to the sensor plugins. The plugins can access the data in the next Gazebo time step.

With the use of the parallel design, the computation of the network should have a similar performance as the sole computation of the slowest node in the network. Thus, when simulating similar nodes, the performance gain should be related to the number of parallel nodes.

To test this hypothesis, multiple tests are designed:

1) **All nodes the same - single** This test simulates one sensor node performing measurements.
2) **All nodes the same - sequential** This test comprises of three identical nodes, each performing the same measurements.
3) **All nodes the same - parallel** The three nodes are run using the parallel computation design.
4) **Networked system - single** In this test each of three different nodes is simulated on its own. The data for nodes two and three is computed by node one and given as input for the simulation.
5) **Networked system - sequential** This tests simulates all three nodes in the network using the sequential approach. The data is generated and encrypted in node one, transmitted over node two, and decrypted and stored in node three.
6) **Networked system - parallel** The three nodes of the networked system are simulated using the parallel simulation design.

The first three tests act as a baseline test for the hypothesis that the simulation performance of the complete simulation is comparable to the simulation of the slowest node.

Test 1 simulates each node separately. As the three nodes are identical the simulation time should be equal as well. Test 2 uses the old connection via Gazebo to test the simulation speed of the sequential case. Each SystemC simulation is identical. As they are executed sequentially, the simulation time should be roughly the sum of the single simulations - in this time three times the duration of Test 1. Test 3 uses the new parallel design to connect the sensors. As all simulations are calculated in parallel, the execution time should be similar to the simulation of one node of Test 1.

The second three tests use three different nodes. One that gathers data, one that transmits the data to the last one, and one that receives and stores the data. The data is continuously transmitted and sent across the nodes. This way all nodes are active all the time (except for the first message). Otherwise, the test would limit the execution to the sequential case.

Test 4 uses precomputed data to test the functionality of each node individually. Each node is simulated separately. Test 5 combines the three nodes using the old connection via Gazebo to test the sequential case. Test 6 uses the new parallel design to connect the nodes.

The resulting simulation represents the data flow between the sensor nodes on the environment scale. Furthermore, as the sensor nodes themselves are simulated using SystemC, the data processing on each sensor node is being calculated.

IV. IMPLEMENTATION

The most notable change to the design of Pieber et al. [6] is that a new plugin has been implemented that performs the communication tasks. In their publication, every sensor plugin communicates with the corresponding SystemC instance. We have implemented another plugin that performs the communication tasks for all sensor plugins. A concept for our implementation can be seen in Figure 4. There, the *sensor plugins* send their data to the *plugin server*. This server handles the communication with all *SystemC* instances. When the SystemC simulations have returned data, the *plugin server* forwards the information to the *sensor plugins* in the next time step.

The communication between the server and the SystemC clients is based on the concept described by Pieber et al. [6]. An additional top-level structure is added to the EXtensible

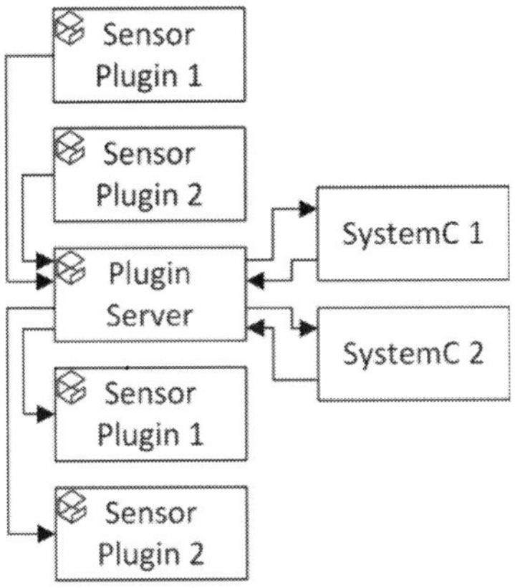

Figure 4. Concept for transmitting data between the sensor plugins, the plugin server, and the SystemC simulations.

Markup Language (XML)-formatted data. This structure specifies the type of message and the according payload. There are two different types of messages that can be sent between the server and client:

1) **Command:** This type specifies a message from the server that the simulation needs as input data. This can be a sensor value, incoming messages, or instructions to change the simulation status (finish the simulation, change the simulation step size).
2) **Status:** The status message can be sent from either side of the communication. If it is sent from the server, it can ask for the identification of the SystemC simulation, request information about the simulation status, or inform the SystemC simulation about its own simulation status. A status message from the client side can contain requested information, or signal the server that the simulation step is finished.

The complete communication structure between the server and a client can be seen in Figure 5. The Gazebo simulation starts the server. The server blocks the simulation until all SystemC clients are connected. After that, the server receives the commands to send from the sensor plugins. This information is relayed to the appropriate client. With this message the client is given the command to start the simulation step. Until all SystemC simulations have finished their step, the server blocks the Gazebo simulation. When all clients are ready, the Gazebo simulation can be resumed. This results in another message to the SystemC client. If the Gazebo simulation is to be ended, the server disconnects from the SystemC client. This triggers the reset of the SystemC simulation. As the simulation system is built to run in a network, simulation clients other than the intended ones could connect to the server. To enable the server to check if the SystemC simulation is required in the current Gazebo simulation run, an ID is requested from the client. This ID specifies the type of simulation. Based on this, the server can decide whether the client should be accepted or rejected. Accepted clients are then logically connected to the appropriate sensor plugin.

During the execution of the SystemC tasks, the plugin server blocks the Gazebo simulation. When all SystemC instances have returned their signal that the simulation step has been finished, the plugin server resumes by distributing the received information to the sensor plugins.

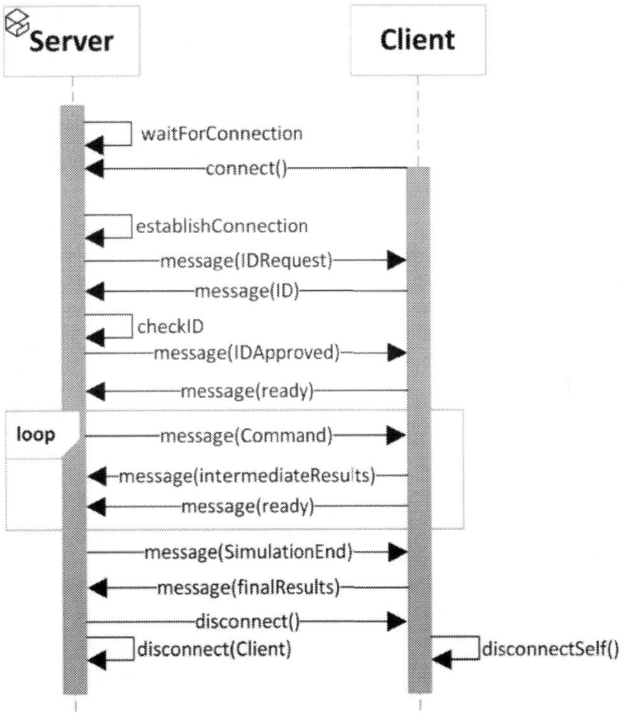

Figure 5. Messages between the server and one SystemC client.

TABLE I. Durations of the test simulations

Test Nr.	Node Nr.	Duration
1	1,2,3	~ 15.34 sec
2	1,2,3	48.0487 sec
3	1,2,3	16.7513 sec
4	1	153.7706 sec
4	2	10.6859 sec
4	3	120.8714 sec
5	1,2,3	284.6381 sec
6	1,2,3	156.1416 sec

V. Results

The results of the experiments introduced in Section III are listed in Table I.

These six experiments show that the final execution time is slightly larger than the longest component simulation. It furthermore shows that the simulation time, compared to the sequential case, can be multiplied with a factor of $\sim \frac{1}{N}$ where N is the number of parallel SystemC simulations where each simulation uses approximately the same amount of time. For simulations that differ in their simulation duration, the final duration is slightly longer than for the slowest simulation. This system therefore provides an extensible and flexible basis to add additional SystemC simulations. The Gazebo server remains independent of any added SystemC simulations while also the client side keeps individual SystemC models separated.

As an additional improvement can be seen that the simulations need not be calculated on the same computer as the Gazebo simulation. Normally, the Gazebo host system would need additional resources to run the Gazebo system and the SystemC simulation. The server-client structure allows the SystemC simulations to be spread over a network. Thus, the amount of possible parallel simulations is not limited to the resources on one machine.

As a limitation to this system, the general network overhead should be mentioned. As the commands and data are sent over a network, additional data is added by the system. This adds to the data size that is to be sent. Furthermore, the data needs to be packed and unpacked at either side of the communication, increasing the latency. This should be considered, when designing the simulation.

VI. Conclusion and Future Work

This paper describes a method to connect multiple SystemC simulations of sensor nodes to a network. These sensor nodes are placed in a virtual environment, simulated with the Gazebo simulator, and communicate via this environment with each other. As the Gazebo simulator processes its components sequentially, the final simulation is inefficient. To improve the performance of this simulation, a server-client structure is proposed and implemented. This connects the server on the Gazebo side to the SystemC simulations via network sockets. The server can then unite the individual calls to the SystemC simulations and start all simulations in parallel. In contrast to the simulation duration being the sum of all component simulations, the duration of the simulation using this structure is only slightly longer than the longest component simulation.

In the current form, the simulation results can only be evaluated when the simulation is finished. Due to the lengthy simulations, this is inefficient. Therefore, live signal plotting can be implemented. Using this, the simulation operator can spot errors in the simulation early and stop the execution prematurely. This would then reduce the simulation time for erroneous runs significantly.

Acknowledgments

This project has received funding from the Electronic Component Systems for European Leadership Joint Undertaking under grant agreement No 692480. This Joint Undertaking receives support from the European Union's Horizon 2020 research and innovation programme and Germany, Netherlands, Spain, Austria, Belgium, Slovakia.

IoSense is funded by the Austrian Federal Ministry of Transport, Innovation and Technology (BMVIT) under the program "ICT of the Future" between May 2016 and April 2019. More information https://iktderzukunft.at/en/

References

[1] Accelera, "SystemC," http://accellera.org/downloads/standards/systemc, 2000. Last accessed on mar 18, 2019.

[2] P. R. Panda, "SystemC - A modelling platform supporting multiple design abstractions," in *Proceedings of the 14th international symposium on Systems synthesis - ISSS*, pp. 75–80, Association for Computing Machinery (ACM), 2001.

[3] P. S. Magnusson, M. Christensson, J. Eskilson, D. Forsgren, G. Hallberg, J. Hogberg, F. Larsson, A. Moestedt, and B. Werner, "Simics: A full system simulation platform," *Computer*, vol. 35, no. 2, pp. 50–58, 2002.

[4] V. Shnayder, M. Hempstead, B.-r. Chen, G. W. Allen, and M. Welsh, "Simulating the Power Consumption of Large-scale Sensor Network Applications," in *Proceedings of the 2Nd International Conference on Embedded Networked Sensor Systems*, SenSys '04, (New York, NY, USA), pp. 188–200, ACM, 2004.

[5] T. W. Pieber, T. Ulz, and C. Steger, "SystemC Test Case Generation with the Gazebo Simulator," in *Proceedings of the 7th International Conference on Simulation and Modeling Methodologies, Technologies and Applications - Volume 1: SIMULTECH*, pp. 65–72, INSTICC, SciTePress, 2017.

[6] T. W. Pieber, T. Ulz, and C. Steger, "Using Gazebo to Generate Use Case Based Stimuli for SystemC," in *International Conference on Simulation and Modeling Methodologies, Technologies and Applications*, pp. 241–256, Springer, 2017.

[7] S. Park, H. Kim, H. Moon, J. Heo, and S. Yoon, "Concurrent Simulation Platform for Energy-Aware Smart Metering Systems," *IEEE transactions on Consumer Electronics*, vol. 56, no. 3, pp. 1918–1926, 2010.

[8] p. Ezudheen, P. Chandran, J. Chandra, B. P. Simon, D. Ravi, *et al.*, "Parallelizing SystemC Kernel for Fast Hardware Simulation on SMP Machines," in *Proceedings of the 2009 ACM/IEEE/SCS 23rd Workshop on Principles of Advanced and Distributed Simulation*, pp. 80–87, IEEE Computer Society, 2009.

[9] C. Schumacher, R. Leupers, D. Petras, and A. Hoffmann, "parSC: synchronous parallel systemc simulation on multi-core host architectures," in *2010 IEEE/ACM/IFIP International Conference on Hardware/Software Codesign and System Synthesis (CODES+ ISSS)*, pp. 241–246, IEEE, 2010.

[10] A. Mello, I. Maia, A. Greiner, and F. Pecheux, "Parallel Simulation of SystemC TLM 2.0 Compliant MPSoC on SMP Workstations," in *Proceedings of the Conference on Design, Automation and Test in Europe*, pp. 606–609, European Design and Automation Association, 2010.

[11] R. Sinha, A. Prakash, and H. D. Patel, "Parallel simulation of mixed-abstraction SystemC models on GPUs and multicore CPUs," in *17th Asia and South Pacific Design Automation Conference*, pp. 455–460, IEEE, Jan. 2012.

[12] B. Chopard, P. Combes, and J. Zory, "A Conservative Approach to SystemC Parallelization," in *International conference on computational science*, pp. 653–660, Springer, 2006.

[13] S. Jones, "Optimistic Pparallelisation of SystemC," *Universite Joseph Fourier: MoSiG DEMIPS, Tech. Rep*, 2011.

[14] R. Dömer, W. Chen, X. Han, and A. Gerstlauer, "Multi-Core Parallel Simulation of System-Level Description Languages," in *Proceedings of the 16th Asia and South Pacific Design Automation Conference*, pp. 311–316, IEEE Press, 2011.

[15] K. Huang, I. Bacivarov, F. Hugelshofer, and L. Thiele, "Scalably distributed SystemC simulation for embedded applications," in *2008 International Symposium on Industrial Embedded Systems*, pp. 271–274, IEEE, 2008.

[16] S. Clement, D. W. McKee, R. Romano, J. Xu, J. Lopez, and D. Battersby, "The Internet of Simulation: Enabling Agile Model Based Systems Engineering for Cyber-Physical Systems," in *2017 12th System of Systems Engineering Conference (SoSE)*, pp. 1–6, IEEE, 2017.

Improving the FLoRa Simulation Framework for the Performance Evaluation of IoT Scenarios

Jose-Manuel Martinez-Caro†, Maria-Dolores Cano
Department of Information Technologies and Communication
Universidad Politécnica de Cartagena
Cartagena, Spain
email: {josem.martinezcaro, mdolores.cano}@upct.es

Abstract— **In the last years, Low-Power Wide Area Network (LPWAN) technologies have increased their presence. Their main characteristic is covering large areas with limited resources. One of the greatest exponents in LPWAN is the entire system composed by Long-Range (LoRa) and (LoRaWAN). LoRa offers an easy deployment, a low-power consumption, a wide-coverage, and a high performance, although it also has several constraints such as a low Data-Rate (DR), a duty-cycle restriction (1%), and a limited application for real-time services. In this paper, we improve the Framework for LoRa (FLoRa) network simulation framework using open-source tools and the programming languages C++ and Python. The incorporated options allow a better adaptation of the simulation to users' requirements (topology, network conditions, or typical LoRa setting parameters, such as Spreading Factor (SF), Transmission Power (TP), Coding Rate (CR), Bandwidth (BW), or Carrier Frequency (CF), among others). As an example, we show the performance of a simulated air-quality monitoring system deployed using LoRa/LoRaWAN with a real dataset. System performance is evaluated in terms of several quality metrics. By using simulation tools like the one we present in this work, IoT (Internet of Things) networks and services can be tested and evaluated in advance, facilitating a better planning of future real deployments.**

Keywords- IoT; LPWAN; LoRa; simulation; OMNeT++; FLoRa Framework.

I. Introduction

The Internet of Things (IoT) concept is described as a dense, large-scale, open and dynamic ecosystem of social-technical entities and applications [1]. This recent concept has shaken the network up with new devices and systems, building a more heterogeneous network, where the interconnection between devices and systems to transmit and receive data is simpler [2]. These data will be further processed to provide information and make decisions. Moreover, IoT will allow an exponential increase of connected devices to the network, rising to almost 31 billion by 2020 and more than 75 billion by 2025 [3].. It will suppose an enormous economic injection to the technology market [3]. IoT is present in many application fields, such as Smart-Home, Smart-City, Industry 4.0, Smart-Grid, etc. [4]. This technology is still in a research and development phase, in spite of the forthcoming massive deployment in short-medium term [5].

IoT features perfectly match with Low-Power Wireless-Area-Network (LPWAN) technologies, which stand out for their resource efficiency, i.e., low-power transmission [6]. IoT and LPWAN share several features such as low-cost, low-power, high-performance, wide-coverage, low Data-Rate (DR), and fast-arrangement, where dense-device deployments could be done in a determined area connected to one or multiple gateways. Over rural areas, LPWAN could achieve communication distances around 30 kilometers between emitter and receptor [7], which means a great enhancement compared to Wireless Local Area Network (WLAN) [8] or Wireless Sensor Networks (WSN) [9]. In addition, LPWAN technologies consume less energy in comparison with cellular networks (2G, 3G, 4G). On the other hand, LPWAN is not suitable for all services and operations because it only sends light and infrequent frames given the limited data rate imposed to fulfill the duty cycle restriction which must not exceed 1% of the time over the Industrial, Scientific and Medical (IMS) band (EU: 868MHz and 433MHz; USA: 915MHz and 433MHz). LoRa/LoRaWAN [10], Weightless [11], NWave [12], Telensa [13], Random Phase Multiple Acces (RPMA) [14], Sigfox [15], and Narrow Band-IoT (NB-IoT) [16] are some of the multiple examples of LPWAN.

One of the LPWAN technologies with a higher popularity is LoRa/LoRaWAN due to its performance. In this work, we present the improvements done in a simulation software to evaluate the performance of LoRa/LoRaWAN networks and services. The modifications are done using different libraries and frameworks at low-level. The base of the simulation tool is the Framework for LoRa (FLoRa) [17] and OMNeT++ [18]. Specifically, our contributions are:

1. FLoRa implements a simplified version of the Okumura-Hata model. However, it is not accurate because it is an approximation based on linear regression whose outcomes do not match the results obtained in the related scientific literature. We introduce a more precise implementation of the Okumura-Hata wireless propagation model.

2. Automatic assignment of some LoRa parameters for static LoRa nodes. We propose a new simple algorithm to automatically set Spreading Factor (SF) and Transmission Power (TP) for each LoRa node according to the LoRa end-nodes location in relation to the LoRa gateway (LoRaGW) position.

3. Introduction of security mechanisms in LoRa. We include encryption/decryption and digital signature in the

communication using Counter Mode (CTR) and the Cipher-based Authentication Code (CMAC) mechanisms, respectively. Both methods are based on Advanced Encryption Standard (AES).

4. Performance evaluation tasks. Using our new implementation, it is possible to change the simulation environment and automatically adapt the parameters to this simulation. After a sample period (Teval), the simulator computes several quality components from numerous quality metrics, namely, Quality of Data (QoD), Quality of Information (QoI), Quality of user Experience (QoE), and Quality-Cost (QC). As an example, we briefly present the performance of a simulated air-quality monitoring system deployed using LoRa/LoRaWAN with a real dataset. An example will be shown under a rural environment, allowing an efficient performance evaluation.

The rest of the paper is organized as follows. In Section 2, we briefly describe LoRa/LoRaWAN and report an overview of the state-of-the-art in computer simulation tools for LoRa. Section 3 describes the software used as the basis for this work. Section 4 details the improvements that we have incorporated and their advantages, with an example of the performance evaluation outcomes. The paper ends summarizing the most important results of this work.

II. Related Works

A. LoRa/LoRaWAN

In a typical LoRa/LoRaWAN deployment (see Figure 1), there are three main devices: LoRa end-nodes, which acquire data from sensors at the application layer (from a simulation perspective) and send these data using LoRa physical layer; one or more LoRaGW that receive LoRa frames and cast them to be forwarded through a wired network; and one or more Network Servers, usually in the cloud, which will process the received data and are likely in charge of decision-making.

LoRa physical-layer uses Chirp Spread Spectrum (CSS) modulation over the Industrial, Scientific and Medical (ISM) frequency band which varies according to the region. Europe uses 868MHz whilst USA adopts 915MHz, though 433MHz is common in both regions. To gain resilience to interference and noise, LoRa spreads a narrowband signal over a wider channel bandwidth [4] and the sensibility of the receiver is 19.5 dB below the noise floor. There are multiple parameters that characterize LoRa communication between LoRa end-nodes and LoRaGW: Spreading Factor (SF), Transmission Power (TP), Carrier Frequency (CF), Coding Rate (CR), and Bandwidth (BW). First, SF varies from 7 to 12 (both included). SF define the coverage area, where higher SF values achieve higher ranges but with lower Data-Rate (DR). Second, TP ranges theoretically from -4dBm to 20dBm. It sets the intensity that LoRa end-nodes use to transmit LoRa data frames to the LoRaGW. Observe that the higher SF and TP, the larger the coverage area. Third, CF is the middle frequency in steps of 61Hz within the range according to the region. Fourth, CR provides security against interferences, where higher values provide higher protection (4/5, 4/6, 4/7 and 4/8) [19]. BW is the frequency width in the transmission band and the wider BW is, the higher DR, though sensibility is lower. Lastly, Time on Air (ToA) is the time to transmit a frame from a LoRa end-node to the LoRaGW and depends on SF and BW, being opposite to the DR parameter. The technology has three degrees of diversity (time, frequency, and SF) [4]. The communication between LoRa end-nodes and LoRaGW can be unidirectional or bidirectional. Unicast, multicast, and broadcast are the three types of communication addressing available in LoRa networks. The duty-cycle is limited and should be lower than 1% of the time, having a high repercussion on the maximum transfer-rate. Depending on the application, this constraint makes this technology inappropriate for many services that require constant data transmission. Some authors propose the implementation of algorithms such as Adaptive Data-Rate (ADR) [20], Distributed Coordination Functions (DCF) particularly Carrier Sense Multiple Access (CSMA) [21], and Channel Activity Detection (CAD) [22][23], with the aim of managing link parameters and getting adequate network processes, providing medium access control mechanisms as CSMA and detecting the LoRa preamble on the channel with maximum power efficiency, respectively.

On the other hand, LoRaWAN [10] specifies the architecture, layers, and protocols operating over LoRa. Mesh or star are the two possible network architectures. There are three LoRa end-node classes (A, B and C), all classes observing the duty-cycle. Class A may open a collecting window to receive acknowledgments or new messages after a specific time lapse. Class B adds scheduled received windows to class A and class C keeps the receive window open at any time. The Network Server deletes duplicate packets if multiples gateways are deployed and redirect the packet to the corresponding Network Server. If the application servers exist, then the Network Server will send the information to them.

B. Simulation tools for LoRa/LoRaWAN

Computer simulators are complete tools to replicate real network operation without the need of acquiring hardware, but programming skills are required to define simulation conditions with a blow of code. Simulators are also useful to test large networks with hundreds or thousands of devices on the network that are too costly in time (by placing and programing) and expenses [24]. For instance, the study done in [25] models the LoRa network efficiency and demonstrates the exponential increase of packet drops with the raising of devices due to interferences in a small area and LoRaWAN access methods. Some well-known network simulators are OMNeT++, NS3 [26], NetSim [27], SimPy [28], and OPNET [29], among others. Moreover, multiple frameworks and libraries are available to be imported such as FLoRa Framework. FLoRa allows recreating a LoRa network scenario under desirable conditions using the OMNeT++ simulator and the INET framework. More details about FLoRa are given in the next section.

Cooja framework is another simulation tool that runs programs to simulate and evaluate the performance of different networks, such as WSN or IoT-based projects such

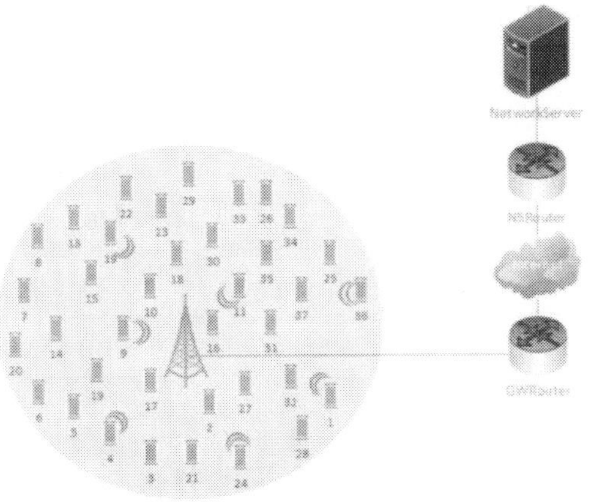

Figure 1. LoRa network and backbone network.

as LoRa using Cooja [24]; it is not a specific framework for LoRa networks though. One of the strengths of Cooja is its simulations taking into account the devices' energy consumption. Cooja is open-source and uses C programming language. It includes low-power protocols to define the simulation settings and uses SimPy to carry out the simulation enabling a graphical interface.

On the other hand, LoRaSim is a discrete event simulator implemented in a 2D scenario. It also uses SimPy to place LoRa end-nodes and LoRa sinks. This framework sets the LoRa parameters described previously and packets payload. LoRaSim uses Semtech SX1301 as the LoRa reference module compatible with Semtech SX1272/SX1276 (used in the FLoRa Framework), which is able to receive 8 concurrent orthogonal signals. Additionally, LoRaSim includes two evaluation metrics: Data Extraction Rate (DER), the ratio of received to transmitted messages over a period of time and Network Energy Consumption (NEC), as the energy spent by the LoRa end-node to successfully achieve the LoRa sink. NEC depends mainly on the transceiver state and time per state, and it should be minimum to extend as much as possible the batteries life of the devices. LoRaSim is open-source and requires additional libraries, e.g., Matplotlib, SimPy, and Numpy, but it has not a graphical interface. Finally, it includes several examples and low-power protocols implementations. Table I summarizes the most important characteristics of the simulation tools for LoRa environments.

III. Baseline Software

We use open-source tools available online to implement the simulator. These resources allow the user to develop a complete LoRa network simulation environment adaptive to any required scenario, getting an exhaustive performance evaluation of the designed topology. The baseline tools used in this work are: OMNeT++, INET Framework, FLoRa Framework, and Crypto++ [30].

A. OMNeT++

OMNeT++ IDE uses Eclipse [31] as the main developer platform and enhances it with new functions such as new editors, views, wizards, and so on. It allows users to create new and/or re-configure existing models using Network Description (NED) language, and configuration files (.ini). Then, the simulator evaluates the performance taking into account the obtained results. All of this is using C++ programming language, git integration, and other open-source tools and components. NED files define and edit the model graphically or by text. Both options are able to create compound modules, channels, and other component classes, as well as other object features. On the other hand, the ini file provides the parameters to adapt and configure models to the simulation, and as the NED files, is edited graphically or by text. An ini file recognizes all NED components from the top-level module to the last inherited module, being possible to define new parameters different to the default ones in all existing modules. Moreover, ini files enable users to define different scenarios according to the set parameters or random number seed.

More than one process can be run at the same time, so the building process is faster. While the simulation process runs in a new window, the user can continue developing the program due to this parallel operation. Once the simulator has finished, the results are preserved into a vector (as a collection of all intermediate results) and scalar files. The default Integrated Development Environment (IDE) or other external tools (e.g. Python) are available to the analysis of the results.

B. INET Framework

New frameworks can be added to OMNeT++ to provide new capabilities to the simulator. Particularly, INET includes agents, protocols, and many other models to create, redefine, or certify new protocols or scenarios. The supplied models in INET are for physical, link, network, transport, and application communication layers for different types of communication networks such as wired, wireless, ad-hoc, or WSN. INET bases its operation on message exchanges between modules.

TABLE I. Comparison of LoRa Simulation Tools

Features	**Simulation Tools**		
	FLoRa Framework	***Cooja Framework***	***LoRaSim***
Base Simulator	OMNeT++	Contiki OS RIOT OS	Python
Programming Language	C++	C	Python
Additional Frameworks	INET	SimPy	Matplotlib SimPy Numpy
Graphical Interface	Yes	Yes	No
Software Licence	Open-source	Open-source	Open-source
Power Awareness	Yes	Yes	Yes
Low-Power protocols	Yes	Yes	Yes
Examples	Yes	Yes	Yes
Last Version	0.8	3.0	0.2.1

C. FLoRa Framework

As INET, FLoRa is a specific framework to test LoRa/LoRaWAN networks. It enables physical and link layer evaluation, defining one (or more) gateways in the network where end-nodes will send data frames to, supporting bi-directional communication, defining the path for messages from source to destination (LoRa end-nodes to Network Server), and estimating the energy consumed by LoRa end-devices. FLoRa sets the main LoRa/LoRaWAN parameters, namely, SF, CF, BW, CR, and TP, which influence the communication coverage and the probability of data frames collision. As LoRa transmission uses the wireless interface, a frame is received correctly if the received power (which depends mainly on SF and TP) is higher than the sensitivity of the LoRaGW. The framework also estimates the energy consumption of each LoRa node according to both the time spent by the LoRa radio module in a specific state (transmit, receive, sleep, and off) and the TP value. Semtech SX1272/73 datasheet provides the consumptions for each state with a supply voltage of 3.3V.

Lastly, a typical deployment is not usually only composed of LoRa end-nodes and LoRaGW. As an example, we usually include in our simulations a backbone network behind the LoRaGW to reach a Network Server (Figure 1). In our case, once the LoRaGW receives a LoRa frame, it encapsulates the frame into an EthernetIIFrame and forwards it to the Network Server using the TCP/IP protocol stack, particularly, User Datagram Protocol (UDP) messages. This part is mainly simulated using the INET modules explained previously. Network Server will discard duplicate packets if the same packet is received by multiple LoRaGWs.

D. Crypto++

Crypto++ is an open-source library based on C++ programming language that includes algorithms for ciphering, message authentication codes, hash generators, public-key cryptosystems, etc. Crypto++ implements multiples methods and schemes such as Diffie-Hellman, Advanced Encryption Standard (AES), RSA, Elliptic Curve Cryptography (ECC), and Digital Signature Algorithm (DSA), among others [30].

IV. Novel Incorporated Tools

This section describes the improvements and modifications that we have incorporated into the simulation software, with the aim of having available an easy to use performance evaluation tool for IoT services and networks based on LoRa/LoRaWAN.

A. Wireless Propagation Model

The FLoRa framework includes an Okumura-Hata implementation. From the FLoRa documentation, it is known that this implemented wireless propagation model is based on an approximation, using a linear regression with three factors, namely, K1, K2, and the distance between a LoRa end-node and the LoRaGW. The first two factors, K1 and K2, take the default values of 127.5 and 35.2, respectively. However, this method is not precise to estimate the Free-Space Path Loss (FSPL), since it reaches a maximum distance of around 6 km (as observed in extensive simulations). It can be verified in the related literature that this distance is too small for this technology [7][32]. Additionally, with this implementation of the Okumura-Hata model, it is not possible to choose one of the three available environments that the original Okumura-Hata provides, namely, rural, sub-urban or urban.

Consequently, we introduce a new Okumura-Hata model implementation in FLoRa to accurately estimate the FSPL in the simulator, taking into account those three possible environments (rural, sub-urban, and urban). FSPL is lower in rural scenarios and higher in urban environments, because in the former there might not be buildings that interfere with the electromagnetic wave propagation, contrary to the urban environment. The main objective of using this type of propagation models is to represent properly the effect of the physical layer in the simulations, providing an environment as real as possible and discarding the use of less accurate regression methods. This new model implementation is defined by (1) [33] and uses more rigorous factors such as frequency (f), the distance between a LoRa end-node and the LoRaGW (d), LoRa end-node height (hm), and LoRaGW height (hb) [33].

$$\begin{aligned} a(h_m) &= 3.2(\log_{10}(11.75 \cdot h_m)^2 - 4.97 \\ L_{urban} &= 69.55 + 26.16\log_{10}(f) - 13.82\log_{10}(h_b) - a(h_m) \\ &\quad + (44.9 - 6.55\log_{10}(h_b)) \cdot \log_{10}(d_m) \\ L_{sub\text{-}urban} &= L_{urban} - 2(\log_{10}(f/28))^2 - 5.4 \\ L_{rural} &= L_{urban} - 4.78(\log_{10}(f))^2 + 18.33\log_{10}(f) - 40.94 \end{aligned} \quad (1)$$

B. Initial settings parameters in LoRa

Additionally, we use Python: a general-purpose programming language to generate automatically an ini file that sets the configuration parameters according to the desired conditions, for instance: the environment (rural, suburban, urban), number of LoRa end-nodes, or performance evaluation period (Teval), among others. Every Teval, the simulation tool will show the calculated performance quality metrics.

In the same script, we define the automatic selection of SF and TP values for each LoRa end-node. These values will depend on two factors: the distance between the LoRa end-node and the LoRaGW and the distance between the farthest LoRa end-node and the LoRaGW. Note that we are working with fixed LoRa nodes and future improvements will be added for mobile nodes. Given that to set SF we have 6 possible options [SF7, SF12], we assume that there are 6 possible distance intervals from 0 until the maximum (farthest) distance, i.e., the LoRa end node that is farther from the LoRaGW. Depending on what interval fits the distance from LoRa end-node i to the LoRaGW, the algorithm assigns the corresponding SF, knowing that lower SF values are used for LoRa end-nodes closer to the LoRaGW, and vice versa. Likewise, we follow the same method to select the appropriate value for the TP, but using

12 possible intervals for 12 possible values [2dB,14dB], assigning lower values to LoRa end-nodes nearer to the LoRaGW.

According to the European case, SF and BW combination results in 7 different DR [DR0, DR6], each one with a specified Maximum Payload Size (M). With all these parameters it is possible to compute the maximum Time-on-Air (ToA) for each DR class impacting in the effective throughput due to data-cycle (1%). We calculate the ToA and the minimum time between packets using a payload of 12 bytes and a duty-cycle of 1% (see Table II).

After the simulation, the Python script processes the results and represents them graphically for a better user comprehension and to facilitate the computation with other environments.

C. *Security*

We have modified the simulation tool so that transmitters and receivers use the AES Counter Mode (CTR) method to encrypt and decrypt messages. CTR is a symmetric encryption method, so it employs a shared private key to encrypt/decrypt messages, whose content will be hidden while flowing through the network. That is, the encrypted message is sent through the wireless channel and it can be only decrypted by those recipients sharing the same private key.

Taking the same shared key (or a different one but also shared), the message is signed using the AES Cipher-based Message Authentication Code (CMAC) method. This digital signature guarantees authentication (the origin of the message is verified) and integrity (the data has not been modified or altered along the communication path). These processes (cipher/decipher and sign) are implemented with Crypto++ libraries imported into OMNeT++. In both algorithms, the key length is 128 bits.

D. *LoRa network*

By default, SimpleLoRaApp is the application module in a LoRa end-node in FLoRa (see Figure 2). This module generates a random number to schedule the messages transmission (e.g., following an exponential distribution) and sends the message to the LoRa physical layer, which is responsible for transmitting the message in plain text. Then, the LoRa end-node sends a RadioFrame to LoRaGW that contains a LoRaAppMessage encapsulated in it.

To compute the number of lost packets and measure the Packet Delivery Rate (PDR) in the LoRa/LoRaWAN, we modify the radio interface of LoRaGW as follows. When LoRaGW receives a new packet, it checks two values: its sequence number and its source ID (LoRa end-node ID). If for a source ID i the received and expected sequence number match, the number of lost packets is 0. In contrast, if for a source ID i the sequence number received is higher than expected, the difference should be the number of lost packets. Since we compute new intermediate metrics in different modules and OMNeT operations is based on message exchange, LoRaAppMessage and LoRaMacFrame modify their payload to carry out the information to the Network Server.

Considering the simplicity of the LoRa end-node application in FLoRa, we redefine it with three submodules with specific functionalities, namely, Read, CipherData, and SimpleLoRaApp, as depicted in Figure 2. The Read module allows each LoRa end-node to read from its own dataset (e.g., from a real one as it will be shown later). Once LoRa end-node acquires the data, it sends a ReadDataPacket message to the CipherData module. This module receives read data and initializes the symmetric encryption process, sending the data to the next module (SimpleLoRaApp) encrypted and signed as explained before. The last module is SimpleLoRaApp, which passes the message to the LoRa physical layer and sends it via the wireless channel. It is important to note that before the physical layer receives the frame, we have also added two throughput meters. The goal is to know the generated and received traffic by each LoRa end-node (bits/s and packets/s).

E. *Backbone Network*

When the LoRaGW receives a new message, it encapsulates the new message into a EthernetIIFrame and forwards it to the Network Server using UDP. This transport protocol implements message delivery through the network with a simple connectionless communication model, without confirmation or flow control. In its original form, the Network Server is defined as StandardHost and when messages arrive to the application module (called udpApp[0]) its only purpose is to count the number of received messages, discarding the message content. The Network Server does not check if the message is duplicated or not, which is insufficient for our needs (Figure 2).

Therefore, we have modified the Network Server splitting it into three independent modules, namely, CommunicationParameters, Decrypt, and Processing. First, CommunicationParameters computes metrics to quantify quality components at different abstraction levels.

TABLE II. LORA PARAMETERS ACCORDING TO SF Y BW

DR	SF	BW (kHz)	M (bits)	Throughput (bps)	ToA (ms)	Min time between Packets (s)
0	12	125	59	250	51	148.3
1	11	125	59	440	51	82.3
2	10	125	59	980	51	41.2
3	9	125	123	1760	115	20.6
4	8	125	250	3125	242	11.3
5	7	125	250	5470	242	6.2
6	7	250	250	11000	242	3.1

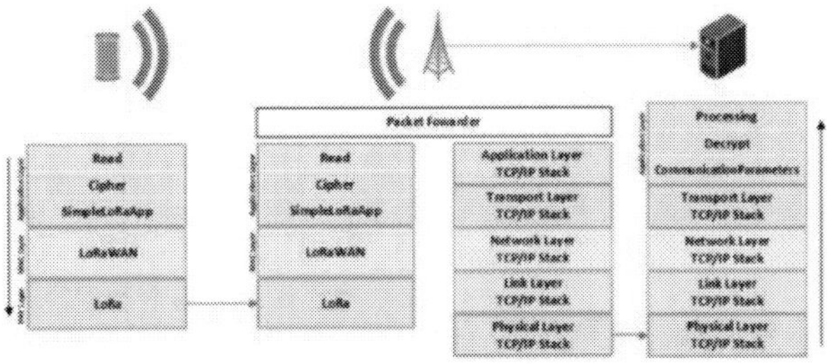

Figure 2. LoRa and backbone network protocol stack in our improved simulation tool.

Particularly, we measure metrics such as precision, accuracy, timeliness, delay, jitter, throughput, PDR, energy consumption, etc., from which we derive QoD, QoI, QoE, and QC. Using these for quality components, the performance of a service based on IoT and LoRa/LoRaWAN can be easily evaluated [34]. The received message and these metrics are sent to the Decrypt module that obtains the plain text from the ciphered text using the shared key and also checks the message signature. In case of a wrong signature, the message is discarded. The last module is Processing, which carries out two functions. First, storing the metrics for each received packet in a T_{eval} and second, when timer (T_{eval}) is over, the simulator processes the metrics and computes the quality components using the received metrics during that period.

F. Use case example

Our example is based on a real air-quality monitoring system, whose dataset measurements will be used in the simulations. The dataset [35] is part of a group of air-quality stations that take multiple measures (Humidity, Temperature, Pressure, CO, NO, etc.), located in a Spanish region. The dataset is preprocessed, splitting it into different files, one per LoRa end-node.

The simulated scenario is composed 53 LoRa end nodes, one LoRaGW, and one Network Server. The location of LoRa end-nodes is set according to the chosen environment (having a higher area of rural environment) and the LoRaGW is located in the center of all LoRa end-nodes. From all the obtained metrics, quality components are derived and normalized for a better comparison (Figure 3), so that the closer to 1 the better the performance. The method to obtain QoD, QoI, QoE, and QC is described in [34][36] and it is out of the scope of this paper.

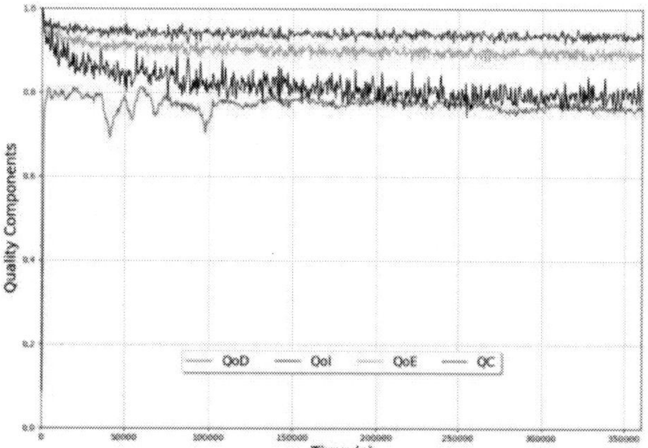

Figure 3. Performance of the LoRa-based air-quality monitoring system in terms of several quality components.

V. CONCLUSIONS

The influence that IoT-based services may have on social and industrial scenarios requires validating the proposed schemes before a real deployment is done. We presented in this paper a LoRa network simulator environment to study the performance of new applications and services under specific conditions, using as a baseline different libraries and frameworks available. Particularly, we used FLoRa and OMNeT, and introduced new features and several modifications. Among others, a new Okumura-Hata model has been implemented improving the accuracy of the simulation tool, and new modules to read, cipher, and send data from the emitter to the receiver have been incorporated. As a future work, we plan to introduce new methods to improve performance evaluation and monitoring based on advanced quality metrics.

ACKNOWLEDGMENT

This work was supported by the AEI/FEDER-UE project grant TEC2016-76465.C2-1-R (AIM).

REFERENCES

[1] G. Fortino, C. Savaglio, and M. Zhou, "Toward opportunistic services for the industrial Internet of Things," *IEEE Int. Conf. Autom. Sci. Eng.*, vol. 2017-Augus, pp. 825–830, 2018, doi:10.1109/COASE.2017.8256205, ISBN: 9781509067800, ISSN:21618089.

[2] A. Al-Fuqaha, M. Guizani, M. Mohammadi, M. Aledhari, and M. Ayyash, "Internet of Things: A Survey on Enabling Technologies, Protocols, and Applications," *IEEE Commun. Surv. Tutorials*, vol. 17, no. 4, pp. 2347–2376, 2015, doi:10.1109/COMST.2015.2444095, ISSN:1553877X.

[3] "Internet of Things (IoT), Connected Devices Installed Base Worldwide From 2015 To 2025," 2015. [Online]. Available: https://www.statista.com/statistics/471264/iot-number-of-connected-devices-worldwide/. [Accessed: 22-Oct-2019].

[4] U. Raza, P. Kulkarni, and M. Sooriyabandara, "Low Power Wide Area Networks: An Overview," *IEEE Commun. Surv. Tutorials*, vol. 19, no. 2, pp. 855–873, 2017, doi:10.1109/COMST.2017.2652320, ISSN:1553877X.

[5] R. Casadei, G. Fortino, D. Pianini, W. Russo, C. Savaglio, and M. Viroli, "Modelling and simulation of Opportunistic IoT Services with Aggregate Computing," *Futur. Gener. Comput. Syst.*, vol. 91, pp. 252–262, Feb. 2019, doi:10.1016/j.future.2018.09.005, ISSN:0167739X.

[6] R. Sanchez-Iborra and M. D. M.-D. Cano, "State of the art in LP-WAN solutions for industrial IoT services," *Sensors (Switzerland)*, vol. 16, no. 5, 2016, doi:10.3390/s16050708, ISBN: 978-3-03842-370-6, ISSN:14248220.

[7] J. Petäjäjärvi, K. Mikhaylov, A. Roivainen, T. Hänninen, and M. Pettissalo, "On the coverage of LPWANs: Range evaluation and channel attenuation model for LoRa technology," *2015 14th Int. Conf. ITS Telecommun. ITST 2015*, pp. 55–59, 2016, doi:10.1109/ITST.2015.7377400, ISBN: 9781467393829.

[8] S. Chieochan, E. Hossain, and J. Diamond, "Channel assignment schemes for infrastructure-based 802.11 WLANs: A survey," *IEEE Commun. Surv. Tutorials*, vol. 12, no. 1, pp. 124–136, 2010, doi:10.1109/SURV.2010.020110.00047, ISSN:1553877X.

[9] L. M. Borges, F. J. Velez, and A. S. Lebres, "Survey on the characterization and classification of wireless sensor network applications," *IEEE Commun. Surv. Tutorials*, vol. 16, no. 4, pp. 1860–1890, 2014, doi:10.1109/COMST.2014.2320073, ISSN:1553877X.

[10] LoRa Alliance, "LoRaWAN - What is it?. A technical overview of LoRa and LoRaWAN," no. November, pp. 1–20, 2015.

[11] "Weightless.," 2019. [Online]. Available: http://www.weightless.org/.

[12] "NWAVE Technology.," 2019. [Online]. Available: https://www.nwave.io/.

[13] "Telensa.," 2019. [Online]. Available: https://www.telensa.com/technology.

[14] Ingenu, "RPMA Technology," 2019. [Online]. Available: https://www.ingenu.com/technology/rpma/.

[15] "Sigfox.," 2019. [Online]. Available: https://www.sigfox.com/en. [Accessed: 09-Sep-2019].

[16] Qualcomm Incorporated, "RP-151621- Narrowband IOT," 2015.

[17] "FLoRa Framework," 2019. [Online]. Available: https://flora.aalto.fi/. [Accessed: 05-Feb-2019].

[18] "OMNeT++ Simulator." [Online]. Available: https://omnetpp.org/. [Accessed: 05-Feb-2019].

[19] M. Bor and U. Roedig, "LoRa transmission parameter selection," *Proc. - 2017 13th Int. Conf. Distrib. Comput. Sens. Syst. DCOSS 2017*, vol. 2018-Janua, pp. 27–34, 2018, doi:10.1109/DCOSS.2017.10, ISBN: 9781538639917, ISSN:2325-2944.

[20] M. Slabicki, G. Premsankar, and M. Di Francesco, "Adaptive configuration of lora networks for dense IoT deployments," *IEEE/IFIP Netw. Oper. Manag. Symp. Cogn. Manag. a Cyber World, NOMS 2018*, pp. 1–9, 2018, doi:10.1109/NOMS.2018.8406255, ISBN: 9781538634165.

[21] J. R. B. Junior, J. Lau, L. De Oliveira Rech, A. S. Morales, and R. Moraes, "Experimental Evaluation of the Coexistence of IEEE 802.11 EDCA and DCF Mechanisms," *Proc. - IEEE Symp. Comput. Commun.*, vol. 2018-June, pp. 847–852, 2018, doi:10.1109/ISCC.2018.8538640, ISBN: 9781538669501, ISSN:15301346.

[22] C. Pham, "Investigating and experimenting CSMA channel access mechanisms for LoRa IoT networks," in *IEEE Wireless Communications and Networking Conference, WCNC*, 2018, vol. 2018-April, pp. 1–6, doi:10.1109/WCNC.2018.8376997, ISBN:9781538617342, ISSN: 15253511.

[23] P. Yuan, X. Wen, H. Lu, and Q. Pan, "Dynamic Backoff Based Access Mechanism for LoRaWAN Class A," in *IEEE International Conference on Energy Internet Dynamic*, 2018, pp. 219–223, doi:10.1109/ICEI.2018.00047, ISBN:9781538641316, ISSN: 15502368.

[24] Y. Song, O. Zendra, and O. Zendra, "Using Cooja for WSN Simulations : Some New Uses and Limits To cite this version : Using Cooja for WSN Simulations : Some New Uses and Limits," pp. 319–324, 2016, ISBN: 9780994988607.

[25] O. Georgiou and U. Raza, "Low Power Wide Area Network Analysis: Can LoRa Scale?," *IEEE Wirel. Commun. Lett.*, vol. 6, no. 2, pp. 162–165, 2017, doi:10.1109/LWC.2016.2647247, ISSN:21622345.

[26] "Discrete Event Network Simulator - NS3." [Online]. Available: https://www.nsnam.org/. [Accessed: 08-May-2019].

[27] "NetSim - Network Simulator & Emulator." [Online]. Available: https://www.tetcos.com/download.html. [Accessed: 08-May-2019].

[28] "SimPy 3.0.11." [Online]. Available: https://simpy.readthedocs.io/en/latest/. [Accessed: 08-May-2019].

[29] "Opnet.com." [Online]. Available: http://www.opnet.com/. [Accessed: 08-May-2019].

[30] "Crypto++ Library 8.0." [Online]. Available: https://www.cryptopp.com/. [Accessed: 05-Feb-2019].

[31] "Eclipse." [Online]. Available: https://www.eclipse.org/. [Accessed: 08-May-2019].

[32] R. Sanchez-Iborra, J. Sanchez-Gomez, J. Ballesta-Viñas, M. D. Cano, and A. F. Skarmeta, "Performance evaluation of lora considering scenario conditions," *Sensors (Switzerland)*, vol. 18, no. 3, 2018, doi:10.3390/s18030772, ISSN:14248220.

[33] J. D. Parsons, *The Mobile Radio Propagation Channel*. 1992, doi:10.1111/1365-2435.13050ISBN:047198857X.

[34] J.-M. Martinez-Caro and M.-D. Cano, "A holistic approach to evaluate the performance of applications and services in the Internet of Things," *Submitt. to Int. J. Commun. Syst.*, no. Special issue on: Emerging ICT Applications and Service-Big Data, IoT, and Cloud Computing, 2019.

[35] "Euskadi air quality (2018)," 2018. [Online]. Available: http://opendata.euskadi.eus/catalogo/-/calidad-aire-en-euskadi-2018/. [Accessed: 09-Sep-2019].

[36] Q. Wu *et al.*, "Cognitive internet of things: A new paradigm beyond connection," *IEEE Internet Things J.*, vol. 1, no. 2, pp. 129–143, 2014, doi:10.1109/JIOT.2014.2311513, ISBN: 2327-4662 VO - 1, ISSN:23274662.

Energy-Aware Grid Based Coverage Path Planning for UAVs

Alia Ghaddar
Department of Computer Science
International University of Beirut, BIU/LIU
Beirut, Lebanon
email: alia.ghaddar@liu.edu.lb

Ahmad Merei
Department of Computer Science
International University of Beirut, BIU/LIU
Beirut, Lebanon
email: 41430485@students.liu.edu.lb

***Abstract*—The usage of Unmanned Aerial Vehicles (UAVs) for different tasks has rapidly increased in recent years. An Unmanned Aerial Vehicle is an unpiloted aircraft that operates by remote control or onboard computers. This technology has become promising in providing new opportunities in many fields, such as smart agriculture, photogrammetry, remote sensing, wireless coverage, rescuing and many others. Controlling the mobility of an Unmanned Aerial Vehicle while monitoring geographical zones is one of the most important problems. In this context, managing the flight route by finding an optimal path that fully covers the Area of Interest with minimum energy consumption is one of the main challenges. In this work, we propose an algorithm to scan an area that reduces completion-time and energy consumption. It also ensures a complete coverage of the area. We consider an Area of Interest without obstacles and non-flying zones.**

Keywords*— *Unmanned Aerial Vehicles; Coverage Path Planning; Energy-Aware Trajectories; Remote Sensings; Cellular Decomposition.

I. Introduction

The rapid technology dissemination and advances in the control field and Micro Electro Mechanical Systems (MEMS) gave rise to a new chain of developments on mini UAVs. The usage of UAVs or drones in remote sensing scenarios has grown fast in the last years. Many application domains address terrain coverage, such as surveillance [1], smart farming [2], photogrammetry [3], disaster management [4–7], civil security, wildfire tracking [8–11] and many others [3][12][13]. Coverage Path Planning (CPP) is basically finding the route that covers every point of a certain Area of Interest (AoI). A main requirement in CPP is to reduce the completion-time of the overall mission and, at the same time, to ensure a complete coverage of the area. The key elements in the scanning mission are the drones types and the trajectory plan.

A. Drone Type and Application domains

UAVs can be divided into three main types: Rotary Wing, Fixed Wing and Hybrid [14–16]. They have different features, sizes and specifications like footprint, weight, power support (gas, electric, nitro, solar, etc.).

Rotory drones, also known as rotary-wings drones, allow vertical take-off and landing. They may hover over a fixed location to produce continuous cellular coverage. This type of aerial platform can also be classified into single-rotor (helicopter) and multi-rotor (quadcopter and hexacopter). Quadcopters are inexpensive and have good maneuverability. They are widely applied in surveillance missions, such as in confined spaces and close-range inspection tasks, marine settings and terrestrial areas with steep terrain, or extensive vegetation cover [14][17].

Fixed wing drones are comparatively weighty, as they need significant battery power. However, they have the advantage of carrying higher payloads. Furthermore, they are suitable to be deployed in a large area because of their high durability and long flight time duration. However, they cannot focus on the same scene for a long period of time due to their high speed. They cannot stop or slow down the speed during the mission. Thus, fixed wing drones cannot be used as remote flying camera controllers as they need high speed sensors to survey [18].

Hybrid drones can switch their flight/operation mode: in one mode they are ready to float, similar to helicopters, and in the alternative mode, they fly, similar to fixed wing drones.

UAVs are used in various fields ranging from the military, humanitarian relief, disaster management to agriculture. Below we present a few typical examples [19–21]:

- Rescue and search: Drones can be used in emergency cases for rescue and search. They can overcome the difficulty of crossing areas that humans cannot reach, bridging isolated areas and enhancing wireless coverage.
- Smart policing: Most of the cities police or private agencies use drones to keep an eye on the crowd during any event. It also provides detailed documentation of a crime and accident scenes.
- Smart transportation and monitoring systems: New UAV application areas are enabled by Internet of Things (IoT). Drone mapping capabilities are helping set the foundation for the future. They offer many services and opportunities that can benefit smart cities applications (medical [22], package delivery, traffic monitoring and firefighting) [23]. Commercial applications are focused on delivering products via new type of smart transportation systems from depots to homes of end-users.
- Smart agriculture: Monitoring the growing process of plants can benefit from the use of drones. Data collected from UAVs can be used for the analysis of soils and drainage. It can also be used for the crop

health assessment. The use of drones gives farmers a richer picture of their fields.

- Entertainment and Media: Advertising, entertainment, aerial photography, shows and special effects [24].
- Security: Monitoring lines and sites, proactive response.
- Telecommunication: Tower maintenance, signal broadcasting.

B. Motivation

The energy constraints and flight limitations of UAVs have attracted significant attention from researches as they directly impact the network performance in Coverage Path Planning missions [25–28]. On-board energy in UAV are consumed for powering the movements of the drone (hovering, horizontal and vertical motions). However, increasing battery size is not an alternative key solution as the energy consumption increases when the drone carries extra payload and has more weight [29][30]. Moreover, additional energy could be consumed in the air in the presence of winds [31–33].

Two main performance metrics mainly reflects energy consumption and completion-time. These metrics are path length (or the traveled distance) [12][34] and the number of turns [18][29]. The number of turns during a mission impacts the time needed to accomplish the entire path. In [35], authors rely on these metrics to find the optimal path. These metrics are compared and investigated in [36]. Studies show that, for UAVs, a path with less turns is more efficient in terms of route length, duration and energy. Lowering the number of turns leads to a lower delay in completion-time and thus to a shorter path. Consequently, lower energy consumption is resulted.

In our work, we consider having one rotary wing drone. We aim to cover an Area of Interest without obstacles and non-flying zones. The main challenges in our work are as follows: achieving minimum completion-time, minimum number of turns, lowering the energy consumption, and having a shortest mission path to cover the whole area. The method described in this paper makes use of grid partitioning to reach its goal.

The rest of this paper is organized as follows. The related works are presented in Section II. In Section III, we present our contribution. The computational experiments and results are discussed in Section IV. Section V concludes our paper.

II. Related Works

The Internet of Flying Robots (IoFR) is a sub-concept of the Internet of Things (IoT) [37] and Internet of Robotic Things [38]. The Rlying Robots (FRs) may refer to drones, UAVs, or airships in different applications [39]. CPP is classified as subtopic of the path planning in robotics. Its objective is to cover a free space in an environment and obtaining a low cost path with minimum overlapping [40]. Various approaches have been proposed to compute a low cost coverage path [41–43] such as mirror mapping method [44], in-field obstacles classification [45], context-aware UAV mobility [46]. Among the different decomposition-based coverage methods that are used for coverage applications, we mention Classical exact cellular decomposition [47], Boustrophedon decomposition [48] and trapezoidal decomposition [49], landmark based topological coverage [50] and grid-based methods [51]. Several research studies focus on the Coverage Path Planning from different perspectives. They propose trajectory solutions with different scenarios taking into consideration different factors: area shape, status of the plan (Online/offline), number of drones, completion-time, energy consumption.

A. Area shape and Plan status

The area shape plays a role in defining the trajectory method for coverage. An AoI could have a regular shape [55][56][60] or an irregular shape [17]. A review of existing approaches resulted in works that explore rectangular areas. Others assume convex polygonal environments with different type of sensors mounted on the UAV (visual sensors, thermal sensors, etc) [36][52][65]. Information about the environment is either available offline or online. Several approaches consider online path plan mainly used to cover mobile sensors in real-time or to modify path depending on sudden changes in the surrounding atmosphere [66]. The basic approach for Offline CPP algorithms is the area decomposition, determining the visiting sequence of the sub regions, and covering decomposed regions to obtain a complete coverage path [43][67][68].

B. Coverage Motion and Path Planning

The large majority of strategies for Coverage Path Planning rely on decomposing the area into cells that must be visited and covered. The whole area is divided using exact or approximate cellular decomposition. Authors in [3][26] adopt grid-based technique to divide the area into squared cells. Each square contains occupancy information of the part of the environment that it covers. Cells are usually explored by back-and-forth motions using single drone such as in [56][62]. Authors in [59][61][68] use multiple drones, and back-and-forth motion to cover the area in offline mode. They aim for less number of turning maneuvers. Other approaches adopt spiral or circular motions. Authors in [54] adopt Spiral motion and use single drone. They aim to cover an area in offline mode in less mission completion-time and shorter distance. Others adopt multiples drones to reduce the path length [57][58]. Authors in [60] relied on Integer Linear Programming for collision avoidance. They try to reduce the flight time and energy consumption. Table I shows a list of CPP related works with the adopted area shape, number of drones, plan status and challenges they tackle.

TABLE I. COVERAGE PATH PLANNING APPROACHES

Ref.	*Area Shape*	*Status*	*Drones*	*Technique/Motion*	*Challenge*
[52]	Circle	NA	Multiple	3D deployment	Increase download link with less power
[53]	Circle	NA	Single	Spiral decomposition	Shorter plans, less runtime
[54]	Irregular	NA	Single	Combine multi data rate scheme	Tracking mobile objects (e.g. bicycles)
[3]	Irregular	Offline	Single	Grid-Based	Minimum completion-time
[26]	Irregular	Offline	Single	Grid-Based	Obtain images to build area map
[55]	Polygonal	Offline	Single	Energy-aware Spiral	Energy consumption
[56]	Polygonal	Offline	Single	Back-and-Forth	reduce turning maneuvers, Path length
[57][58]	Polygonal	Offline	Multiple	Spiral	Path length
[59]	Polygonal	Offline	Multiple	Back-and-Forth	Number of turning maneuvers
[60]	Rectangular	NA	Multiple	Mixed Integer Linear Programming	Flight time
[61]	Rectangular	Offline	Multiple	Back-and-Forth (Line Formation)	Target detection, Search time, # of UAVs and info. exchange
[62]	Rectangular	NA	Single	Back-and-Forth, Square	Fixed and mobile target detection, Coverage rate
[63]	Square	NA	Multiple	Multi objective	Minimum cost, lowest altitude possible
[28]	Graph Grid	Online	Multiple	Edge Counting and Patrol-GRAPH*	Path length; Robots distance average
[64]	Rectangular	Online	Multiple	Reinforced Random Walk	Coverage time; Global detection efficiency

III. CONTRIBUTION

In this work, we are going to use one rotary wing drone to cover an area in an offline mode without obstacles and non-flying zones. We planned the path using Grid based technique with tractor mobility path pattern. We applied sub-division on the main heatmap to tune the path and reduce the number of turns and save energy. The main phases in our path planning method are presented below:

A. Cellular decomposition

- *Generate Grid-cells*: We consider having an image of the Area of Interest in binary format (black/white image). We generate a matrix representation (heatmap) of the area (Figure 1(a)) and map it to a grid-based form (Figure 1(b)). The required matrix dimensions (i.e, length and width) are given by the path planner. It depends on the UAV footprint and determines the size of each grid cell in our work.

  Concerning the scan direction, we choose it to be parallel to the longest side of the grid (length or width). Using principal axis transformation, the longest side of the area is aligned parallel to the Y-axis of the image. Each value on the heatmap represents a percentage of the area covered in a grid cell.

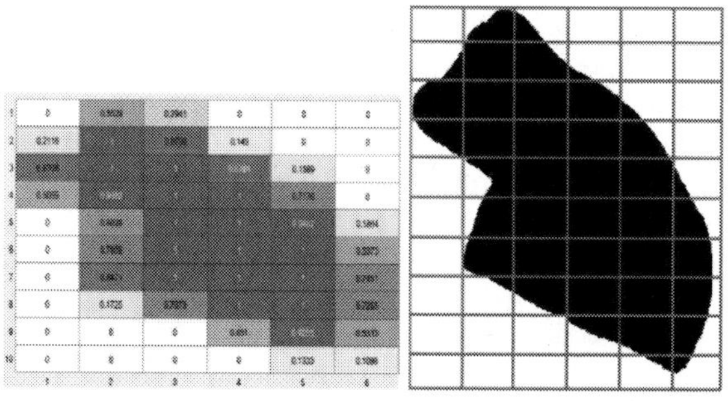

(a) *Heatmap format* (b) *Area mapped to a grid*

Figure 1. Binary image representation using Heatmap of the matrix

- *UAV coverage range*: The path planer defines the coverage range for the UAV. Basically, a UAV's coverage projection (or footprint) is circular shape. However, due to the usage of grid-based method in our work (i.e, grid-cells have rectangular shape), we consider the rectangle inscribed in the footprint circle (see Figure 2). Each rectangle is going to represent a grid-cell entity.

Figure 2. UAV footprint

B. Path Pattern and trajectory generation

1) Basic approach

A tractor mobility pattern covers all nodes without leaving any gap [69]. It pursues parallel tracks to the grid dimensions, as shown in Figure 3(a). The turn angle is always 90°. However, the path crossing points v_1, v_2, v_3 passes through unneeded cell (example cell A1). Since point v_3 is higher than v_1, a UAV has to move to point v_2 and make the rectangular angle.

In our basic plotting approach, we modify the turn angles to get trapezoidal tracks (see Figure 3(b)). By this modification, the path length is shorter. The track's end-point is the center of the last non-zero value cell on the track. A path track crosses the center of the grid cells that have non-zero values.

For example, in Figure 3(b), assume that the UAV is positioned at v_1 and is moving upward. Instead of moving to cell A1, a turn is to be done at point v_2 (cell A2) which

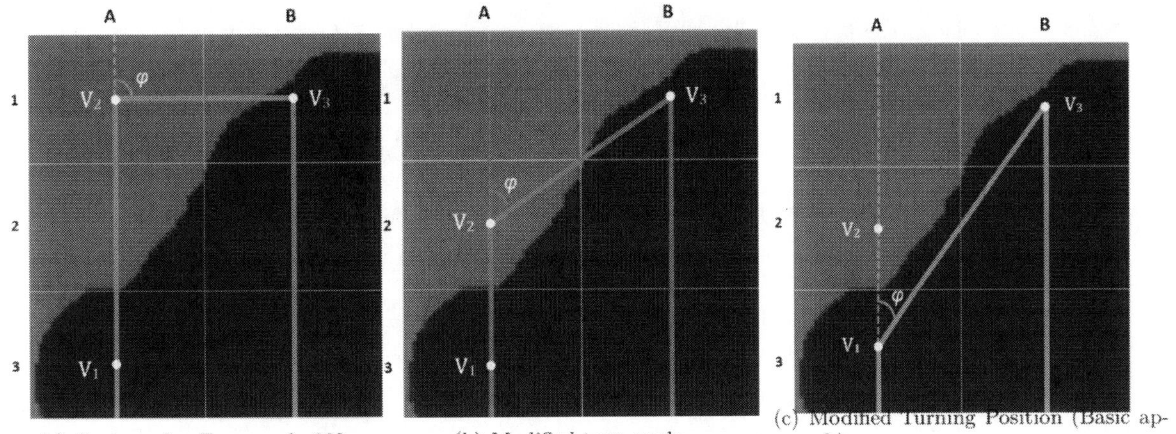

(a) *Rectangular Turn-angle 90°* (b) Modified turn angle (c) Modified Turning Position (Basic approach)

Figure 3. Tractor mobility- Trapezoidal and Rectangular Turns

is the center of the last non-zero-value cell. The calculation of the turn angle is explained in section III-B3.

Another concern can be raised when the grid cell contains small portion of the area. Is it possible to cover the portion without moving to the center of the grid as this avoids long path? In Figure 3(b), cell A2, a small portion of the area exists. the same portion of the area can be covered by moving directly from v_1 to v_3 as shown in Figure 3(c). This can reduce the energy consumed during the movement. The below section explains how we plan the new trajectory. The main ideas discussed below are (a) the selection of the turning positions, (b) the selection of the start point and the direction of the trajectory.

2) Path turning and plotting points

In order to determine the accurate position at which a turning is to be done, we divide each grid cell into a group of 4 subcells. The new heatmap of the area in Figure 1(a) is presented in Figure 4.

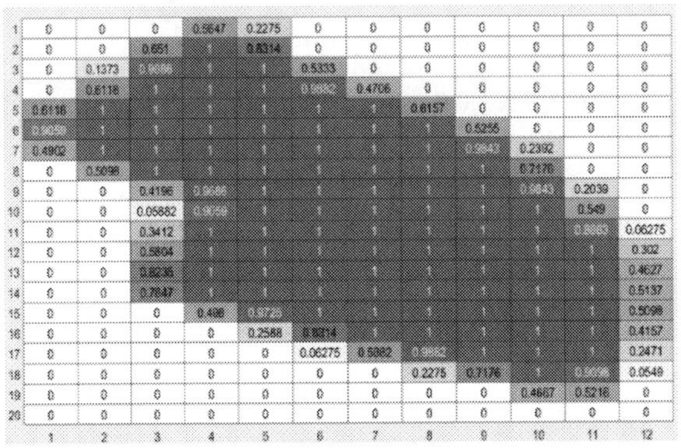

Figure 4. Resulted Heat-Map after the subdivision (grid: 20 x12)

Figure 5(b) represents the heatmap of Figure 3(c) after subdivision. We investigate the heatmap values of the subcells to determine at which side the portion of the area is located in the cell, as well as, the turning position and degree.

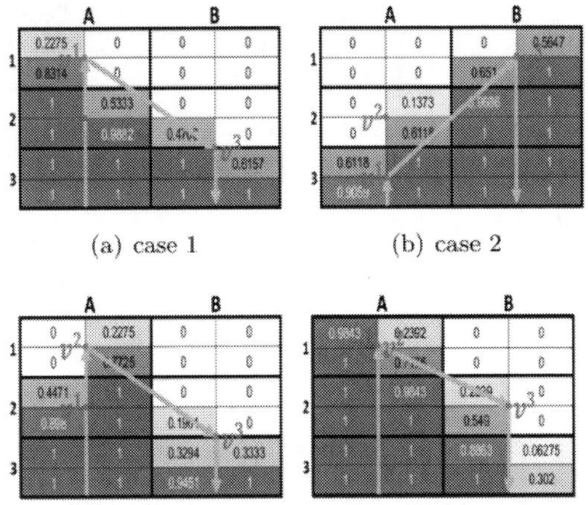

(a) case 1 (b) case 2 (c) case 3 (d) case 4

Figure 5. Subdivision of a grid cell

The main steps in the trajectory generation are:

- **Step 1:** Perform the subdivision of the original grid cells and generate the new heatmap. Assume the original dimensions are L x W, the new grid dimensions are $L' = max\{2W, 2L\}$ and $W' = min\{2W, 2L\}$. We denote by $\mathscr{H}$ the matrix as follows:

$$\mathscr{H} = \{h_{ij} \in [0,1] | i \in [1, L'] \wedge j \in [1, W']\}$$

Each grid cell has a positive value in the heatmap $\mathscr{H}$.

- **Step 2:** We denote by ζ the set of non-zero columns in the grid ($|\zeta| <= W'$). A column p (denoted ζ_p) belongs to ζ if and only if the following holds:

$$\zeta_p \in \zeta \Leftrightarrow \exists h_{ip} > 0 \wedge i \in [1, L']$$

$$\zeta_p = \{h_{ij} \in \mathscr{H} | j = p \wedge i \in [1, L']\}$$

thus,

$$\zeta = \{\zeta_p | p \in [1, W']\}$$

Let F_p denotes the first non-zero cells in column ζ_p (see Figure 6):

$$F_p = \{h_{ip} \in \zeta_p | h_{ip} > 0 \wedge i < i', \forall i' \in [1, L']\}$$

Let L_p denote the Last non-zero cells in column ζ_p as follows:

$$L_p = \{h_{ip} \in \zeta_p | h_{ip} > 0 \wedge i > i', \forall i' \in [1, L']\}$$

The cardinalities of F_p and L_p are $|F_p| = |L_p| = 1$. For example, in Figure 4, ζ_3 has F_3 located at row 2 and L_3 located at row 14.

We start the trajectory planning from the first column in ζ. Each path track (denoted q) is going to be the vertical middle line between two adjacent columns in the grid. Track q_1 is the vertical middle line between ζ_1 and ζ_2. Track q_2 is the middle line between ζ_3 and ζ_4 and so on. We are going to

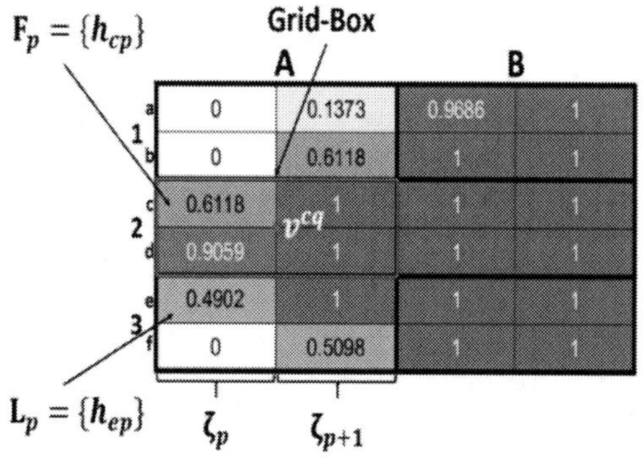

Figure 6. Notations

investigate the positions of F_p and L_p in order to determine the turning points of each track. It should be noted that the two points of a track segment are the track start-point and turning-point. Except for the last track that has only a start-point and a stop-point.

- **Step 3:** Formally, a grid is represented as graph $G(V, E)$, where V is the set of nodes and E is the set of edges. The center of the grid box (or range) formed by 4 adjacent cells represents a node v in the graph (see Figure (6)). These nodes (once determined) will be linked together to form the final path.

In general, for two columns ζ_p and ζ_{p+1}, the range at row r and row (r+1), is denoted

$$[h_{rp}: h_{(r+1)(p+1)}]$$

, where r$\in [1, L'[$. Let v^{rq} be the center of this range.

Two cases occurs (see Figure 7):

(1) If the end-point of a track q is located from the side of the first elements of ζ_p and ζ_{p+1}, the two possible turning points (or nodes) are:

- The center of the range that contains the first element in ζ_p.
- The center of the range that contains the first element in ζ_{p+1}.

(2) If the end-point of a track q is located from the side of the last elements of ζ_p and ζ_{p+1}, the ranges for the turning points are calculated from the Last elements of ζ_p and ζ_{p+1}. In this case, the two points are:

- The center of the range that contains the Last element in ζ_p.
- The center of the range that contains the Last element in ζ_{p+1}.

The range is the same as defined above.

If $h_{(r+1)(p+1)} = 0$ or $h_{(r+1)p} = 0$ or $r = L'$, the range becomes:

$$[h_{(r-1)p} : h_{r(p+1)}]$$

- **Step 4:** To tune the path and choose between the two possible turning points on a track q, we follow the steps presented in Figure 8. Assume that the start direction of track q is vertical ascending, the algorithm indicates the turning point as well as, the next node on the coming track (q+1). This point is the start point of the new track. The algorithm checks the position of each node in the grid in order to draw the path link from one track to another. This link forms an edge of the graph.
- **Step 5:** According to our trajectory pattern, for each track, there are two options for the direction:
Option1: UAV moves vertically ascending from the side of last element (L_p) of the track q to the first element (F_p). In this case, a turning point is located on the side of the First element. The corresponding path planning was described in the previous sections.
Option2: UAV moves vertically descending from the side of the first element of the track p (F_p) to the last element (L_p). In this case, the turning point of track q and the start point of track (q+1) are located on the side of the last element. The same steps described in the previous presented algorithm (Figure 8) are applied. We reverse the operators in the conditions.

3) Turn angle calculation

Let's go back to Figure 3(c), the turn angle at point v_2 is the exterior angle between nodes v_1, v_2, v_3. We denote it φ_{123}.

Each node $v \in V$ has coordinate (x, y) in the cartesian plan. Let v_i, $v_j \in V$ denote specific nodes and $e_{ij} \in E$ denotes an edge between nodes v_i and v_j. $d(v_i, v_j)$ is the distance between them.

$$d(v_i, v_j) = \sqrt{\left(x_{v_i} - x_{v_j}\right)^2 + \left(y_{v_i} - y_{v_j}\right)^2} \quad (1)$$

The turn angle at point v_j can be calculated from the internal angle $\angle v_i v_j v_k$ as follows:

$$\varphi_{ijk} = \pi - \cos^{-1}(\angle v_i v_j v_k) \quad (2)$$

where $\cos^{-1}(\angle v_i v_j v_k)$ is found using the law of cosines in the triangle $\Delta v_i v_j v_k$. Consequently,

Algorithm 1

Input: $\zeta_p \wedge \zeta_{p+1}$
Output: Two possible turning points on a track q
{**If end-point of q is from the side of** F_p **&** F_{p+1} }
Find F_p for ζ_p
$r_1 \leftarrow$ row of F_p
Find F_{p+1} for ζ_{p+1}
$r_2 \leftarrow$ row of F_{p+1}
{1^{st} possible turning point}
$v^{r_2q} \leftarrow$ center of grid box $[h_{r_2p} : h_{(r_2+1)(p+1)}]$
{2^{nd} possible turning point}
$v^{r_1q} \leftarrow$ center of grid box $[h_{r_1p}: h_{(r_1+1)(p+1)}]$
{**If end-point of q is from the side of** L_p **&** L_{p+1} }
Find L_p for ζ_p
$r_1 \leftarrow$ row of L_p
Find L_{p+1} for ζ_{p+1}
$r_2 \leftarrow$ row of L_{p+1}
{1^{st} possible turning point}
if $(r_1 == L')$ **then**
  $v^{r_1q} \leftarrow$ center of grid box $[h_{(r_1-1)p} : h_{r_1(p+1)}]$
else
  if $(h_{(r_1+1)(p+1)} == 0)$ **then**
    $v^{r_1q} \leftarrow$ center of grid box $[h_{(r_1-1)p} : h_{r_1(p+1)}]$
  else
    $v^{r_1q} \leftarrow$ center of grid box $[h_{r_1p}: h_{(r_1+1)(p+1)}]$
  end if
end if
{2^{nd} possible turning point}
if $(r_2 == L')$ **then**
  $v^{r_2q} \leftarrow$ center of grid box $[h_{(r_2-1)p} : h_{r_2(p+1)}]$
else
  if $(h_{(r_2+1)p} == 0)$ **then**
    $v^{r_2q} \leftarrow$ center of grid box $[h_{(r_2-1)p} : h_{r_2(p+1)}]$
  else
    $v^{r_2q} \leftarrow$ center of grid box $[h_{r_2p}: h_{(r_2+1)(p+1)}]$
  end if
end if

Figure 7. Algorithm 1 generates two possible turning points

$$\varphi_{ijk} = \pi - \cos^{-1}\left[\frac{(d(v_i, v_j)^2 + d(v_j, v_k)^2 - d(v_k, v_i)^2)}{2d(v_i, v_j)d(v_j, v_k)}\right] \tag{3}$$

It has been mentioned earlier that UAV's power consumption decreases when the number of turns performed during the mission decreases [67]. We aim to have a compromise between the length of the generated path and the number of turn in such a way to cover the whole area with minimum energy consumption and completion-time. We took different scenarios to evaluate the time and energy consumption. The results are shown in Section IV.

Algorithm 2

Input: $v^{r_1q} \wedge v^{r_2q} \wedge \zeta$
Output: The turning point on track q and the start point on track (q+1)
$r_3 \leftarrow$ row of F_{p+2}
$v^{r_3(q+1)} \leftarrow$ center of grid box $[h_{(r_3)(p+2)} : h_{(r_3+1)(p+3)}]$
{for simplification}
$v_1 \leftarrow v^{r_1q}$
$v_2 \leftarrow v^{r_2q}$
$v_3 \leftarrow v^{r_3(q+1)}$
{Below Case refers to Figure 5(a)}
if $(r_1 > r_2)$ **then**
  The turning point $\leftarrow v_1$
  Move from v_1 to v_3
end if
{Below Case refers to Figure 5(b)}
if $(r_1 < r_2) \wedge (r_2 < r_3)$ **then**
  The turning point $\leftarrow v_1$
  Move from v_1 to v_3
end if
{Below Case refers to Figure 5(c)}
if $(r_1 < r_2) \wedge (r_2 >= r_3)$ **then**
  The turning point $\leftarrow v_2$
  Move from v_2 to v_3
end if
{Below Case refers to Figure 5(d)}
if $(r_1 == r_2)$ **then**
  The turning point $\leftarrow v_1$
  Move from v_1 to v_3
end if

Figure 8. Tuning the trajectory from track q to track q+1

IV. COMPUTATIONAL EXPERIMENTS AND RESULT

In this section, we perform a set of comparisons with different flight patterns. We demonstrate the performance of our proposed method for the CPP problem.

The performance metrics are completion-time and energy consumption.

- *Completion-Time:* We adopt the formula [3] below to compute the completion-time:

$$T = \frac{S}{V} + \sum_{u=1}^{k} \frac{\varphi_u}{\omega} \tag{4}$$

where completion-time is denoted by T, S for route length, V is UAV movement speed, while k is the number of turns, φ is the angle of uth turn and ω is the UAV rotation rate.

- *Energy model:* We adopt the following energy model [67] to evaluate our work. Below we give a quick recapit-

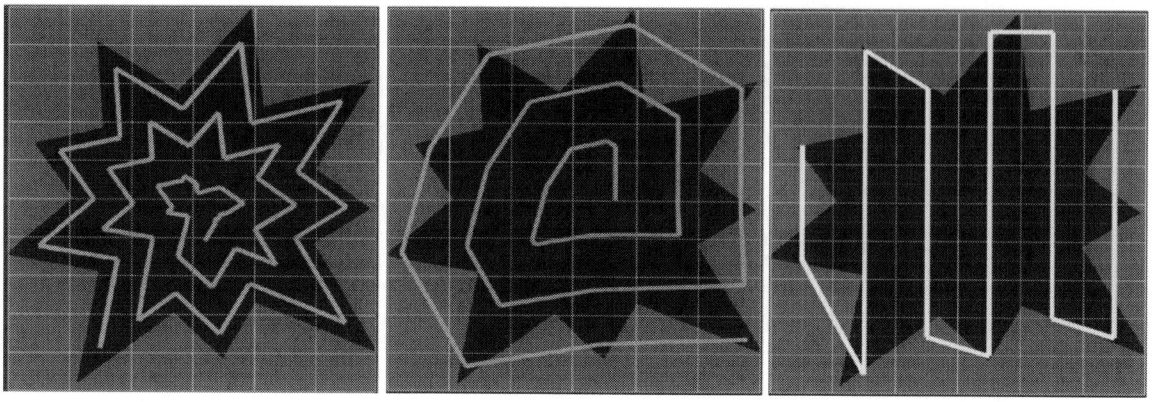

(a) *Trajectory by Basic Spiral motion* (b) Trajectory by Spiral convex hull (c) Trajectory by our work

Figure 9. Trajectory planning in Spiral motion v/s our work

ulation on the model components. Let $c(e_{ij})$ denotes the energy cost of traversing the edge e_{ij} between these nodes.

$$c(e_{ij}) = \lambda d(v_i, v_j) \quad (5)$$

where λ denotes the energy consumption per unit length. It is related to the UAV characteristics.

Let $c(\varphi_u)$ be the cost associated with a feasible turn. It is proportional to the angle of the turn φ_u.

$$c(\varphi_u) = \gamma \frac{180}{\pi} \varphi \quad (6)$$

The total energy E consumed is the sum of two terms. The first term is proportional to the distance traveled and the second term is proportional to the sum of turn angles.

$$\mathrm{E} = \sum_{i \in V} \sum_{j \in V} c(e_{ij}) + \sum_{i \in V} \sum_{j \in V} \sum_{k \in V} c(\varphi_{ijk}) \quad (7)$$

In our experimentation, we assume that $\lambda = 0.1164$ KJ/unit length and $\gamma = 0.0173$ KJ/degree.

(i) Scenario 1: We compared our algorithm to the basic spiral and spiral convex hull patterns on irregular star area shape. The grid is 10rows*6columns. The grid cell dimension is (0.98274 x 1.39335 $unit^2$). The paths are presented in Figure 9.

We assume that the UAV speed = 0.5 unit/sec and UAV rotation rate ω= 30 degree/sec. The paths are compared according to completion-time and energy consumption. The comparative results are presented in Table II. The table shows that our path length is 15.499% shorter than the spiral path pattern in Figure 9(a). It is also 6.666% shorter than the path in Figure 9(b) with reduction of 81.725% and 15.01% in number of turns in degree. This means our approach achieves better energy saving. Results show that the mission completion-time is reduced by 54.27% by our work over Figure 9(a) and by 8.76% over Figure 9(b), with energy saving of 76.85% and 12.92% compared to Figure 9(a) and Figure 9(b) respectively. In

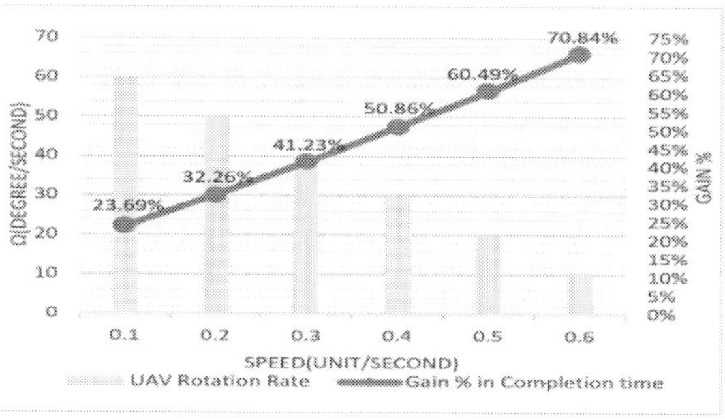

Figure 10. Gain in completion-time in our work compared to Spiral path in Figure 9(a)

TABLE II. SPIRAL MOTIONS V/S OUR WORK

	Spiral Figure 9(a)	*Spiral Figure 9(b)*	*Our work*
Route length S in units	58.1238	52.6216	49.1151
UAV speed V in unit/sec	0.5	0.5	0.5
Number of Turns k	48	27	24
Turns in degree	4925	1059	900
Rotation rate ω in degree/sec	30	30	30
Completion-time T in sec	280.4143	140.5432	128.2302
Energy consumption E in KJ	91.97282	24.44687	21.28786

Figure 10, we present the gain percentage in completion-time in our work over the results of Figure 9(a). We take different UAV speed and rotation rate values. Results show mission time reduction up to 70.84%.

In Figure 11, we present the gain percentage in completion-time in our work over the results of Figure 9(b). We take different UAV speed and rotation rate values. Results show mission time reduction up to 11.23%.

- **More irregular shapes:** We explore the performance of our algorithm on other irregular shapes. In

TABLE III. ENERGY CONSUMPTION AND MISSION COMPLETION-TIME COMPARED TO SPIRAL TECHNIQUE

Shapes	*Path Length (unit)*		*Sum of Angles (degree)*		*Completion-time* (sec.)		*Energy consumed (KJ)*		*Energy Saving*
	(a)	*(b)*	*(a)*	*(b)*	*(a)*	*(b)*	*(a)*	*(b)*	
L Shape (Figure 12)	160	187.3	450	540	350	404.6	34.2	37.4	8.55%
U Shape (Figure 13)	200	209.8	540	540	430	449.6	38.8	40	3%
Y Shape (Figure 14)	130	158.2	540	540	290	346.4	30.7	34	9.7%

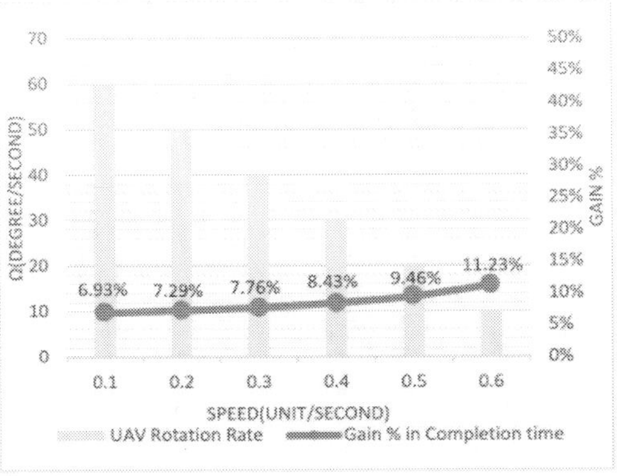

Figure 11. Gain in completion-time in our work compared to Spiral convex hull in Figure 9(b)

this section, we compare our work to other irregular shapes (L, U, Y shapes).

Figure 12, Figure 13 and Figure 14 show the trajectory planning in L shape, U shape and Y shape area respectively. The comparison is between our approach and Spiral technique. The scenarios are tested with a speed v=0.5 *unit/sec* and a rotation degree ω= 30 *degree/sec* assuming that the grid cell dimension is 10*10 $unit^2$.

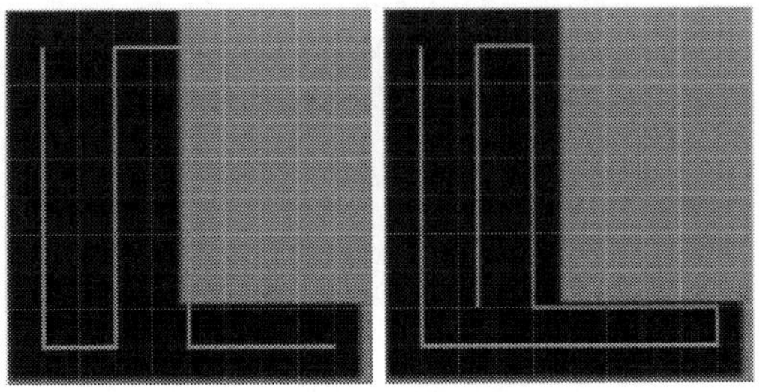

(a) Trajectory by our work (b) *Trajectory by Basic Spiral motion*

Figure 12. L Shape - Trajectory planning

The performance of our algorithm is presented in Table III. The table shows the energy consumed and completion-time while covering the different area shapes. Our algorithm performs between 3% and 9% energy saving over spiral technique.

(ii) Scenario 2: We compared our method to trajectory

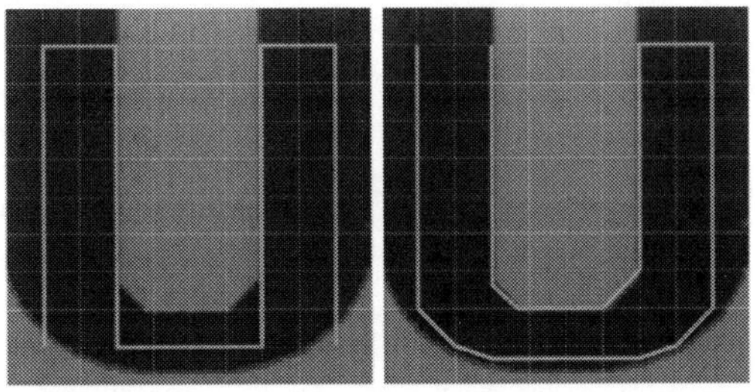

(a) Trajectory by our work (b) Trajectory by Basic Spiral motion

Figure 13. U Shape - Trajectory planning

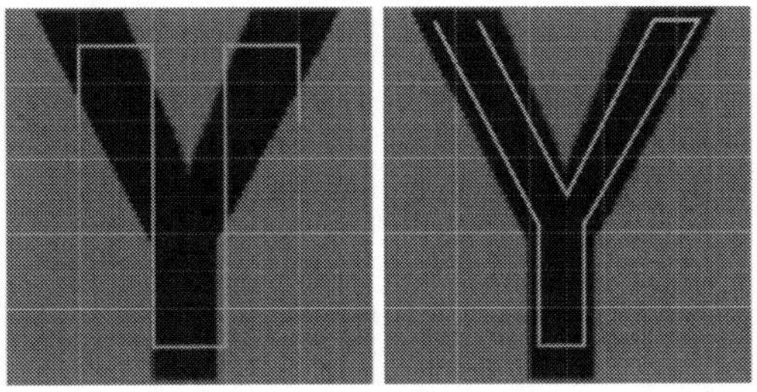

(a) Trajectory by our work (b) Trajectory by Basic Spiral motion

Figure 14. Y Shape - Trajectory planning

plan proposed in [3]. The grid dimensions are 10 rows x 6 columns. The path patterns are shown in Figure 15, where the cell dimension is (0.9894 x 1.3934 $unit^2$). The values are shown in Table IV. We assume that the UAV speed = 0.5 unit/sec and UAV rotation rate ω= 30 degree/sec.

TABLE IV. RESULTS OBTAINED BY THE TRAJECTORY PLAN IN in FIGURE 15(a) AND FIGURE 15(b)

	(a) Ref.[3]	*(b) Our work*
Route length S in units	50.2747	41.2304
UAV speed V in unit/sec	0.5	0.5
Number of Turns k	17	10
Total Turns in degree	1530	900
Rotation rate ω *in degree/sec*	30	30
Completion-time T in sec	151.5494	112.4608
Energy consumption E in KJ	32.32034	20.36884484

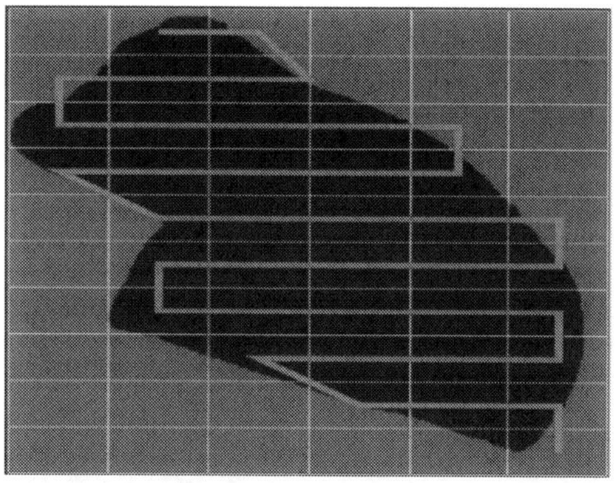

(a) Trajectory plan by the work done in Ref. [3]

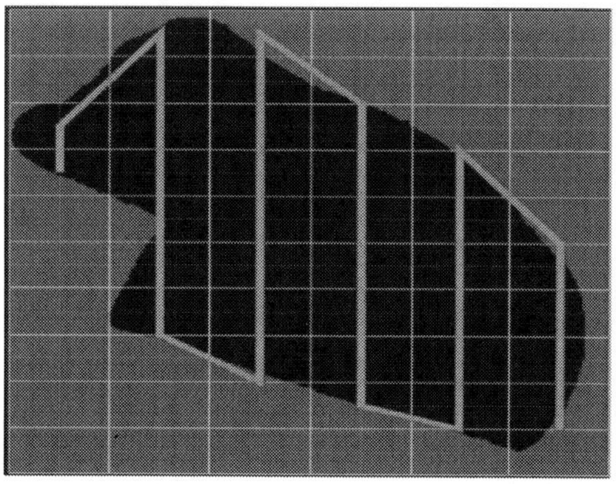

(b) Trajectory plan by our work

Figure 15. Trajectory planning in our work v/s CPP's algorithm in Ref. [3]

Table IV shows that our path is 17.989% shorter than the path in Figure 15(a) with reduction of 41.17% in number of turns. This means better energy saving. Results show that the mission completion-time is reduced by 25.79% in our work, with energy saving of 36.98% compared to the results obtained in [3]. It should be noted that the area is not totally covered by the work in [3]. There are two cells in Figure 15(a) that are part of the area and the drone didn't cover them. However, in our work all required cells are covered.

In Figure 16, we present the gain percentage in completion-time in our work over the work in [3]. We take different UAV speed and rotation rate values. Results show mission time reduction up to 32.97%.

(iii) Scenario 3: We compared our trajectory plan to work presented in [26] on an area grid of dimension 6rowsx10columns. The obtained path patterns are presented in Figure 17. The cell dimension is 1 x 1 $unit^2$. The resulted values are shown in Table V.

Table V shows that our path is 8.301% shorter than the path in [26] with reduction in number of turns by 61.904%. As for the completion-time, it is reduced by 29.37% in our work, with a 53.53% less in energy consumption.

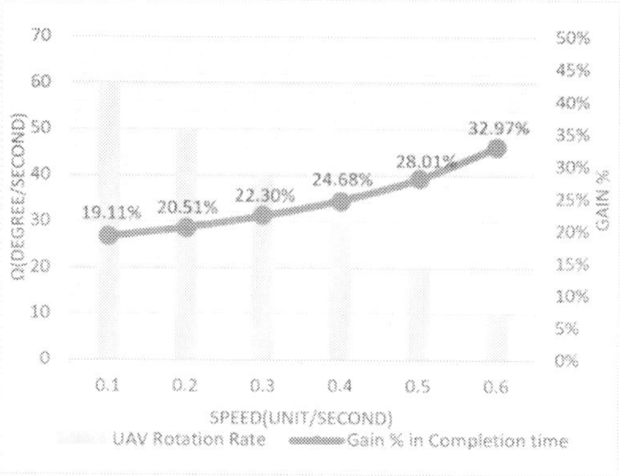

Figure 16. Gain in completion-time in our work compared to Ref. [3]

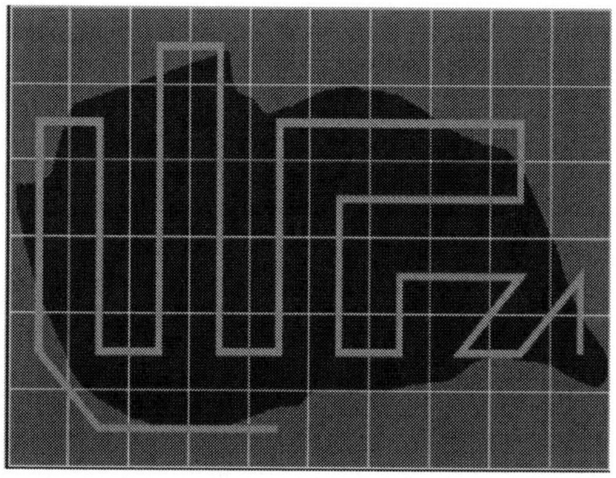

(a) Trajectory plan by the work done in Ref. [26]

(b) Trajectory plan by our work

Figure 17. Trajectories obtained by the CPP in Ref. [26] and our CPP method

In Figure 18, we present the gain in completion-time in our work over the work in [26]. We take different speed values and rotation rates. Results show a gain up to 45.82% in time reduction in our work.

TABLE V. RESULTS OBTAINED BY THE PLAN IN FIGURE 17(a) AND FIGURE 17(b)

	(a)Ref.[26]	*(b)Our work*
Route length S in unit length	48.6268	44.5875
UAV speed V in unit/sec	0.5	0.5
Number of Turns k	21	8
Total Turns in degree	1890	720
Rotation rate ω in degree/sec	30	30
Completion-time T in sec	160.2536	113.175
Energy consumption E in KJ	36.22407	16.833379

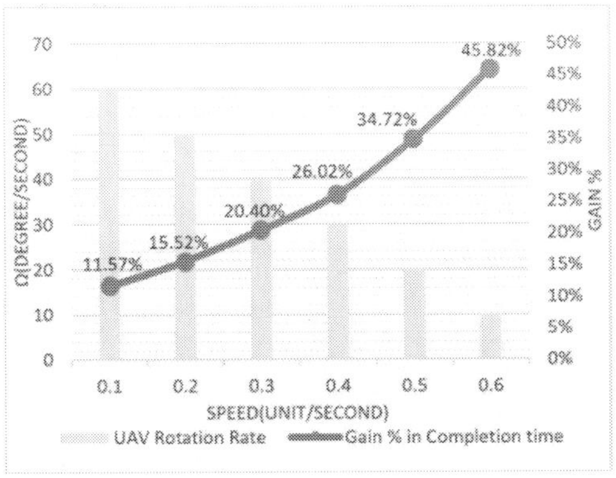

Figure 18. Reduction in completion-time in our work over the work in Ref. [26]

V. CONCLUSION

We proposed an energy aware coverage path planning method. In our work, we use one drone to cover areas without obstacles and nonflying zones in an offline mode. The results show that our work covers the whole area and has lower completion-time and energy consumption in comparison to the state of the art and the test cases used. In the future work, we plan to extend the proposed method to study the CPP in the presence of obstacles in the Area of Interest.

REFERENCES

[1] N. Basilico and S. Carpin, "Deploying teams of heterogeneous uavs in cooperative two-level surveillance missions," in *2015 IEEE/RSJ International Conference on Intelligent Robots and Systems (IROS)*, Sep. 2015, pp. 610–615.

[2] P. Lottes *et al.*, "Uav-based crop and weed classification for smart farming," in *2017 IEEE International Conference on Robotics and Automation (ICRA)*, May 2017, pp. 3024–3031.

[3] L. H. Nam, L. Huang, X. J. Li, and J. F. Xu, "An approach for coverage path planning for uavs," in *2016 IEEE 14th International Workshop on Advanced Motion Control (AMC)*, April 2016, pp. 411–416.

[4] L. Chunbo *et al.*, "Unmanned aerial vehicles for disaster management," in *Springer*, 08 2019, pp. 83–107.

[5] A. Hansen, "Applying visitor monitoring methods in coastal and marine areas – some learnings and critical reflections from sweden," *Scandinavian Journal of Hospitality and Tourism*, pp. 1–18, 03 2016.

[6] K. Park and R. Ewing, "The usability of unmanned aerial vehicles (uavs) for measuring park-based physical activity," *Landscape and Urban Planning*, vol. 167, pp. 157–164, 11 2017.

[7] D. Leary, "Drones on ice: an assessment of the legal implications of the use of unmanned aerial vehicles in scientific research and by the tourist industry in antarctica," *Polar Record*, vol. 53, pp. 1–15, 05 2017.

[8] H. X. Pham, H. M. La, D. Feil-Seifer, and M. Deans, "A distributed control framework for a team of unmanned aerial vehicles for dynamic wildfire tracking," in *2017 IEEE/RSJ International Conference on Intelligent Robots and Systems (IROS)*, Sep. 2017, pp. 6648–6653.

[9] L.-P. Chrétien, J. Théau, and P. Menard, "Visible and thermal infrared remote sensing for the detection of white-tailed deer using an unmanned aerial system," *Wildlife Society Bulletin*, vol. 40, pp. 181–191, 02 2016.

[10] S. Wich, D. Dellatore, M. Houghton, R. Ardi, and L. Koh, "A preliminary assessment of using conservation drones for sumatran orang-utan (pongo abelii) distribution and density," *Journal of Unmanned Vehicle Systems*, vol. 4, pp. 45–52, 11 2015.

[11] D. Stark, I. P. Vaughan, L. Evans, H. Kler, and B. Goossens, "Combining drones and satellite tracking as an effective tool for informing policy change in riparian habitats: A proboscis monkey case study," *Remote Sensing in Ecology and Conservation*, pp. 44–52, 07 2017.

[12] W. Ken *et al.*, "Remote sensing of the environment with small unmanned aircraft systems (uass), part 2: Scientific and commercial applications," *Journal of Unmanned Vehicle Systems*, vol. 2, pp. 86–102, 09 2014.

[13] P. Vihervaara *et al.*, "How essential biodiversity variables and remote sensing can help national biodiversity monitoring," *Global Ecology and Conservation*, vol. 10, pp. 43 – 59, 2017.

[14] J. Jiménez López and M. Mulero-Pázmány, "Drones for conservation in protected areas: Present and future," *Drones*, vol. 3, no. 1, 2019. [Online]. Available: https://www.mdpi.com/2504-446X/3/1/10

[15] I. Petkovic, D. Petkovic, and r. Petkovics, *IoT Devices vs. Drones for Data Collection in Agriculture*, 01 2017, pp. 063–080.

[16] A. Fotouhi, H. Qiang, M. Ding, M. Hassan, L. G. Giordano, A. García-Rodríguez, and J. Yuan, "Survey on UAV cellular communications: Practical aspects, standardization advancements, regulation, and security challenges," *CoRR*, vol. abs/1809.01752, 2018. [Online]. Available: http://arxiv.org/abs/1809.01752

[17] E. Grøtli and T. Johansen, "Path planning for uavs under communication constraints using splat! and milp," *Journal of Intelligent and Robotic Systems*, vol. 65, pp. 265–282, 08 2012.

[18] C. Di Franco and G. Buttazzo, "Coverage path planning for uavs photogrammetry with energy and resolution constraints," *Journal of Intelligent & Robotic Systems*, vol. 83, pp. 445–462, 02 2016.

[19] PwC, "global report on the commercial applications of drone technology," https://www.pwc.pl/pl/pdf/clarity-from-above-pwc.pdf, 09 2017.

[20] M. Khan, B. A. Alvi, E. Safi, and I. Khan, "Drones for good in smart cities:a review," *International Conference on Electrical, Electronics, Computers, Communication, Mechanical and Computing (EECCMC)*, 01 2018.

[21] J. C. Rosser, V. Vignesh, B. A. Terwilliger, and B. C. Parker, "Surgical and medical applications of drones: A comprehensive review." *JSLS Journal of the Society of Laparoendoscopic Surgeons*, vol. 22, no. 3, p. e2018.00018, 2018.

[22] N. R. Zema, E. Natalizio, M. Poss, G. Ruggeri, and

A. Molinaro, "MeDrone: On the use of a medical drone to heal a sensor network infected by a malicious epidemic," *Ad Hoc Networks*, vol. 50, pp. 115–127, Nov. 2016. [Online]. Available: https://hal.archives-ouvertes.fr/hal-01396858

[23] F. Mohammed, A. Idries, N. Mohamed, J. AlJaroodi, and I. Jawhar, "Uavs for smart cities: Opportunities and challenges," *International Conference on Unmanned Aircraft Systems (ICUAS)*, pp. 267–273, 05 2014.

[24] N. R. Zema, E. Natalizio, and E. Yanmaz, "An Unmanned Aerial Vehicle Network for Sport Event Filming with Communication Constraints," in *BalkanCom 2017 First International Balkan Conference on Communications and Networking*, Tirana, Albania, May 2017. [Online]. Available: https://hal.archives-ouvertes.fr/hal-01731379

[25] O. Artemenko, O. J. Dominic, O. Andryeyev, and A. Mitschele-Thiel, "Energy-aware trajectory planning for the localization of mobile devices using an unmanned aerial vehicle," in *2016 25th International Conference on Computer Communication and Networks (ICCCN)*, Aug 2016, pp. 1–9.

[26] J. Valente, D. Sanz, J. Cerro, A. Barrientos, and M. de Frutos, "Near-optimal coverage trajectories for image mosaicing using a mini quad-rotor over irregular-shaped fields," *Precision Agriculture*, vol. 14, pp. 115–132,, 02 2013.

[27] D. Li, X. Wang, and T. Sun, "Energy-optimal coverage path planning on topographic map for environment survey with unmanned aerial vehicles," *Electronics Letters*, vol. 52, no. 9, pp. 699–701, 2016.

[28] C. Recchiuto, C. Nattero, A. Sgorbissa, and R. Zaccaria, "Coverage algorithms for search and rescue with uav drones - abstract," in *In Workshop of the XIII AIIA Symposium on Artificial Intelligence*, 12 2014.

[29] C.-M. Tseng, C.-K. Chau, K. Elbassioni, and M. Khonji, "Flight tour planning with recharging optimization for battery-operated autonomous drones," 03 2017. [Online]. Available: https://arxiv.org/abs/1703.10049

[30] C. Di Franco and G. C. Buttazzo, in *Energy-aware Coverage Path Planning of UAVs*, 04 2015, pp. 111–117.

[31] J. Ware and N. Roy, in *An analysis of wind field estimation and exploitation for quadrotor flight in the urban canopy layer*, 05 2016, pp. 1507–1514.

[32] W. Al-Sabban, L. Gonzalez, and R. Smith, "Wind-energy based path planning for electric unmanned aerial vehicles using markov decision processes," in *Proceedings of the IEEE/RSJ International Conference on Intelligent Robots and Systems. IEEE*, 01 2013.

[33] M. Coombes, W.-H. Chen, and C. Liu, in *Boustrophedon coverage path planning for UAV aerial surveys in wind*, 06 2017, pp. 1563–1571.

[34] J. Gross, S. Goetz, and J. Cihlar, "Application of remote sensing to parks and protected area monitoring: Introduction to the special issue," *Remote Sensing of Environment*, vol. 113, pp. 1343–1345, 07 2009.

[35] C. Imen *et al.*, "Design and performance analysis of global path planning techniques for autonomous mobile robots in grid environments," *International Journal of Advanced Robotic Systems*, vol. 14, 04 2017.

[36] H. Xu, L. Shu, and M. Huang, "Planning paths with fewer turns on grid maps," in *Proceedings of the Sixth International Symposium on Combinatorial Search*, 2013, pp. 193–201.

[37] J. Gubbi, R. Buyya, S. Marusic, and M. Palaniswami, "Internet of things (iot): A vision, architectural elements, and future directions." *Future Generation Comp. Syst.*, vol. 29, no. 7, pp. 1645–1660, 2013. [Online]. Available: http://dblp.uni-trier.de/db/journals/fgcs/fgcs29.htmlGubbiBMP13

[38] P. Simoens, M. Dragone, and S. A., "The internet of robotic things: A review of concept, added value and applications." *International journal of Advanced Robotic Systems*, vol. 15, no. 1, p. 1729881418759424, 2018. [Online]. Available: https://doi.org/10.1177/1729881418759424

[39] S. Chandrasekharan *et al.*, "Designing and implementing future aerial communication networks," *IEEE Communications Magazine*, vol. 54, no. 5, pp. 26–34, May 2016.

[40] H. Choset, "Coverage for robotics–a survey of recent results," *Annals of mathematics and artificial intelligence*, vol. 31, no. 1-4, pp. 113–126, 2001.

[41] S. Bochkarev, S.and Smith, "On minimizing turns in robot coverage path planning." in *Proceedings of the 2016 IEEE International Conference on Automation Science and Engineering (CASE)*, August 2016, p. 18–20.

[42] E. Galceran and M. Carreras, "A survey on coverage path planning for robotics," *Robotics and Autonomous systems*, vol. 61, no. 12, pp. 1258–1276, 2013.

[43] A. Majeed and S. Lee, "A new coverage flight path planning algorithm based on footprint sweep fitting for unmanned aerial vehicle navigation in urban environments," *Applied Sciences (Switzerland)*, vol. 9, 04 2019.

[44] S. Nasr, H. Mekki, and K. Bouallegue, "A multi-scroll chaotic system for a higher coverage path planning of a mobile robot using flatness controller," *Chaos Solitons Fractals*, vol. 118, p. 366–375, 2019.

[45] K. Zhou *et al.*, "Agricultural operations planning in fields with multiple obstacle areas," *Computers and Electronics in Agriculture*, vol. 109, pp. 12–22, 2014.

[46] A. Montanari, F. Kringberg, A. Valentini, C. Mascolo, and A. Prorok, "Surveying areas in developing regions through context aware drone mobility," in *Proceedings of the 4th ACM Workshop on Micro Aerial Vehicle Networks, Systems, and Applications*, ser. DroNet'18. New York, NY, USA: ACM, 2018, pp. 27–32. [Online]. Available: http://doi.acm.org/10.1145/3213526.3213532

[47] F. Lingelbach, "Path planning using probabilistic cell decomposition." in *Proceedings of the 2004 IEEE International Conference on Robotics and Automation, ICRA'04*, vol. 1, 2004, p. 467–472.

[48] H. Choset, "Coverage of known spaces: The boustrophedon cellular decomposition." *Autonomous Robots*, vol. 9, p. 247–253, 2000.

[49] H. Choset *et al.*, "Principles of robot motion: Theory, algorithms, and implementation," *MIT Press*, 2005.

[50] S. Wong, "Qualitative topological coverage of unknown environments by mobile robots," *Doctoral Dissertation, The University of Auckland, New Zealand*, 2006.

[51] V. Shivashankar *et al.*, "Real-time planning for covering an initially-unknown spatial environment," in *Proceedings of the Twenty-Fourth International Florida Artificial Intelligence Research Society Conference*, May 2011, p. 18–20.

[52] R. Díaz-Delgado, G. Ónodi, G. Kröel-Dulay, and M. Kertész, "Enhancement of ecological field experimental research by means of uav multispectral sensing," *Drones*, vol. 3, no. 1, p. 7, 2019.

[53] M. Mozaffari, W. Saad, M. Bennis, and M. Debbah, "Efficient deployment of multiple unmanned aerial vehicles for optimal wireless coverage," *IEEE Communications Letters*, vol. 20, 06 2016.

[54] W. Yue and Z. Jiang, "Path planning for uav to collect sensors data based on spiral decomposition," *Procedia Computer Science*, vol. 131, pp. 873–879, 01 2018.

[55] T. M. Cabreira, C. D. Franco, P. R. Ferreira, and G. C. Buttazzo, "Energy-aware spiral coverage path planning for uav photogrammetric applications," *IEEE Robotics and Automation Letters*, vol. 3, no. 4, pp. 3662–3668, Oct 2018.

[56] M. Torres, D. A. Pelta, J. L. Verdegay, and J. C. Torres, "Coverage path planning with unmanned aerial vehicles for 3d terrain reconstruction," *Expert Systems with Applications*, vol. 55, pp. 441–451, 2016.

[57] F. Balampanis, I. Maza, and A. Ollero, in *Area decomposition, partition and coverage with multiple remotely piloted aircraft systems operating in coastal regions*, 07 2016, pp. 275–283.

[58] Balampanis, Fotios and Maza, Ivan and Ollero, Anibal, "Area partition for coastal regions with multiple uas," *Journal of Intelligent and Robotic Systems*, vol. 88, no. 2, pp. 751–766, Dec 2017. [Online]. Available: https://doi.org/10.1007/s10846-017-0559-9

[59] J. Fortuna, S. P.B, and J. Sousa, in *Multiple UAV area decomposition and coverage*, 04 2013, pp. 30–37.

[60] E. J. Forsmo, E. Grøtli, T. Fossen, and T. Johansen, in *Optimal search mission with Unmanned Aerial Vehicles using Mixed Integer Linear Programming*, 05 2013, pp. 253–259.

[61] J. Acevedo, B. Arrue, I. Maza, and A. Ollero, "Distributed approach for coverage and patrolling missions with a team of heterogeneous aerial robots under communication constraints," *International Journal of Advanced Robotic Systems*, vol. 10, pp. 1–13, 01 2013.

[62] H. L. Andersen, "Path planning for search and rescue mission using multicopters," 2014.

[63] C. Caillouet and T. Razafindralambo, in *Efficient deployment of connected unmanned aerial vehicles for optimal target coverage*, 10 2017, pp. 1–8.

[64] D. Albani, D. Nardi, and V. Trianni, in *2017 IEEE/RSJ International Conference on Intelligent Robots and Systems (IROS)*, Sep. 2017, pp. 4319–4325.

[65] J. J. Acevedo, B. C. Arrue, I. Maza, and A. Ollero, "Cooperative large area surveillance with a team of aerial mobile robots for long endurance missions," *Journal of Intelligent & Robotic Systems*, vol. 70, no. 1, pp. 329–345, Apr 2013. [Online]. Available: https://doi.org/10.1007/s10846-012-9716-3

[66] C. Wenkai *et al.*, "Development of a power line inspection robot with hybrid operation modes*," in *2017 IEEE/RSJ International Conference on Intelligent Robots and Systems*, 09 2017, p. 973–978.

[67] J. Modares, F. Ghanei, N. Mastronarde, and K. Dantu, in *UB-ANC planner: Energy efficient coverage path planning with multiple drones*, 05 2017, pp. 6182–6189.

[68] G. Öst, "Search path generation with uav applications using approximate convex decomposition," Master's thesis, Linköping UniversityLinköping University, Automatic Control, The Institute of Technology, 2012.

[69] S. Rashed and M. Soyturk, "Analyzing the effects of uav mobility patterns on data collection in wireless sensor networks," *Sensors*, vol. 17, 02 2017.

Energy-aware Cross-level Model for Wireless Sensor Networks

Michel Bakni, Guillaume Terrasson, Octavian Curea, Alvaro Llaria, Jessye Dos Santos
Univ. Bordeaux, ESTIA Institute of Technology
F-64210 Bidart, France
e-mail: {m.bakni, g.terrasson, o.curea, a.llaria, j.dossantos}@estia.fr

Abstract— **In the design stage, Wireless Sensor Network developers generally need simulation tools to save both time and costs. These simulators require accurate models to precisely describe the network components and behaviours, such as energy consumption. Nevertheless, although the model has grown in complexity over last years, from layered-stack to cross-level, the energy aspects are not yet well implemented. In this paper, we suggest an energy-aware cross-level model for Wireless Sensor Networks. Our modelling approach allows for parameters that belong to different levels to interact with each other and to analyse their impact on energy consumption. To validate this approach, the energy-aware cross-level model for network radiofrequency activities is first provided. The results obtained using suggested scenarios are compared with those collected from a well-known simulator: NS2. Finally, the usefulness of our model in Wireless Sensor Network design process is demonstrated thanks to a case study aimed at comparing and selecting the most energy-efficient wireless link protocol.**

Keywords-Energy-aware design; Cross-level; Energy modelling; Wireless Sensor Networks.

I. INTRODUCTION

A Wireless Sensor Network (WSN) is a set of nodes, which embed sensors coupled with processing units and wireless communication devices. This kind of network is used to monitor physical phenomena in the deployment area or to trace targets moving inside it. Thanks to battery-powered and wireless connectivity features, WSNs are both highly flexible and scalable. These two characteristics make WSNs a technology that provides innovative applications in a wide variety of domains, such as healthcare, industry, and agriculture [1].

Nevertheless, node energy resources are strictly limited, making the power-aware design of WSNs a major research issue, whose relevance has increased in recent years [2]. In this regard, at the very early stages of the design process, engineers and researchers involved in the development of WSN applications must take the right decisions in terms of energy efficiency and also consider overall application performances. Usually, simulators and emulators are used to accomplish this task.

The scientific literature review reveals a wide variety of simulators generally designed for a specific-level such as network or node levels. However, this review shows that there is a lack of analysis tools dedicated to the early design stages, especially from a power awareness point of view. For example, there is no model that is able to show how a given parameter impacts energy consumption, not only from a specific-level perspective but from a multilevel one as well [3].

In this context, the work presented defines an energy-aware cross-level model for WSNs which tries to mitigate the limitations mentioned above. The suggested model is applied to the radiofrequency (RF) activities of the network, a vital part of the node that is generally responsible for a high-energy consumption in WSN applications [4]. The goal of our model is to accurately estimate RF module consumption based on cross-level parameter impacts.

This paper is organised as follows. Section II provides an overview of the development of WSN models and the associated simulators. In Section III, a global description of the proposed cross-level approach together with its application to WSN RF activities is provided. The first results using the implemented energy-aware model are presented and discussed in Sections IV and V. Finally, Section VI concludes this paper.

II. WSN MODELLING AND SIMULATION

To better address the modelling issue, a review of the evolution of WSN models is first provided. Then, for WSN simulators based on these models, an energy-aware level-based classification is introduced.

A. WSN Models: from Layered-stack to Cross-level Design

Classical data network models, such as Open Systems Interconnection (OSI), propose a design approach consisting of a set of layers that are stacked together. In a layered-stack model, the layers are separated according to their functionality. Every layer offers interfaces only towards adjacent layers in the stack [5]. However, in WSNs, parameters from different layers interact with each other, and services are provided across the stack layers rather than a specific layer. Thus, the traditional stack-layered model is difficult to adapt to the requirements of this kind of network [6].

Several years ago, many works dealt with the modelling issue, developing various solutions. In [5], the authors propose a modelling approach based on a cross-layer design. This approach supports adaptivity and optimisation across multiple layers of the protocol stack. A similar cross-layered model is proposed in [7]. Moreover, security considerations from a cross-layer point of view are added to this cross-layered model in [8].

Another strategy is to propose the “tier” or “level” concept [9], where a level represents a group of parameters that belong to different functions and features of WSNs, and not only to the network model. In parallel to the previous approaches, the solution described in [10] groups the model layers into two levels. The first is mainly concerned with non-physical parameters related to software and the application. The second is dedicated to hardware where the protocols are implemented, mainly routing and linking, as well as sensors and RF unit parameters.

Subsequently, different evolutions were proposed to develop a cross-level model following the multi-level approach. This led to the development of a new approach to model WSNs, extending the traditional layered-stack model to include not only software and hardware levels that make up the nodes, but also parameters from the surrounding environment. In this way, a wireless medium level was attached to the model in [11] and [12]. In [13], a description of how the multiple-level model is used to design and develop WSN from a cross-level perspective is also carried out.

Nevertheless, as demonstrated in [13], not all the proposed approaches are actually employed in an effective cross-level manner. Moreover, as mentioned above, the energy aspect of WSNs is not always well implemented, despite this being a crucial issue in WSN design.

B. *WSN Simulators: a Level-based Overview*

In general, WSNs simulators are dedicated to a specific level of abstraction and are built over the previously discussed models. Thus, they focus on simulating parameters related to one particular level [2]. A parameter is a numeric value describing one property of a given level, such as power levels or bit rate.

For example, Network simulator 2 (NS2) [14] is oriented to network protocol simulation and provides poor support for hardware. On the contrary, TOSSIM [15] emulates hardware in detail, but it provides an abstract perspective of network protocols. Furthermore, there are multi-level simulators. In this case, the simulator uses parameters belonging to different levels at the same time. For instance, Jsim [16] is a multi-level WSN simulator because it simulates both environment and network parameters. Finally, some simulators are described as cross-level, because they provide the ability for parameters belonging to different levels to interact with each other. COOJA [17] is an example of this category of simulators.

All the previously mentioned simulators are non-energy-oriented. This does not mean they cannot simulate energy aspects, but rather they were not built for this purpose. Based on this, another classification can be proposed, as illustrated in Figure 1. Simulators are first divided based on energy with two main branches, energy-oriented and non-energy-oriented simulators [3]. Then, a level-based classification is added.

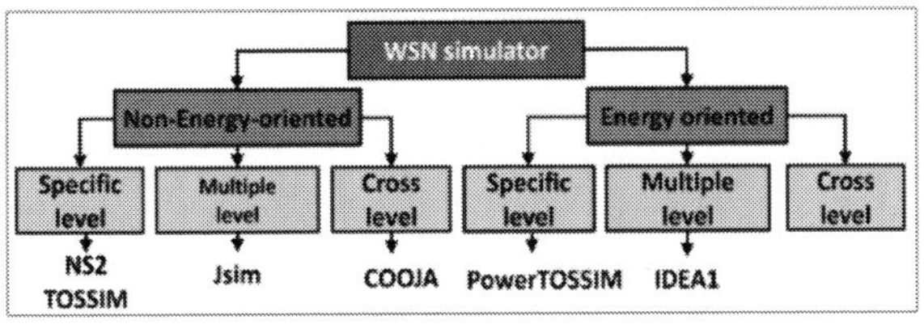

Figure 1. Energy-aware level-based classification for WSN simulators.

Overviewing the energy-oriented simulators, on the one hand, PowerTOSSIM [18] is an energy-oriented TOSSIM extension dedicated to the emulation of energy in hardware. On the other hand, IDEA1 [19] is an example of an energy-oriented multi-level simulator. IDEA1 divides the network into three abstract levels: the environment, the node, and the wireless medium. Although the simulator allows cross-level interaction for some parameters, this feature is not fully supported, and there are still parameters that are not treated in a cross-level manner, such as the environment parameters.

This review shows that many non-energy-oriented multi or cross-level models and simulators of WSNs have been proposed. However, from an energy point of view, the cross-level approach is not fully adopted. Therefore, with existing simulators, it is difficult to analyse the impact of parameters that belong to different levels on both the overall node energy consumption and WSN lifetime.

III. CROSS-LEVEL ENERGY MODEL

In this section, to address the problems described above, we propose a model for WSNs that is both energy-aware and cross-level.

A. *Global Model*

In our model, the implementation of the cross-level concept allows parameters from different levels to interact with each other affecting the performances of WSNs. In this work, we are only concerned with the impact of the parameters on energy performance such as network lifetime and node autonomy. Figure 2 provides an overview of the proposed model.

The model's levels can be described as follows:

- The Use case Level (UL) is the most abstract level of the model. It is related to the design stage of the WSN application. Parameters, such as frequency of the pattern F_p of the nodes, to be defined later, or payload length reside in this level.

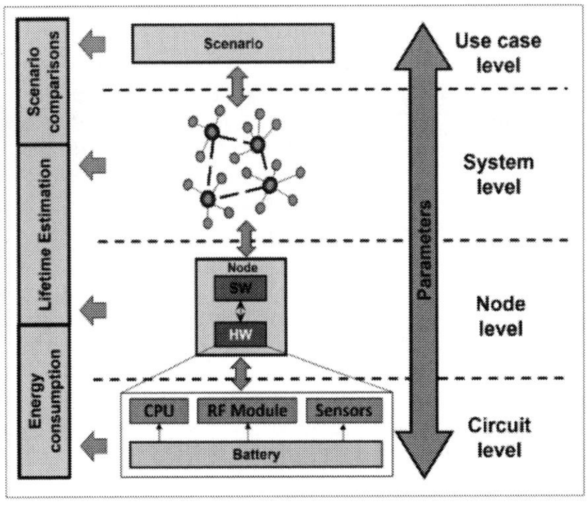

Figure 2. The Proposed Cross-level model for Wireless Sensor Networks.

- The System Level (SL) reflects a topological point of view of the network. It focuses on how high-level protocols and algorithms affect WSN performances. Parameters related to the network topology, like the distance between nodes or high-level protocols headers, belong to this level.
- The Node Level (NL) concerns the interaction between software (node operating system) and onboard hardware (RF circuit). As illustrated in Figure 3, the parameters related to the link protocol, such as the bit rate and the link layer header fit in this level, as well as the parameters related to channel access or acknowledgment process.
- The Circuit Level (CL) is particularly used to describe node hardware. Modelling and description of electronic circuits reside in this level. It includes RF module, sensors, CPU and battery as well as hardware-specific parameters, such as power level or supply voltage.

Consequently, in this model, the higher the level is, the more abstract and general the parameters are. For example, parameters belonging to the UL are related to the scenario description and theoretically fit into any WSN application. On the other hand, CL parameters are very specific and describe only particular electronic circuits.

As illustrated in Figure 2, the use of the cross-level feature enables not only energy consumption of the nodes or the system's lifetime to be estimated, but also provides a basis for different scenario comparisons.

B. Energy-aware Model Applied to RF Activities

The proposed model is first applied to describe RF activities in a WSN. Based on the afore mentioned classification, the parameters related to RF activities are categorised as illustrated in Figure 3. Note that the colour of each parameter corresponds to its parent level.

In the first stage, the total number of bits to send is calculated. This includes the payload (UL) created by the sensors or other applications that generate data on the node, as well as high-level protocol headers (SL) and the link layer protocol header (NL).

After this, the total amount of data is confronted against the fragmentation threshold (NL) identified by the wireless link protocol. If fragmentation is needed, the process will take place in this stage, and will result in two or more data frames. Next, the preamble (NL) is added to each data frame. Then, the length of each frame is calculated in terms of seconds, thanks to the bitrate(s) (CL) provided by the selected chipset.

The next step is to build the energy consumption pattern for the node's RF activities. In our approach, we assume the energy consumption in each node takes place based on a repeated pattern. The pattern is defined as a set of sequenced activities or phases with their corresponding power levels. In this context, the frequency of the pattern F_p (UL) corresponds to the ratio between the number of occurrences of the pattern and the considered simulation time.

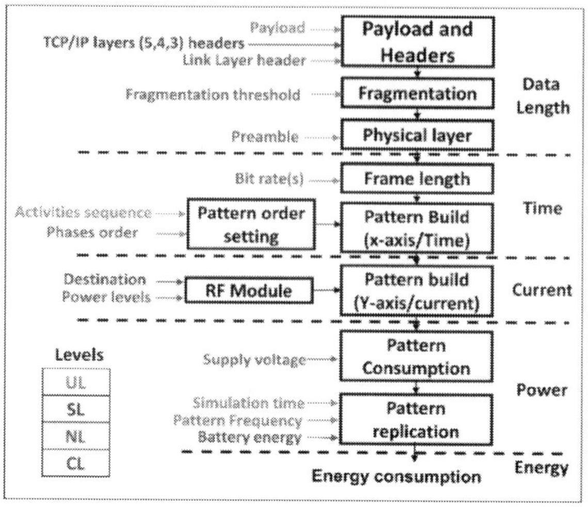

Figure 3. An energy-aware cross-level model for RF activities.

Then, to build this RF consumption pattern, activities sequence (UL) and phases order (NL) are to be considered. The activity sequence helps to specify the actions taking place, i.e. sending or receiving frames, while the link protocol defines the phases and their order within each activity. For example, in the sending activity, the order of phases is: accessing the channel (ph_{acc}), exchanging data frames (ph_{exch}) and then waiting for acknowledgment (ph_{ack}).

After that, the sequence of activities is to be matched with the power levels (CL) provided by the RF module datasheet. This includes the consideration of the distance (SL) that has a direct impact on the power level of the sending activity. Then, the energy consumed is calculated.

In the last stage, the total simulation time (UL), the frequency of the pattern F_p (UL), as well as the initial amount of the energy stored in the battery (CL) are considered in our model to estimate the system's lifetime.

IV. MODEL COMPARISON WITH NS2

A. Scenario Definition

Simulation scenarios are suggested to compare the results obtained from the proposed model with those of a well-known simulator, namely NS2. These scenarios take place in an open area measuring 25x25 m2. Within this area, there are two wireless nodes, 10m apart, named Node A and Node B. Periodically, Node A sends a fixed-length payload to Node B through the wireless medium using its RF module. As soon as Node B receives the payload, it replies by sending the received payload to Node A through the wireless medium. Node A and Node B use the same protocol stack.

Each node applies a TCP/IP network model. The implementation of the protocols starts at the network layer where Internet Protocol version 4 (IPv4) has been chosen. The Internet Control Message Protocol (ICMP), which is an integral part of IPv4, is employed to create echo messages. Consequently, whenever the IPv4 module receives a data packet, it sends the same data back to the original source. In all scenarios, the length of IPv4 and ICMP headers are 20 and

4 bytes respectively, as defined by the standards. Table I displays the scenario settings.

Next, the link layer parameters are set. We decided to implement two wireless link protocols. 802.11a is used in the first set of scenarios, while 802.15.4 is applied in the second set. The energy specification for the 802.11a RF module is derived from an implementation of a chipset named HDG204 (H&D wireless). For 802.15.4, the CC2420 transceiver (Texas Instruments) is selected. Table II shows the settings of the two wireless link protocols.

For each simulation, the considered time used to calculate energy consumption is 100 seconds, and it begins after initialising the nodes. For each protocol, three different values of F_P: 0.1, 1 and 2 Hz, and ten values for the payload length ranging between 10 to 100 bytes are used. Each scenario requires a combination of the three parameters mentioned above. As a result, there are 30 scenarios to be run for each wireless link protocol. These scenarios are configured both in NS2 and in the proposed model implemented in Matlab aimed at comparing the results.

B. Results and Discussion

The obtained results are the energy consumed by different activities of the RF module. These activities are categorised into 4 phases:

- Access phase (ph_{acc}): RF module tries to access the wireless channel.
- Exchange phase (ph_{exch}): RF module sends or receives data frames.
- Acknowledge phase (ph_{ack}): RF module sends or receives acknowledgment frames.
- Complementary phase (ph_{com}): The RF module is in sleep state.

In these phases, the cross-level interaction between parameters takes place, i.e. the energy consumed in each phase is the result of interplay between parameters related to different levels. For example, in the exchange phase, the consumed energy is a function of the header lengths, payload length and bit rate, which belongs to the following levels: UL, SL and NL respectively.

TABLE I. GENERAL SETTINGS FOR THE PROPOSED SCENARIOS

Parameter	Value
Number of the nodes	2
Node positions	(10,10), (10,20) [m]
Scenario duration T_{Sce}	100 [s]
Pattern Frequency F_p	0.1, 1, 2 [Hz]
Payload length	10, 20, …, 100 [Byte]
Link protocol	802.11a, 802.15.4

TABLE II. WIRELESS LINK PROTOCOLS SETTINGS

Parameter	802.11a (HDG204)	802.15.4 (CC2420)
Bitrate [bps]	12 M	250 K
Carrier Sense Mechanism	Pure CSMA/CA	CCA-ED
Transmitter power [mW]	725	52
Receiver Power [mW]	220	59
Sleep Power [mW]	0.2	0.06

The results obtained by implementing the previously described scenarios in NS2 and Matlab using our model can be found in Table III. The upper part shows the obtained results from 802.11a and the lower part for 802.15.4. Each part is further divided into two subparts, corresponding to scenarios with 10 and 100 bytes for the payload length respectively. Figure 4 shows the energy consumption patterns of Node B, extracted from our model, for the two protocols when the payload length is 100 bytes. Compared to NodeB, Node A has the same activities, thus, it has an identical energy consumption.

For the two protocols, when comparing results obtained from NS2 and our proposed model, the following differences and similarities can be found. The energy consumed in ph_{acc} or ph_{ack} is identical and there is a slight difference in the energy consumed in ph_{com}. In ph_{exch}, the difference is notable but fix and this is due to different interpretations of the link protocol specifications. For example, in our model, the ICMP header is considered to be part of the data packet, contrary to NS2 where this header is added to the data packet later on.

Figure 5 shows the relative errors between the results obtained from NS2 and those obtained from the proposed model. The left side of the figure is dedicated to 802.11a and the right side to 802.15.4. Different values of F_p are displayed, namely 0.1, 1, and 2 Hz. For each of these values, a set of corresponding errors is provided, each of which is also related to a simulation where the payload length is 10, 50, or 100 bytes.

TABLE III. ENERGY CONSUMPTION OF THE PHASES IN DIFFERENT SCENARIOS FOR NODE B(F_P = 1 Hz)

Simulation	The consumed energy by phase [μJ]				
	ph_{acc}	ph_{exch}	ph_{ack}	ph_{com}	Total
802.11a					
10 Bytes					
Matlab	51.03	50.08	23.63	199.959	324.69
NS2	51.03	55.76	23.63	199.950	330.37
100 Bytes					
Matlab	51.03	106.79	23.63	199.935	381.38
NS2	51.03	112.46	23.63	199.927	387.04
802.15.4					
10 Bytes					
Matlab	18.89	145.73	39.07	59.78	263.47
NS2	18.88	152.84	39.07	59.78	270.47
100 Bytes					
Matlab	18.89	465.37	39.07	59.44	582.77
NS2	18.88	472.42	39.07	59.45	589.82

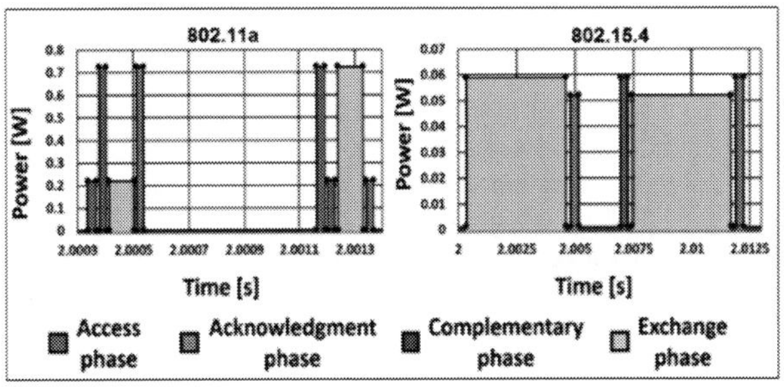

Figure 4. Energy consumption patterns for different wireless link protocols (Node B, Payload length = 100 Bytes, F_p = 1 Hz).

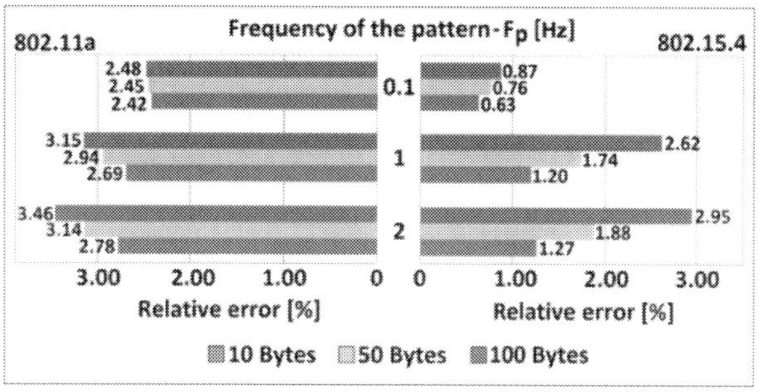

Figure 5. Relative error between the proposed model and NS2.

In all the simulation results, the relative errors obtained from 802.11a are greater than those of the corresponding scenarios of 802.15.4. This difference can be explained by unplanned and non-periodic radio activities that appear periodically in NS2 802.11a simulations. These activities have a fixed duration regardless of F_p and the payload length. Each of these activities appears as a single pulse of transmission or reception causing an additional energy consumption around of 5 µJ and 2 µJ respectively.

Finally, as illustrated in Figure 5, the value of the relative error between NS2 and the proposed model did not exceed 3.5%. Based on this, we can consider the proposed model is validated with NS2. Although not shown in this scenario, our proposed WSN model also allows adding energy consumption phases with other hardware on the node, such as CPU or sensors. As a result, an accurate pattern can be constructed precisely representing the real consumption of the node contrary to NS2 that has poor support for hardware, as mentioned above.

V. Application of the Model: A Case Study

To demonstrate the usefulness of the proposed model, the previous scenarios, suggested in Section IV.A, are used to compare wireless link protocol performance in terms of energy consumption. The interaction between two parameters with regard to energy consumption is observed. These two parameters are the pattern frequency F_p and the payload length.

Figure 6 presents the difference, in Joules, between the energies ($E_{pat802.11a}$ - $E_{pat802.15.4}$) consumed by the two link protocols respectively. There are three distinguishable situations:

- The red curve: this represents the equal-energy boundary, i.e. for the scenarios that are positioned on the curve, the two protocols consume the same amount of energy.
- The area above the curve (cyan): in this area, 802.11a is more energy-efficient than 802.15.4. For all the scenarios that are positioned inside this area, using 802.11a as the wireless link protocol is recommended from an energy point of view.

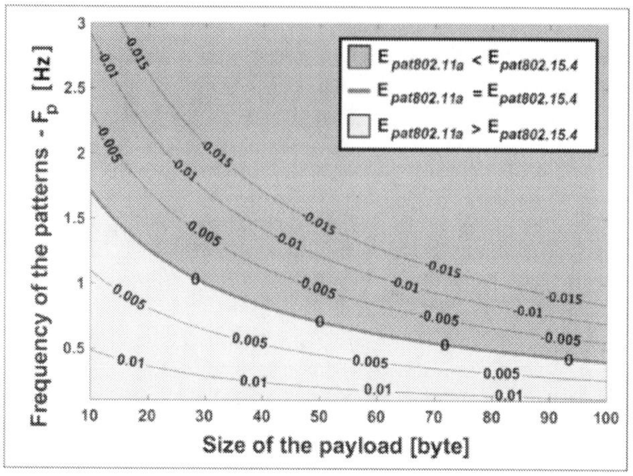

Figure 6. The Equal-energy caurve of the 802.11a and 802.15.4 in the proposed scenarios.

- The area below the curve (yellow): in this area, 802.15.4 is more energy-efficient than 802.11a. For all the scenarios that are positioned inside this area, using 802.15.4 as the wireless link protocol is recommended.

As illustrated in Figure 6, when F_p is 2 Hz, using 802.11a is more efficient in terms of energy consumption. On the contrary, when F_p is 0.1 Hz, the use of 802.15.4 is more energy efficient. In the case where F_p is 1 Hz, the choice is a function of the payload size. If it is less than 30 bytes, the use of 802.15.4 is more efficient. Conversely, when the payload size is greater than 30 bytes, using 802.11a is more effective from an energy perspective.

Finally, this case study demonstrates how the proposed model could be used in the early design stage, as a tool to select, for example, the most energy-efficient protocol for a given case study. Moreover, it shows the energy-aware aspect of our model, namely, its ability to observe how a given parameter could impact energy consumption.

VI. Conclusion

This paper has presented the principles of a cross-level energy model for power-aware WSN design, mainly aimed at WSN designers. First, the model was implemented to describe the RF activities and the obtained results were compared with NS2. This comparison showed a relative error percentage below 3.5% for the considered scenarios. The model's usefulness has also been illustrated by comparing two wireless link protocol from an energy point of view, using a basic case study.

Although the results are promising, other hardware activities, such as the CPU and sensors, are to be implemented in the proposed model as well. Furthermore, for future work, a simulation tool which implements the complete cross-level energy-aware model is also to be developed. This tool will first be validated using more complex scenarios that cover, for example, a number of different network topologies with more than two nodes. Then, the results obtained from this tool will be also compared to experimental case studies to demonstrate the accuracy of our cross-level approach.

ACKNOWLEDGMENT

The work presented in this paper has been financially supported by the New Aquitaine Regional Council, Bordeaux, France (as part of the Call for 2016 Project funds), within the framework of the OUDINI research project.

REFERENCES

[1] J. Yick, M. Biswanath, and G. Dipak, "Wireless sensor network survey," Computer networks, Elsevier, pp. 2292-2330, vol. 52, no. 12, Aug. 2008, doi: 10.1016/j.comnet.2008.04.002.

[2] R. Chéour, M. W. Jmal, O. Kanoun, and M. Abid, "Evaluation of simulator tools and power-aware scheduling model for wireless sensor networks," IET Computers & Digital Techniques, vol. 11, pp. 173-182, Aug. 2017, doi: 10.1049/iet-cdt.2017.0003.

[3] J. Haase, J. M. Molina, and D. Dietrich, "Power-aware system design of wireless sensor networks: Power estimation and power profiling strategies," IEEE Trans. on Industrial Informatics, vol. 7, pp. 601-613, 2011, doi: 10.1109/TII.2011.2166793.

[4] G. Terrasson, R. Briand, S. Basrour, V. Dupé, and O. Arrijuria, "Energy Model for the Design of Ultra-Low Power Nodes for Wireless Sensor Networks", Procedia Chemistry, Vol. 1, Issue 1, pp. 1195-1198, 2009, doi 10.1016/j.proche.2009.07.298.

[5] H. Zimmermann, "OSI Reference Model - The ISO Model of Architecture for Open Systems Interconnection," in IEEE Trans. on Communications, vol. 28, no. 4, pp. 425-432, April 1980, doi: 10.1109/TCOM.1980.1094702.

[6] A. J. Goldsmith and S. B. Wicker, "Design challenges for energy-constrained ad hoc wireless networks," IEEE Wireless Communications, vol. 9, pp. 8-27, Aug. 2002, doi: 10.1109/MWC.2002.1028874.

[7] I. F. Akyildiz, W. Su, Y. Sankarasubramaniam, and E. Cayirci, "Wireless sensor networks: a survey," Computer Networks, vol. 38, no. 4, pp. 393-422, Mar. 2002, doi: 10.1016/S1389-1286(01)00302-4.

[8] W. Charfi, M. Masmoudi, and F. Derbel, "A layered model for wireless sensor networks," Proc. of 6th International Multi-Conference on Systems, Signals and Devices, IEEE, Mar. 2009, pp. 1-5, doi: 10.1109/SSD.2009.4956693.

[9] E. Egea-López, J. Vales-Alonso, A. S. Martínez-Sala, P. Pavón-Mariño, and J. García-Haro, "Simulation tools for wireless sensor networks," International Symposium on Performance Evaluation of Computer and Telecommunication Systems (SPECTS05), Society for Modeling & Simulation International, Jul. 2005, pp. 1-8, ISBN: 9781622763504.

[10] M. Kuorilehto, M. Kohvakka, M. Hännikäinen, and T. D. Hämäläinen, "High abstraction level design and implementation framework for wireless sensor networks," International Workshop on Embedded Computer Systems: Architectures, Modeling, and Simulation (SAMOS 2005), Lecture Notes in Computer Science Springer, Jul. 2005, pp. 384-393, doi:10.1007/11512622_41.

[11] M. Korkalainen, M. Sallinen, N. Kärkkäinen, and P. Tukeva, "Survey of wireless sensor networks simulation tools for demanding applications," 2009 Fifth International Conference on Networking and Services, IEEE, Apr. 2009, pp. 102-106, doi: 10.1109/ICNS.2009.75.

[12] W. Du, D. Navarro, F. Mieyeville, and F. Gaffiot, "Towards a taxonomy of simulation tools for wireless sensor networks," Proc. of the 3rd Int. Conf. on Simulation Tools and Techniques, ICST, Mar. 2010, pp. 52-59, doi: 10.4108/ICST.SIMUTOOLS2010.8659.

[13] M. Imran, A. M. Said, and H. Hasbullah, "A survey of simulators, emulators and testbeds for wireless sensor networks," 2010 International Symposium on Information Technology, IEEE, Jun. 2010, pp. 897-902, doi: 10.1109/ITSIM.2010.5561571.

[14] T. Issariyakul and E. Hossain, "Introduction to Network Simulator 2 (NS2)," in Introduction to Network Simulator NS2. Springer US, pp. 21-40, 2012, doi: 10.1007/978-0-387-71760-9_2.

[15] P. Levis, N. Lee, M. Welsh, and D. Culler, "TOSSIM: Accurate and scalable simulation of entire TinyOS applications," Proc. of the 1st Int. Conf. on Embedded Networked Sensor Systems, ACM, Nov. 2003, pp. 126-137, doi: 10.1145/958491.958506.

[16] A. Sobeih et al., "J-Sim: A simulation and emulation environment for wireless sensor networks," IEEE Wireless Communications, vol. 13, pp. 104-119, Aug. 2006, doi: 10.1109/MWC.2006.1678171.

[17] F. Osterlind, A. Dunkels, J. Eriksson, N. Finne, and T. Voigt, "Cross-Level sensor network simulation with COOJA," Proc. of the 31st Conf. on Local Computer Networks, IEEE, Nov. 2006, pp. 641-648, doi: 10.1109/LCN.2006.322172.

[18] E. Perla, A. Ó. Catháin, R. S. Carbajo, M. Huggard, and C. McGoldric, "PowerTOSSIM z: Realistic energy modelling for wireless sensor network environments," Proc. of the 3rd ACM Workshop on Performance Monitoring and Measurement of Heterogeneous Wireless and Wired Networks, ACM, Oct. 2008, pp. 35-42, doi: 10.1145/1454630.1454636.

[19] W. Du, D. Navarro, F. Mieyeville, and I. O'Connor, "IDEA1: A validated system C-based simulator for wireless sensor networks," Proc. of the 8th Int. Conf. on Mobile Ad-Hoc and Sensor Systems, IEEE, Oct. 2011, pp. 825-830, doi: 10.1109/MASS.2011.95.

A Bandwidth-Efficient Soft-Decision Scheme for Distributed Binary Detection in Sensor Networks

Victor W. Cheng
Dept. of Comp. Sci. and Information Eng.
National Chi Nan University
Taiwan
Email: vicwk@csie.ncnu.edu.tw

Tsang-Yi Wang
Inst. of Communications Eng.
National Sun Yat-sen University
Taiwan
Email: tcwang@mail.nsysu.edu.tw

Hao Wang
Inst. of Communications Eng.
National Sun Yat-sen University
Taiwan
Email: u0222130@gmail.com

***Abstract*—The soft-decision fusion scheme on sensor detection in wireless sensor networks is able to improve the detection performance on the final decision made at the Fusion Center (FC). In this paper, a bandwidth-efficient transmission scheme using the soft-decision fusion scheme is proposed for distributed binary detection. In the scheme, the source coding is through the quantization process, but the output of the quantizer is analogously transmitted to the FC. In the FC, the Maximum-a-Posteriori (MAP) fusion rule is adopted to make the final decision. The problem of huge channel bandwidth demand can be avoided by using the considered data transmission scheme. The proposed scheme is illustrated with numerical examples highlighting its significant improvement in error performance at the FC as compared with the hard-decision scheme.**

Keywords–Distributed detection; bandwidth efficiency; fusion rule; wireless sensor networks.

I. Introduction

Distributed detection fusion using multiple sensors has a lot of applications in Wireless Sensor Networks (WSNs) [1] [2]. Conventionally, in the distributed parallel fusion network, a phenomenon in a specified environment is first observed by a sensor, and a decision based on the observation is made without exchanging the information with other local sensors. Then, each sensor transmits a signal to the Fusion Center (FC), where the final decision is made.

In contrast to the binary local decision case [3], many works have also studied the case of soft-decision fusion, in which the sensor observation is divided into M regions, where M is an arbitrary integer with $M > 2$ [4]–[11]. However, all the works mentioned above assume that the information of soft local decision is digitally transmitted to the FC, in which the information of each quantization level is mapped to several digital bits and the local quantizer output corresponding to the received quantization level is then utilized by the FC to make its final decision. As opposed to the existing works mentioned above, this study considers bandwidth-efficient transmission between the local sensors and FC in designing the soft-decision fusion scheme on the sensor observation. Specifically, the output of the quantizer is analogously transmitted to the FC. In the FC, the Maximum-a-Posteriori (MAP) fusion rule is adopted to make the final decision. Hence, by the proposed scheme, the problem of huge channel bandwidth demand can be avoided.

In the proposed scheme, the detection on the phenomenon is divided into M regions, where M is an arbitrary integer with $M \geq 2$. When the detection falls within a specific region, a conditional mean is adopted as a representation of the observation in the region. The goal of the proposed scheme is to minimize the decision errors at the FC with the MAP fusion rule via optimizing the region allocation.

The rest of this paper is organized as follows. Section II first depicts the proposed M-ary scheme for binary distributed detection problem. Section III shows the error performance of the M-ary scheme and its comparison with that of the conventional hard-decision scheme. Section IV concludes this work and discusses possible directions in the future.

II. Design of Soft-decision Fusion Scheme

In a binary detection environment under binary hypothesis H_0 and H_1 shown in Figure 1, assume a phenomenon A either $H_0 : A = \gamma$ or $H_1 : A = -\gamma$, where $\gamma > 0$, occurs symmetrically with equal prior probability $P[H_0] = P[H_1] = 0.5$. L sensors observe the measurements generated from H_0 or H_1 and the observation value by the l-th sensor is denoted by W_l, where $l = 1, \ldots, L$. W_l is independent and identically distributed (i.i.d.) from sensor to sensor. Also, assume H_0 : $W_l = \gamma + \eta_l$; $H_1 : W_l = -\gamma + \eta_l$, where η_l is a standard normal random variable. The probability density function (PDF) of W_l conditioned on H_0 or H_1 is $f_{W_l|H_0}(w) = e^{-(w-\gamma)^2/2}/\sqrt{2\pi}$ or $f_{W_l|H_1}(w) = e^{-(w+\gamma)^2/2}/\sqrt{2\pi}$. In the considered parallel fusion networks, the l-th sensor makes its own decision X, independent of all other nodes.

In this study, an M-ary source coding algorithm is applied on the observation at each sensor, where W_l at the l-th sensor is divided into M equally spaced regions, as shown in Figure 1. When M is even ($M = 2N$), the $2N$ regions are $I_{-N}, I_{-(N-1)}, \ldots, I_{-1}, I_1, \ldots, I_N$, and the $(2N-1)$ boundaries are $-(N-1)\Delta, -(N-2)\Delta, \ldots, -\Delta, 0, \Delta, \ldots, (N-1)\Delta$. Δ is the width of each region except for the two end regions I_{-N} and I_N. Similarly, when M is odd ($M = (2N+1)$), the $2N+1$ regions are $I_{-N}, I_{-(N-1)}, \ldots, I_{-1}, I_0, I_1, \ldots, I_N$, and the $2N$ boundaries are $-(N-\frac{1}{2})\Delta, -(N-\frac{3}{2})\Delta, \ldots, -\frac{1}{2}\Delta, \frac{1}{2}\Delta, \ldots, (N-\frac{1}{2})\Delta$. We define $p_n = P[W_l \in I_n|H_0] = Q(d_{low} - \gamma) - Q(d_{up} - \gamma)$, where $n = -N, -(N-1), ..., N$, d_{low} and d_{up} denote the lower and upper bounds of I_n, i.e., $I_n = \{W_l | d_{low} < W_l < d_{up}\}$, Q denotes the Q-function, and P denotes the probability function. p_n is the probability that W_l falls within region I_n when H_0 occurs. $(d_{up} - d_{low})$ is Δ except for I_{-N} and I_N,

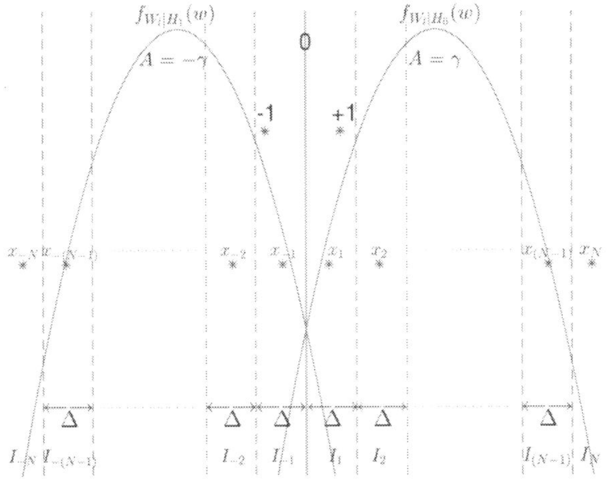

Figure 1. WSN with M-ary source coding on sensor detection

where $d_{low} = -\infty$ for I_{-N} and $d_{up} = \infty$ for I_N. From symmetry, $P[W_l \in I_n|H_1] = P[W_l \in I_{-n}|H_0] = p_{-n}$.

M-level quantization X is applied on the observation and $X = x_n$ is the representation value of the n-th region I_n. At the l-th sensor, x_n is defined as the conditional mean when W_l falls in I_n, i.e., $x_n = E[W_l|W_l \in I_n] = P[H_0]E[W_l|H_0, W_l \in I_n] + P[H_1]E[W_l|H_1, W_l \in I_n]$. From symmetry, $x_{-n} = -x_n$ and $x_0 = 0$.

The signal s_l transmitted to the FC by the l-th sensor is $x_n\sqrt{E}$, according to the decision on $W_l \in I_n$. Given γ and E/N_0, the goal of the proposed algorithm is to minimize the error rate P_e of the final decision at the FC via varying Δ to obtain the optimal region allocation. The average consumed energy $\bar{E}$ of the transmitted signal is $\bar{E} = \sum_{n=-N}^{N} p_n x_n^2 E$.

III. Results

The received signal from the l-th sensor at the FC is $R_l = s_l + n_l$, and the PDF of R_l is

$$f_{R_l|H_0}(r_l) = \sum_{n=-N}^{N} \frac{p_n e^{-(r_l - x_n\sqrt{E})^2/N_0}}{\sqrt{\pi N_0}}$$

$$f_{R_l|H_1}(r_l) = \sum_{n=-N}^{N} \frac{p_{-n} e^{-(r_l - x_n\sqrt{E})^2/N_0}}{\sqrt{\pi N_0}} = \sum_{n=-N}^{N} \frac{p_n e^{-(r_l + x_n\sqrt{E})^2/N_0}}{\sqrt{\pi N_0}} = f_{R_l|H_0}(-r_l)$$

After all the received signals $R_1, R_2, , R_L$ have been collected at the FC from each of the sensors, the optimal Maximum-a-Posteriori (MAP) rule is applied to obtain the final decision $\hat{A} = \pm\gamma$, i.e., H_0 or H_1.

$$f_{R_1,R_2,\ldots,R_L|H_0}(r_1, r_2, \ldots, r_L) \underset{\hat{A}=-\gamma}{\overset{\hat{A}=\gamma}{\gtrless}} f_{R_1,R_2,\ldots,R_L|H_1}(r_1, r_2, \ldots, r_L).$$

Since $R_1, R_2, \ldots, R_L$ are assumed i.i.d., the MAP fusion rule at the FC is the combination of the log-likelihood.

$$\sum_{l=1}^{L} \log(f_{R_l|H_0}(r_l)) \underset{\hat{A}=-\gamma}{\overset{\hat{A}=\gamma}{\gtrless}} \sum_{l=1}^{L} \log(f_{R_l|H_1}(r_l)). \quad (1)$$

Without loss of generality, assume H_0 occurs, i.e., $A = \gamma$, and thus the error probability P_e of the final decision is

$$P_e = P\left[\sum_{l=1}^{L} \log\left(\frac{f_{R_l|H_0}(r_l)}{f_{R_l|H_1}(r_l)}\right) < 0\right]. \quad (2)$$

No closed form of P_e is obtained. Nevertheless, given γ, N, L, Δ, and E/N_0, P_e is derived via numerical analysis, and is optimized, i.e., minimized, by revising Δ iteratively.

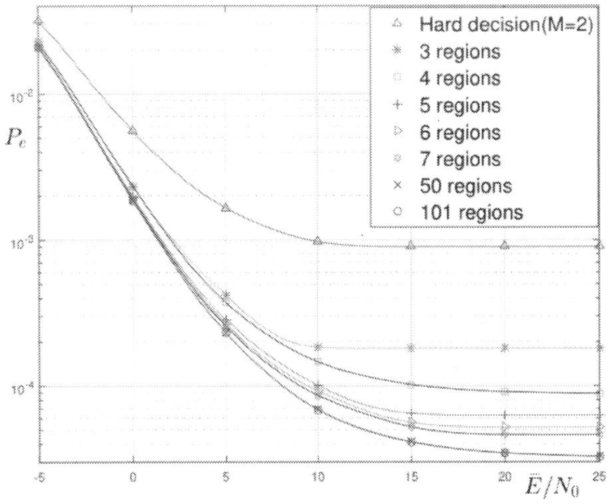

Figure 2. Fusion performance of the proposed soft-decision fusion scheme

We conduct the performance comparison of the proposed soft-decision scheme and the hard-decision scheme. Figure 2 illustrates P_e of the WSN under the proposed soft-decision fusion scheme with $\gamma = 1$. As it can be seen, P_e is lower than that of the hard-decision fusion system and is improved as M increases. No significant difference exists between $M = 50$ and $M = 101$. Furthermore, the flooring of the curves is observed at high signal-to-noise ratio (SNR), which is due to the fact that the erroneous behavior of the transmitted signal to the FC vanishes as SNR increases and hence the error performance is from the decision made by each sensor only.

IV. Conclusion

In this paper, a new M-ary scheme on the decentralized detection in WSN using analog transmission is proposed and examined. The problem of huge channel bandwidth demand is avoided by using the considered M-ary scheme. The goal of minimizing the decision errors at the FC via optimizing the region allocation is achieved. The error performance of the M-ary scheme is better than that of the hard-decision scheme. The behavior of the M-ary scheme when the transmitted signal to the FC is under a fading environment is open to further study.

ACKNOWLEDGMENT

This work is sponsored by the Ministry of Science and Technology of Taiwan (MOST) under grant MOST 106-2221-E-110-016-MY3.

REFERENCES

[1] Q. Cheng, P. K. Varshney, J. H. Michels, and C. M. Belcastro, "Fault detection in dynamic systems via decision fusion," IEEE Transactions on Aerospace and Electronic Systems, vol. 44, no. 1, January 2008, pp. 227–242.

[2] Q. Ling, Z. Tian, and Y. Li, "Distributed decision-making in wireless sensor networks for online structural health monitoring," Journal of Communications and Networks, vol. 11, no. 4, August 2009, pp. 350–358.

[3] P. K. Varshney, Distributed Detection and Data Fusion. New York: Springer, 1997.

[4] S. C. A. Thomopoulos, R. Viswanathan, and D. C. Bougoulias, "Optimal decision fusion in multiple sensor systems," IEEE Transactions on Aerospace and Electronic Systems, vol. AES-23, no. 5, September 1987, pp. 644–653.

[5] S. Saha, A. Kumar, Priyanka, and R. Bhattacharya, "An LLR based cooperative spectrum sensing with hard-soft combining for cognitive radio networks," in 32nd International Union of Radio Science General Assembly Scientific Symposium (URSI GASS), Montreal, Canada, August 2017, pp. 1–4.

[6] M. Xiang and C. Han, "Global optimization for distributed and quantized bayesian detection system," in Proceedings of the Third International Conference on Information Fusion, Paris, France, July 2000, pp. ThC4 25–30.

[7] H. Varaee, G. Mirjalily, and A. Pouramini, "An analytical technique to determine the decision thresholds of multi-bit distributed detection in sensor networks," in 2009 Second International Conference on Computer and Electrical Engineering, Dubai, United Arab Emirates, December 2009, pp. 32–35.

[8] X. Fan, D. Duan, and L. Yang, "Multi-bit cooperative spectrum sensing strategy in closed form," in 2013 Asilomar Conference on Signals, Systems and Computers, Pacific Grove, CA, November 2013, pp. 1473–1477.

[9] A. M. Aziz, "A soft-decision fusion approach for multiple-sensor distributed binary detection systems," IEEE Transactions on Aerospace and Electronic Systems, vol. 47, no. 3, July 2011, pp. 2208–2216.

[10] E. Nurellari, D. McLernon, and M. Ghogho, "Distributed two-step quantized fusion rules via consensus algorithm for distributed detection in wireless sensor networks," IEEE Transactions on Signal and Information Processing over Networks, vol. 2, no. 3, September 2016, pp. 321–335.

[11] H. Kasasbeh, L. Cao, and R. Viswanathan, "Soft-decision-based distributed detection with correlated sensing channels," IEEE Transactions on Aerospace and Electronic Systems, vol. 55, no. 3, June 2019, pp. 1435–1449.

Design and Development of Medical Sensor Networks for Differently Abled Persons

Veeraprathap Veerabharaiah, Fazaluddeen Doddahosur Mohammad Jamal and Narendra Kumar Gurumurthy
Dept. of Electronics & Communication Engineering,
University Visvesvaraya College of Engineering, Bangalore University,
Bangalore, India

Email: veeraprathap2001@gmail.com, fazaluddeen.dm@gmail.com, gnarenk@yahoo.com

Abstract— **13% of the global population is elderly and that percentage is estimated to increase to 16.4% by 2030 as life expectancy keeps increasing due in a great part to modern medical technologies. Serving the elderly and the paralytic persons is a noble cause; it is our responsibility to respect, care and fulfill their needs. Communication for a person having a speech disorder thoroughly relies upon the movement of their fingers, hands and articulations. In this paper, we propose a glove based Sign To Speech (STS) system that uses gestures of fingers and hand to convert the American Sign Language (ASL) into a Speech Signal synthesized to adapt for English and different Indian languages. To improve the services to the people in need of mobility assistance, a Sensor Controlled Wheelchair (SCW) is proposed with capabilities of navigating, detecting obstacles and moving automatically by utilizing Gesture and Ultrasonic Sensors that establish Ad-hoc Sensor Networks. The wheelchair is intended for elderly, medically challenged and paralytic patients, so they can lead a peaceful and satisfying life.**

Keywords-Sign to Speech; American Sign Language; Sensor Controlled Wheelchair.

I. Introduction

Wheelchair assistive technology provides the opportunity for people with mobility impairments, such as imperfect limbs, weakness, muscle atrophy, stroke and other symptoms, to move through indoor and outdoor environments [1]-[3]. Depending on the lifestyle and mobility of the wheelchair user, there are many types of wheelchairs available including basic, lightweight, folding, multi-function, special types, etc. Wheelchairs can be divided into manual wheelchairs and automatic wheelchairs. Sensor Controlled Wheelchairs designed as traditional and automatic wheelchairs are not always suitable for elderly people.

Muteness is commonly referred to as an inability to speak often caused by speech disorders and hearing loss. Normally, people have the ability to freely communicate between each other vocally without any barriers but cannot communicate with people with a speech disorder. Researchers have been focusing on hand gestures detections and have been developing applications in the field of robotics [4]-[6], in the extended area of artificial or prosthetic hands, that can mimic the behaviour of a natural human hand using American Sign Language (ASL).

American Sign Language is a natural predominant sign language that has the same linguistic properties as spoken languages with grammar that differs from the English expressed by movements of the hands and face. It is the primary language of Deaf and Mute communities in the United States and Canada. The dialects of ASL and ASL-based creoles are used in many countries around the world. The movement of fingers is converted into alphabets using American Sign Language, as shown in Figure 1.

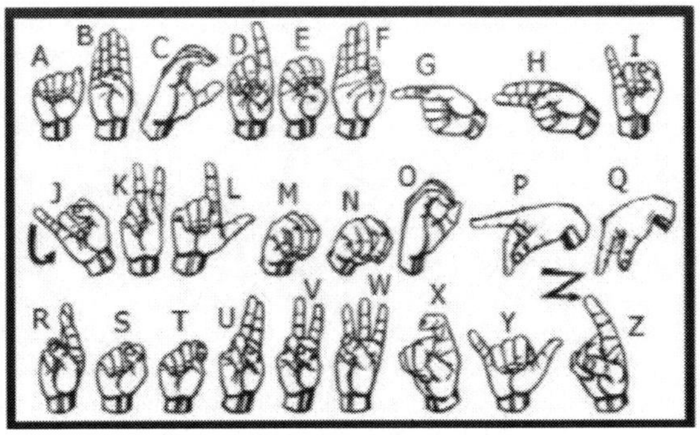

Figure 1. American Sign Language Alphabets [6].

Gesture recognition is classified into a pair of main categories: vision and glove based techniques. The vision based system fails during no visible light and it includes challenges in image and video processing in varying lighting conditions, backgrounds, field of scan constraints and occlusion.

Our proposed system adopted a glove based technique and will efficiently translate each gesture into speech. Thus, it can be used by patients who are not able to speak, but are able to move their fingers and hand.

The paper is organized as follows. Section II presents a brief literature review and its implications. Section III presents the proposed system for differently abled persons based on Medical Sensor Networks. The model presented in this section includes block diagrams. Section IV presents the system implementation. The model presented in this section includes a flowchart of Sign to Speech and Sensor Controlled Wheelchair. Section V presents some of the results obtained from the hardware module described in Section IV. Conclusion and future scope are presented in Sections VI and VII.

II. Literature Review

A. Hartman et al. [1] has proposed autonomous vehicle technology in the field of medical mobility where wheelchair users can advance their movement using a smart human and machine interface. The research focused on the design of such robotic wheelchair, which is a multilayered task incorporating hardware and software with sensor technology, computer processing and power distribution. The system described the design and development of a smart wheelchair for autonomous path planning and high- performance computing for real time data processing.

S. Umchid et al. [2] have developed a Voice Controlled Automatic Wheelchair. In general, due to many reasons such as injury from accident, age and health problems, physical disability occurs. The wheelchair is needed for handicapped people travelling to other places by themselves; however, people with hands and arms impairment find it difficult to use a typical wheelchair. The system's objective was to design, develop and construct a voice controlled automatic wheelchair.

T. Gomi et al. [3] have developed an Intelligent Wheelchairs for the handicapped. A standardized autonomy management system that can be installed on readily available power chairs, which have been well-engineered over the years, has been developed and tested. A behavior based approach was used to establish sufficient onboard autonomy at minimal cost and material usage while achieving high efficiency, sufficient safety, transparency in appearance and extendibility.

S. Faiz Ahmed et al. [4] have described Electronic Speaking Glove for Speechless Patients. The electronic speaking glove was designed to facilitate easy communication through synthesized speech for the benefit of speech impaired patients. Commonly, a mute person communicating through sign language is not understood by the majority of people. The gesture of fingers of a user is converted into synthesized speech to convey an audible message to other people.

M. M. Abdel-Aziz et al. [5] have invented a Smart Communication System as deaf and mute people find a difficulty in communicating with normal people. The sign language translator system is used for reducing the communication barrier between the deaf-mute people and the people who do not have this impairment. The system deals with all these problems and supports the Arabic sign language and Arabic vocal language as well as efficient and friendly communication between deaf-mute people and the rest.

A. Al Mamun et al. [6] have described a Flex Sensor Based Hand Glove for deaf and mute people. As sign language is the only way to communicate for listening and talking with disabled people, the designed system uses a hand glove that will make the sign language understandable to all. An Android mobile phone app is used to receive a voice, which will generate a speech signal and send it to the hand glove through a wireless communication system.

III. PROPOSED WORK

The proposed Medical Sensor Networks (MSN) based system provides an opportunity for elderly people with mobility impairment to move through indoor and outdoor environments and enables communication for persons having a speech disorder, i.e. mute people. The Medical Sensor Networks based system has a Sign to Speech node and Sensor Controlled Wheelchair node.

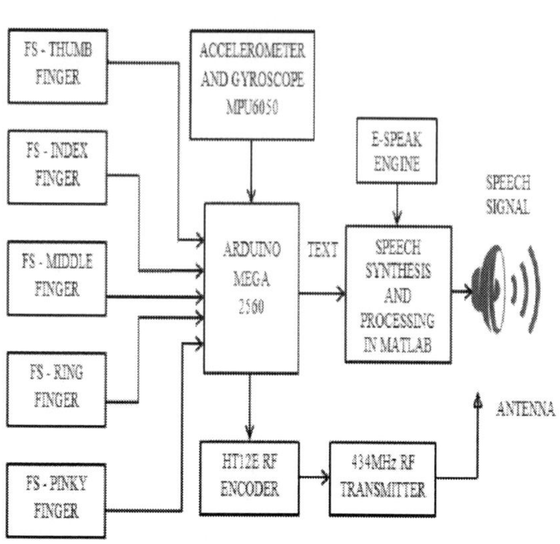

Figure 2. Block diagram of Sign to Speech system.

The Sign to Speech system starts with obtaining a signal proportional to the movement of fingers. Fingers can interpret different hand gestures. Research showed that Flex and MPU6050 sensors based on finger and hand gesture are best suited to convert sign to the text as it is more reliable and cost effective solution. However, to convert the obtained text into a speech signal, the E-Speak Synthesis Engine enables the user to get a speech signal in English, or predefined different Indian language, as shown in Figure 2.

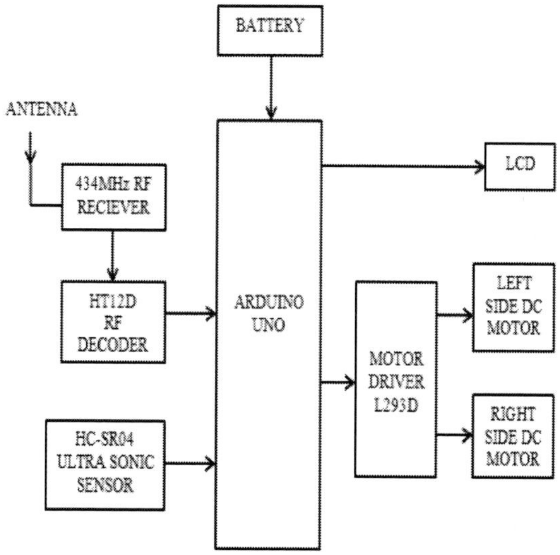

Figure 3. Block diagram of Sensor Controlled Wheelchair.

The block diagram of the developed sensor controlled automatic wheelchair is shown in Figure 3. The MPU6050 based hand gesture of the user is transmitted through 434 MHz RF (Radio-Frequency) transceiver to operate and move the Sensor Controlled Wheelchair in different directions. The Ultrasonic Sensors are employed for automatic obstacle detection to stop the wheelchair during object detection.

A. E-Speak Speech Synthesis Engine

E-Speak [11] is a compact open source software speech synthesizer for English and other languages, for Linux and Windows, and uses a "formant synthesis" method. E-Speak coverts text into speech signal for the following languages: Afrikaans, Albanian, Aragonese, Armenian, Bulgarian, Cantonese, Catalan, Croatian, Czech, Danish, Dutch, English, Esperanto, Estonian, Farsi, Finnish, French, Georgian, German, Greek, Hindi, Hungarian, Icelandic, Indonesian, Irish, Italian, Kannada, Kurdish, Latvian, Lithuanian, Lojban, Macedonian, Malaysian, Malayalam, Mandarin, Nepalese, Norwegian, Polish, Portuguese, Punjabi, Romanian, Russian, Serbian, Slovak, Spanish, Swahili, Swedish, Tamil, Turkish, Vietnamese, Welsh.

Methods of accessing E-Speak:

- The command line program of Linux and Windows to speak the text from a file or from a standard input.
- On Windows, a shared DLL library of E-Speak.

The features of E-Speak:

- Includes many languages with different voices whose characteristics can be altered.
- It provides flexibility to generate WAV file for Synthesized Speech Output.
- Provides program and data memory of about 2 Mbytes.
- Converts text to phonemes with pitch and length information and can be used as a front-end to MBROLA diphone voices.
- Modifies as a front end for another speech synthesis engine.
- Used with screen-readers and other programs supporting the Windows SAPI5 interface.
- Supports Speech Synthesis Markup Language (SSML) and HTML language and other platforms including Android, Mac OSX and Solaris.

B. Matrix Laboratory (MATLAB)

MATLAB [12] is a multi-paradigm numerical computing environment and patented programming language developed by MathWorks. It allows matrix manipulations, plotting of functions for data, implementation of algorithms, creation of user interfaces and interfacing with programs written in other languages including C, C++, C#, Java, Fortran and Python.

C. Flex Sensor

The Flex Sensor, also known as Bend Sensor, measures the amount of bending. The resistance of the sensor element is proportional to the amount of bending; it is used as goniometer and often called flexible potentiometer.

TABLE I. CHARACTERISTICS OF FLEX SENSOR.

Range of Resistance	1.5-40 kΩ depending on sensor type. Flex point claims a 0-250 kΩ resistance range.
Range of Temperature	-35 to +80 degrees Celsius
Lifetime	Lifetime greater than one million life cycles
Hysteresis	Hysteresis 7%
Voltage	Voltage 5 to 12 V
Size	Approximately 0.28" wide and 1"/3"/5"

The Flex Sensor contains carbon resistive elements within a thin flexible substrate. The characteristics are described in Table I. The sensor produces a resistance output relative to the bend radius. Practically, the deflection in degrees of 0, 20, 40, 45, 50, 70 and 90 will give 10 kΩ, 14.5 kΩ, 18.8 kΩ, 20 kΩ, 21.1 kΩ, 25.5 kΩ and 30 kΩ of resistances, respectively.

D. Motor Driver

The Motor Driver L293D is a Dual H-bridge IC; it allows the DC motor to drive in either direction and can control a set of two DC motors simultaneously in any direction. The clockwise and anti-clockwise rotation of the DC motor depends on the polarity of the applied voltage. A 9-volt battery is used to power the motor driver for driving the DC motors.

E. MPU6050 Sensor Module

The MPU6050 Sensor Module is a 6-axis Motion Tracking Device and combines 3-axis gyroscope, 3-axis accelerometer and Digital Motion Processor in a single package with the additional feature of on-chip Temperature Sensor. It has I2C bus interface to communicate with the microcontrollers and auxiliary I2C bus to communicate with the sensor devices magnetometer, pressure sensor, etc.

F. Ultrasonic Sensor

The Ultrasonic Sensor measures the distance of the nearest object. HC-SR04 is employed for the automatic obstacle detection and its range is from 2 cm to 3 meters.

$$\text{Distance} = (\text{Echo Pulse Duration} * .0343)/2 \quad (1)$$

The Ultrasonic Sensor detects the nearest object by emitting a short pulse and receiving the reflected echo. The time spent by the pulse signal to reach the object and return is used to determine the relative distance (1).

IV. SYSTEM IMPLEMENTATION

The working principle of the developed Sign to Speech system is presented in a flowchart, as shown in Figure 4. After the hand glove is powered up, every fingers and hand movement is analyzed each time to detect word or character for its given American Sign Language pattern. The gesture of fingers is obtained by Flex Sensor and hand by MPU6050 Sensor. Depending on the degree of bending, the Flex Sensor values are mapped onto eight different values 0, 1, 2, 3, 4, 5, 6 and 7.

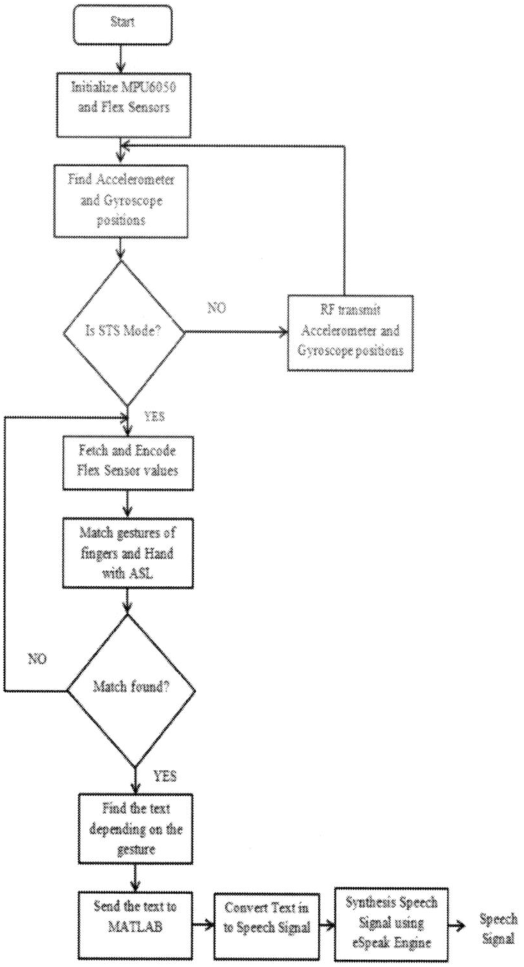

Figure 4. A flowchart of Sign to Speech System.

The words and characters of the English language are recognized based on values of Flex Sensor and orientation of MPU6050. These are described in Tables II and III.

TABLE II. WORD FORMATION.

Word	PF	RF	MF	IF	TF	MPU6050 Orientation
FOOD	2|3	2|3	4|5	4|5	2|3	X>5
NEWSPAPER	1|2	1|2	1|2	1|2	1|2	X>5, Y<5
WASHROOM	4|5	3|4	4|5	3|4	2|3	X>5
SICK	1|2	1|2	3	1|2	1|2	X>5
MEDICINE	1|2	1|2	4|5	1|2	1|2	X>5
EMERGENCY	5|6	4|5	4|5	4|5	4|5	X>5
WATER	4|5	1|2	1|2	1|2	4|5	X>5

The system provides flexibility to convert multiple signs into text depending on the combination of American Sign Language words and characters. However, the obtained text is processed in MATLAB using E-Speak to get a synthesized speech signal in English and other Indian languages. This speech signal is used by a mute patient to communicate with other people to inform or their needs, desires and any other problems.

TABLE III. CHARACTER FORMATION.

Character	PF	RF	MF	IF	TF	MPU6050 Orientation
A	5|6	5|6	5|6	5|6	1|2	X>5
B	1|2	1|2	1|2	1|2	4|5	X>5
C	2|3	2|3	2|3	2|3	2|3	X>5
D	3|4	3|4	3|4	1|2	2|3	X>5, Y>2
E	5|6	5|6	5|6	5|6	5|6	X>5
F	1|2	1|2	1|2	4|5	3|4	X>5
G	4|5	4|5	4|5	1|2	1|2	X>0, Y>5
H	4|5	4|5	1|2	1|2	2|3	X>0, Y>5
I	1|2	4|5	4|5	4|5	4|5	X>5, Y<5
J	1|2	4|5	4|5	4|5	4|5	X>5, Y>5
K	4|5	4|5	1|2	1|2	2|3	X>5
L	5|6	4|5	5|6	1|2	1|2	X>5
M	5	4	4	4	4	X>5
N	5	5	4	4	4	X>5
O	4	4	4	4	3	X>5
P	3|4	3|4	3|4	1|2	2|3	X<5, Y<5
Q	4|5	4|5	4|5	2|3	2|3	X<5, Y<5
R	4|5	4|5	1|2	3|4	4|5	X>5
S	4|5	4|5	4|5	4|5	4	X>5
T	4|5	4|5	4|5	4|5	3	X>5
U	4|5	4|5	2|3	1|2	4|5	X>5, Y<2
V	4|5	4|5	1|2	1|2	4|5	X>5, Y>2
W	4|5	1|2	1|2	1|2	4|5	X>5
X	5|6	4|5	5|6	3|4	4|5	X>5
Y	1|2	5|6	5|6	5|6	1|2	X>5
Z	5|6	4|5	5|6	1|2	2|3	X>5, Y<-2

Note: PF=Pinky Finger, RF=Ring Finger, MF=Middle Finger, IF=Index Finger, TF=Thumb Finger, | = Logical – OR

The movement of the Sensor Controlled Wheelchair is dependent on the orientation of the MPU6050 dictated in Table IV. A single MPU6050 is shared between the nodes in the Medical Sensor Network.

TABLE IV. WORKING STATUS OF SENSOR CONTROLLED WHEELCHAIR.

MPU6050 Orientation	RF Bits	Movement of Wheelchair
X<0	1000	FORWARD
X>0	0001	BACKWARD
Y>0	0100	RIGHT
Y<0	0010	LEFT
X=0 & Y=0	0000	STOP

The Sensor Controlled Wheelchair has five types of motions, namely, moving forward, moving backward, moving to the left, moving to the right and stop motion. The Ultrasonic Sensors have been included to stop the wheelchair during obstacle detection.

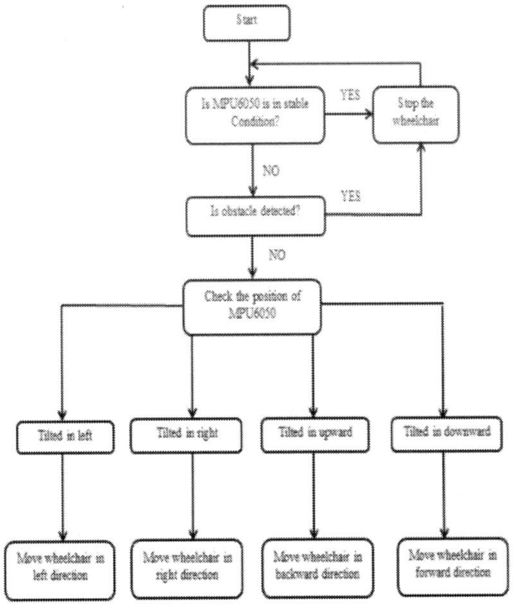

Figure 5. A flowchart of Sensor Controlled Wheelchair.

The working principle of the developed Sensor Controlled Wheelchair is presented in a flowchart, as shown in Figure 5. The orientation of MPU6050 is transmitted to the Sensor Controlled Wheelchair through RF wireless communication includes RF Encoder and Decoder to encrypt the data and remove noise. The Motor Driver L293D controls the rotation of the DC motors in clock and anti-clock wise direction so that the required movement of the wheelchair is achieved.

V. RESULT EVALUATION

The implementation of Medical Sensor Networks for differently-abled persons has shown good results in encouraging the patients during recovery transition.

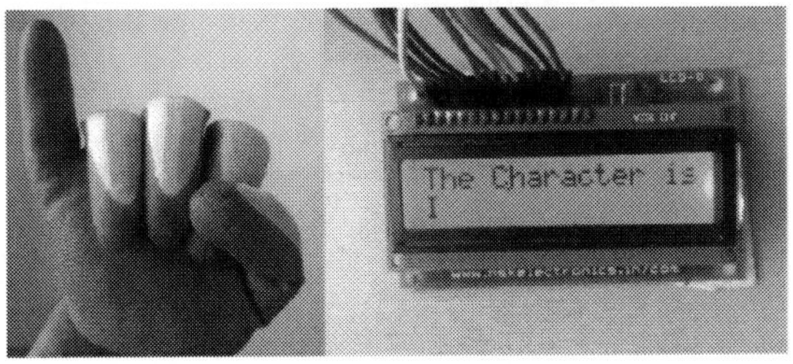

Figure 6. Sign for the English Alphabet 'I'

Figure 6 shows the sign for English Alphabet letter 'I' based on American Sign Language, getting converted into the corresponding text on the right-hand side by processing the obtained values of Flex and MPU6050 Sensors.

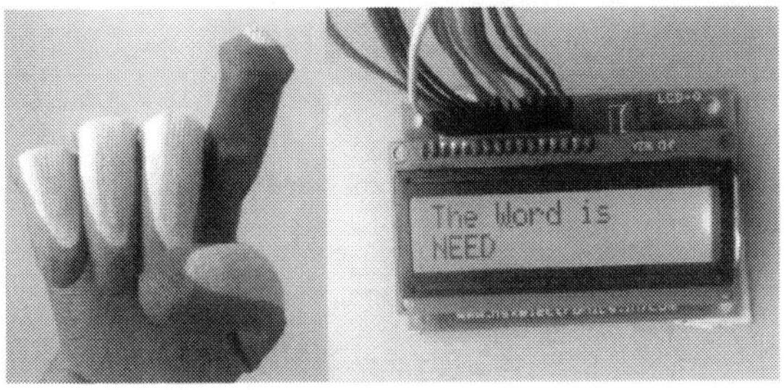

Figure 7. Sign for The English Word 'NEED'

Figure 7 shows the sign for the English word 'NEED' based on the American Sign Language getting converted into the corresponding text on the right-hand side.

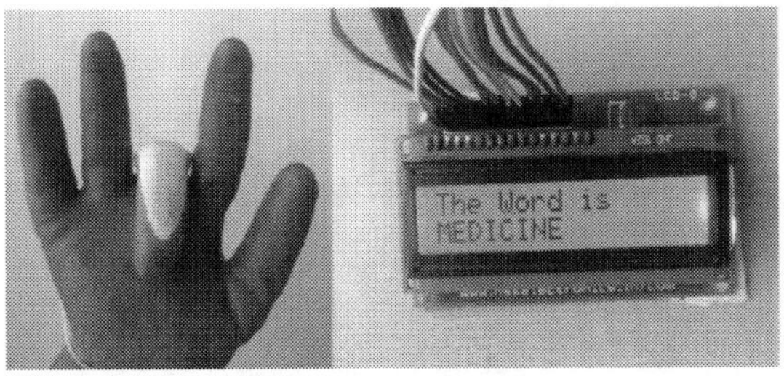

Figure 8. Sign for The English Word 'MEDICINE'

Figure 8 shows the sign for the English word 'MEDICINE' based on American Sign Language, getting converted into the corresponding text on the right-hand side.

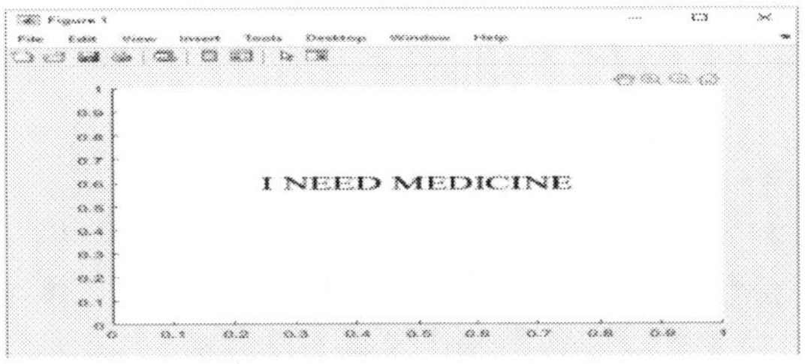

Figure 9. Signs to Speech Conversion in the English Language

Based on the words and characters of American Sign Language, the obtained text is synthesized in MATLAB using Speech API to generate a Speech Signal in the English language, as shown in Figure 9.

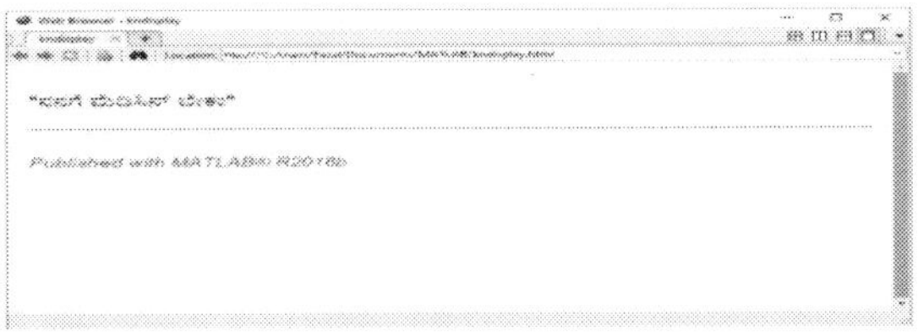

Figure 10. Signs to Speech Conversion in the Kannada Language

The obtained text in the English language is converted into the Kannada language and then synthesized using E-Speak to generate a Speech Signal in the Kannada language, as shown in Figure 10.

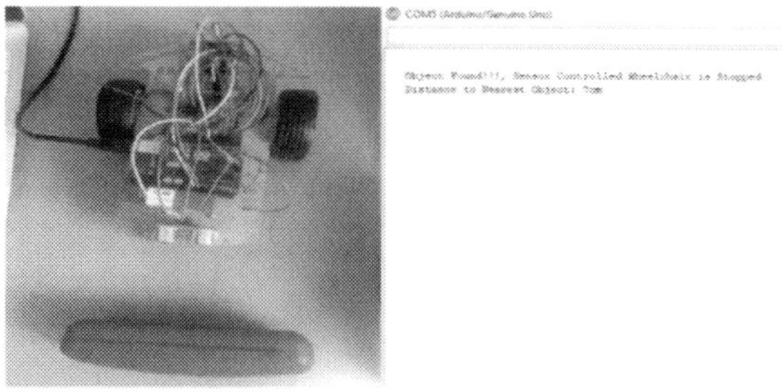

Figure 11. Object Detection in Sensor Controlled Wheelchair

The Sensor Controlled Wheelchair gets stopped automatically as it finds any object in the path it moves using the Ultrasonic Sensors and displays the corresponding message on the right side, as shown in Figure 11.

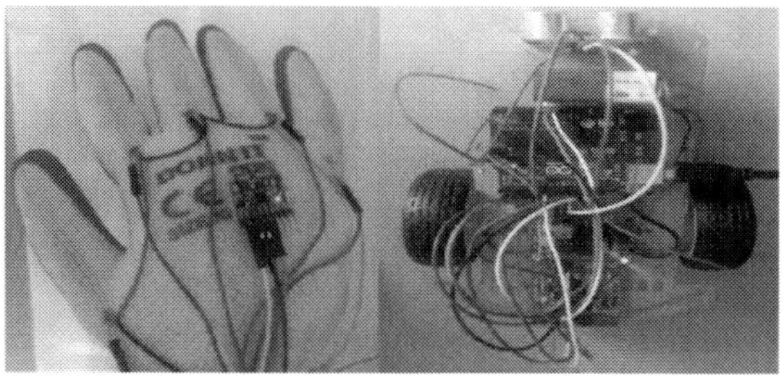

Figure 12. Moving Sensor Controlled Wheelchair in Forward Direction

The Sensor Controlled Wheelchair moving in forward direction as the horizontal orientation of MPU6050 is less than zero makes the RF bits equal to 1000, as shown in Figure 12.

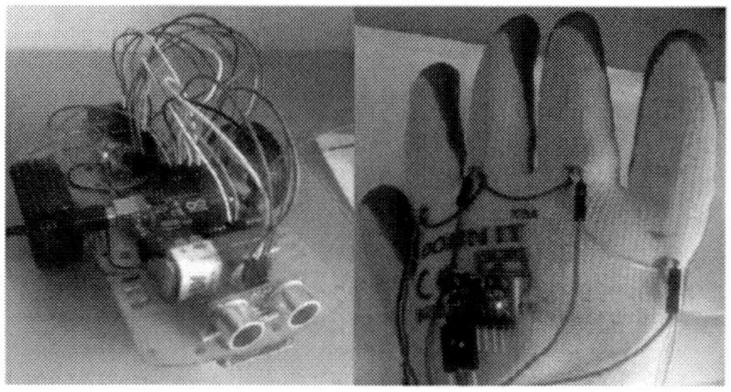

Figure 13. Moving Sensor Controlled Wheelchair in Left Direction.

The Sensor Controlled Wheelchair moving towards left as the vertical orientation of MPU6050 is less than zero makes RF bits equal to 0010, as shown in Figure 13.

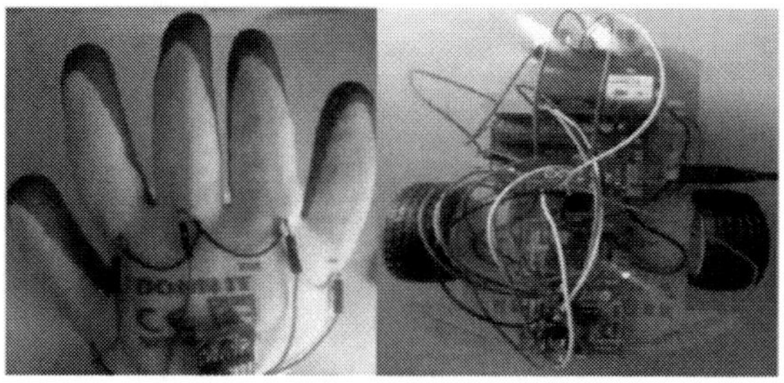

Figure 14. Moving Sensor Controlled Wheelchair in Backward Direction

The Sensor Controlled Wheelchair moving in the backward direction as the horizontal orientation of MPU6050 is greater than zero makes RF bits equal to 0001, as shown in Figure 14.

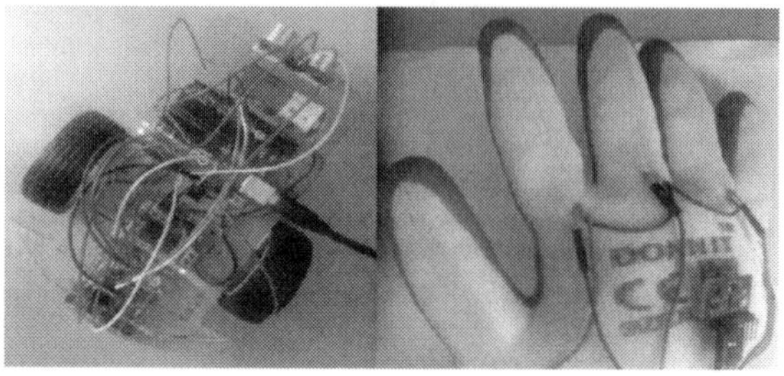

Figure 15. Moving Sensor Controlled Wheelchair in Right Direction

The Sensor Controlled Wheelchair moving towards the right as the vertical orientation of MPU6050 is greater than zero makes RF bits equal to 0100, as shown in Figure 15.

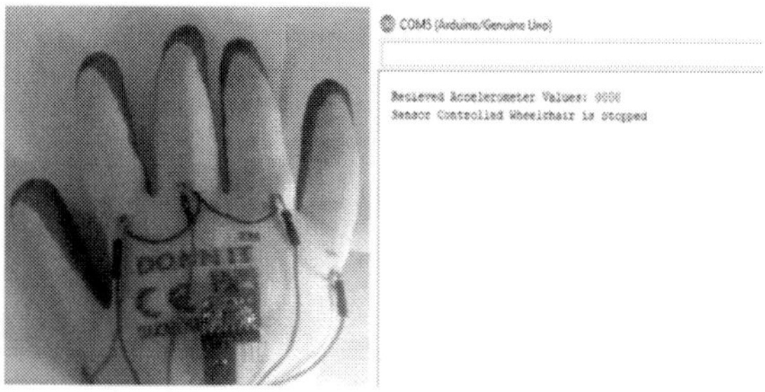

Figure 16. Sensor Controlled Wheelchair is Stopped

The Sensor Controlled Wheelchair gets stopped as the vertical and horizontal orientation of MPU6050 is equal to zero makes RF bits equal to 0000 and displays the corresponding message on the right side, as shown in Figure 16.

VI. CONCLUSION

Our proposed system uses Sign to Speech, which converts American Sign Language into a Speech Signal useful for speech impaired elderly patients to fill the communication gap between patients, doctors and relatives. The output speech can be in English or other Indian languages for the mute patient to express their needs by using gestures.

The Sensor Controlled Wheelchair operated by the gestures of hand provides the opportunity for the old age patients with mobility impairment to move through indoor and outdoor environments. The automatic obstacle detection is implemented in the system to stop the movement of the wheelchair automatically, providing easy access for elderly people and automatic protection from obstacle collision.

VII. FUTURE SCOPE

The Flex Sensors based hand glove can be replaced by an E-Textile make hand glove that is light weight and less wiring is required; however, it can be very expensive.

The K-Nearest Neighbors Algorithm can be adopted as the graphical view of the characters, words and sensor values change with different persons.

REFERENCES

[1] A. Hartman, R. Gillberg Jr, C. T. Lin, and V. K. Nandikolla, "Design and development of an autonomous robotic wheelchair for medical mobility," IEEE, 2018.

[2] S. Umchid, P. Limhaprasert, S. Chumsoongnern, T. Petthong, and T. Leeudomwong, "Voice Controlled Automatic Wheelchair," The 2018 Biomedical Engineering International Conference, 2018.

[3] T. Gomi and A. Griffith, "Developing Intelligent Wheelchairs for the Handicapped," Springer, 2006.

[4] S. Faiz Ahmed, S. M. Baber Ali, and S. S. Munawwar Qureshi, "Electronic Speaking Glove for Speechless Patients - A Tongue to a Mute," IEEE Conference on Sustainable Utilization and Development in Engineering and Technology, 2010.

[5] M. M. Abdel-Aziz, M. M. Abdel-Masieh, and M. M. Nasief, "Smart Communication System for Deaf- Dumb People," Int'l Conf. Embedded Systems, Cyber-physical Systems, & Applications, 2017.

[6] A. Al Mamun, M. Sarwar Jahan Khan Polash, and F. Mashuque Alamgir, "Flex Sensor Based Hand Glove for Deaf and Dumb People," International Journal of Computer Networks and Communications Security VOL. 5, NO. 2, February 2017, 38–48

[7] N. Ambika, G. K. Rama Murali, S. Sheka, and G. Narendra Kumar, "TTS System for Coal Miners in MANET Based Disaster Management System," 2nd Intl Multi-Conference on Complexity, Informatics and Cybernetics, Mar 2011.

[8] C. K. Huang, Z. W. Wang, G. W. Chen, and C. Y. Yang, "Development of a Smart Wheelchair with Dual Functions: Real-time Control and Automated Guide," 2nd International Conference on Control and Robotics Engineering, 2017

[9] T. Arsan, "Sign Language Converter," International Journal of Computer Science & Engineering Survey (IJCSES) Vol.6, No.4, August 2015.

[10] D. Wang and H. Yu, "Development of the control system of a voice-operated wheelchair with multi-posture characteristics," 2nd Asia-Pacific Conference on Intelligent Robot Systems (ACIRS), 2017, pp. 151-155.

[11] E-Speak, http://espeak.sourceforge.net/ [retrieved Oct. 2019]

[12] MATLAB, https://www.mathworks.com/products/matlab.html [retrieved Oct. 2019]

Proposition of a Smart Environment Architecture for Ressources Monitoring and Rural Activities Management

Thierry Antoine-Santoni
UMR CNRS 6134 SPE
University of Corsica
Corte, France
e-mail: antoine-santoni_t@univ-corse.fr

Bastien Poggi
UMR CNRS 6134 SPE
University of Corsica
Corte, France
e-mail: poggi_b@univ-corse.fr

Dominique Federici
UMR CNRS 6134 SPE
University of Corsica
Corte, France
e-mail: federici_d@univ-corse.fr

François-Marie Manicacci
UMR CNRS 6134 SPE
University of Corsica
Corte, France
e-mail: manicacci_fm@univ-corse.fr

Gualtieri Jean-Sébastien
SITEC
Techno Park
Furiani, France
e-mail: gualtieri_js@sitec.fr

Aiello Antoine
UMS CNRS 3514 Stella Mare
University of Corsica
Corte, France
e-mail: aiello_a@univ-corse.fr

***Abstract*— We can find different examples of declared Smart Cities in the world: Barcelona, London, Santander, Padova, Paris, Stockholm, etc. In a Smart Planet context, what is the place of the rural territories? We develop a scientific program called Smart Village - Smart Paese: emergence of Smart territories in a small village of 250 people in Corsica island. The goal is to include rural areas is the global Smart Planet by the development of a robust management system for resources and rural activities management. In this paper, we introduce our definition of a Smart Village and we propose a global architecture with 3 parts: (1) a Wireless Sensors Network (WSN) deployment of 20 nodes (with several sensors) according to different activities (smart water, smart buildings, smart farm, smart agriculture), (2) Data storage and Visualization tools and (3) a prediction system. We describe the wireless network deployment using Long Range (LoRa) technology, the used sensors, and the developed dashboards for the dynamic data display. We introduce also the first development ways of the smart approach with Machine Learning algorithms called Smart Entity Model (SEM) using Smart Village data.**

Keywords- Smart city; Smart village; WSN; Data; LoRa; ML.

I. INTRODUCTION

The emergence of Smart Cities cannot be considered sudden, but as a natural transition brought about by technological developments in the service of citizens, new environmental constraints and the reduction of planetary resources. The Smart Planet vision of [1] is possible by the task automation and the acceleration of Information Technologies (I.T.) development positioned to ensure the realization of revolutionary, real-time, and real-world people-centric applications and services. Nowadays, this common term of Smart City allows (3) us to talk about urban and social innovation, citizen participation and all others common fundamentals. Smart City appears sometimes as a marketing term and it is difficult to discern the reality of these projects.

The WSN take an important place in the development of Smart Cities. The ever more reducing cost of WSNs is allowing to embed them everywhere to monitor and control virtually any space and environment and to form a part of the Internet of Things (IoT) [2]. In the last 10 years, we have seen the development of platforms using WSN in urban space [3] to collect data, to manage the resources, interact with the citizen and provide a model of sustainable development or e-citizenship.

In this context of Smart Planet, it is important to find a place for the rural areas. We can perceive in India and Indonesia a real development of Smart Village concept; a definition of Smart Village could be assigned to Ghandi: a Smart Village accounts a bundle of services delivered effectively to the residents of the village in an efficient manner. We can find the same objective between a Smart Village and a Smart City with the citizen in the heart of the development strategy of the territory thanks, in particular, to robust I.T. infrastructures (communication, storage, security, responsiveness, sensor networks, etc.). The creation of digital, participatory and inclusive services is a permanent goal to control natural, energy, human and economic resources. In this paper, we introduce an WSN architecture and Machine Learning tools for rural resources and activities management.

We provide in this paper, a first global overview of Smart Village applications. Section III, we present the experimental area of Cozzano, a small Corsican village. In Section IV, we introduce the complete architecture for our developed system, which uses LoRa communication, a data visualization tool and a Machine Learning approach for rural activities and resources management. In Section V, we present the first results of our machine learning system called SEM.

II. The Smart Village overview applications

It is difficult to find robust researches on the Smart Village concept. However, the European commission introduces two important working definitions of rural communities and Smart Village[4]:

- Communities in rural areas can include one or several human settlements, without any restrictions regarding the number of habitants. Rural areas are defined as "predominantly rural areas" according to the urban-rural typology used by the Organization for Economic Co-operation and Development (O.E.C.D.) and Statiscal Office of the European Communities (EUROSTAT).
- "Smart Villages are communities in rural areas that develop smart solutions to deal with challenges in their local context. They build on existing local strengths and opportunities to engage in a process of sustainable development of their territories. They rely on a participatory approach to develop and implement their strategies to improve their economic, social and environmental conditions, in particular by promoting innovation and mobilizing solutions offered by digital technologies. Smart Villages benefit from cooperation and alliances with other communities and actors in rural and urban areas. The initiation and the implementation of Smart Village strategies may build on existing initiatives and can be funded by a variety of public and private sources".

Based on the potential of WSN and the previous definitions, we decide to focus on the WSN possible applications using smart technologies [5] for rural communities needs. Digital agriculture [6], Smart farming or Precision Agriculture (PA) [7] aim to optimize agricultural processes in order to give growers a more detailed overview of the ongoing situation in their cultivation area, and/or coordinate the actions in such way that optimizes energy consumption, water use and the use of chemicals.

Recent works have focused on these research activities and developed different solutions using WSN [8][9] or a combination of IoT- Machine Learning algorithms [10]-[12]

The development of animal tracking solutions can help to manage rural activities. Indeed, since the 1960s the scientists have used electronic tags to track animals [13].

Nowadays, the low cost and the performance of devices clearly favor the use of WSN to collect different kinds of data (GPS, Temperature, acceleration) to help the breeders to adapt their exploitation (animal health, crossing alert) [14][15].

The need to know the environment conditions is important in the development of rural activities and economy: natural water quality [16]-[18], air quality [19][20], etc.

In the previous works and examples, we can observe that telemetry is the main axis in the use of WSNs, and the list of activities is not exhaustive. However, we can distinguish different possibilities offered by the WSNs. We propose in the following section a deployment of WSN for telemetry using LoRa communication in a small village in Corsica.

III. Experimental area and Smart village definition

The village of Cozzano is located in the center of the Corsica island at 650m, surrounded by a pines forest, chestnut trees and oaks, in a green valley with many streams illustrated in Figure 1. With 250 people, the municipality tried to lead a strategy towards a sustainable development. As a result of this last point, the village is organized around four power generation systems: a hydroelectric power plant on drinking water, a hydroelectric power plant on a river, biomass boiler for communal buildings and solar panel on social housing.

Figure 1. Village of Cozzano (Corsica island)

According to the definitions in the previous sections, we build the concept of Smart Village around four axes:

1. Sustainable development: to promote development of renewable energies, to manage natural resources, to reduce global energy consumption;
2. Infrastructure and digital services: to develop a wireless network and different services around this network;
3. Rural activities: to improve agricultural activities to promote precision agriculture and smart farming;
4. Education and citizenship: to include school and citizens in the project, to inform citizens, to develop inclusive, participatory and collaborative actions.

To contribute to these objectives in the Smart Village context, we propose different steps in Smart Village building:

1. Build a wireless network infrastructure that has low energy consumption to connect different kinds of devices;
2. Deploy of a WSN to collect environmental data such smart water, smart building, smart weather, and smart rural activities;

3. Display data for decision support in the several activities, to inform the people, and to include the citizens in the Smart Village strategy;
4. Improve the system with prediction algorithms of the observed system evolution;
5. Create services for the data users.

These 5 axes are presented in the following section.

IV. APPROACH OF SMART VILLAGE ARCHITECTURE

According to our previous development process, we present the developed approach for the Smart Village. In Figure 2, we provide a basic representation of the different systems in the Smart Village:

- smart water
- smart farm
- smart agriculture
- smart public buildings

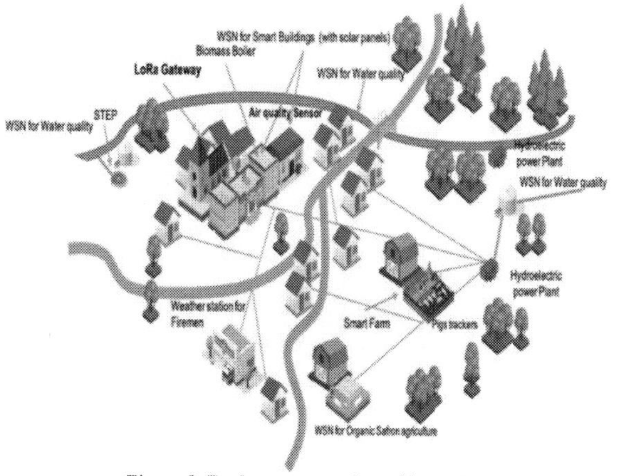

Figure 2. Basic representation of Smart Village

To reach these objectives, we build a WSN based on LoRa communication. Our architecture is divided in five blocks, as illustrated in Figure 3:

- Collect environmental data with a LoRa WSN (including people's survey);
- Store data in an indexed datacenter;
- Display the data with different dashboards according to the different activities of Smart Village (smart water, smart agriculture, smart building, etc.) or citizen categories (children, elderly, mayor and municipal council);
- Use the database for the evolution prediction of the observed systems;
- Create services for the citizens according to the dashboards: air and water quality with real-time information, real-time weather and prediction, information for the activities school.

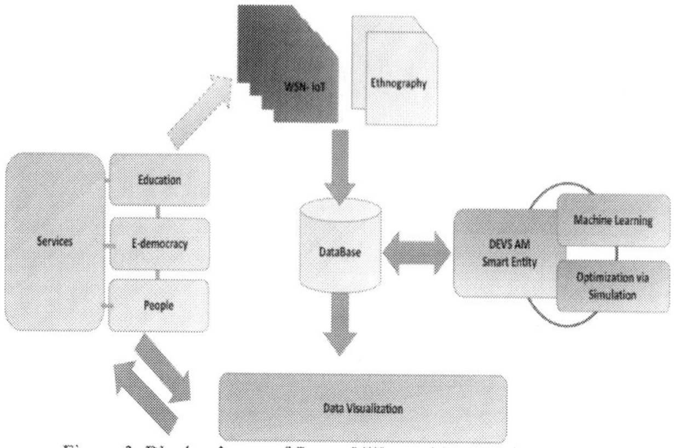

Figure 3. Block scheme of Smart Village objectives interactions

A. LoRa Network infrastructure

The wireless network is built around a central sink based on the church roof using LoRa technologies, as illustrated in Figure 4. In this program, we would like to build a homogeneous, robust and long-range network with a low power consumption technology. LoRa develops an approach based on the following two distinct layers: (1) a physical layer, based on the radio modulation technique (868 MHz for Europe), called CSS (Chirp Spread Spectrum) and (2) a MAC layer protocol (LoRaWAN) that provides access to LoRa architecture [21].

Figure 4. LoRa Antenna for the Smart Village on the church roof (left) and second rescue antenna with solar panel (right)

The technology offers a mix of long range, low power consumption and secures data transmission. The choice of LoRa is clearly in the philosophy of the Smart Village program and allows us to manage the network and devices performances. The network deployed is a local private network and we manage the global system using a carrier grade network server. This choice allows us to study the best possible coverage and to adapt the network. To supplement the main antenna, a second LoRa Gateway visible in Figure 4 is deployed on a distant hill about 4 km from the village of Cozzano to offer greater network coverage. In our system, we collect different kinds of data from a WSN and the collected data is stored in a database. The data are stored in a database according to the different applications of the Smart Village, as illustrated in Table I and Figure 5.

TABLE I. SENSORS FOR SMART VILLAGE APPLICATIONS

Application	Type	Input	Precision	Operating temperature	Accuracy
Smart Agriculture	Soil temperature	Negative temperature coefficient		-30°C to 80°C	0,4°C
Smart Agriculture	Soil humidity	Electric Voltage	Capacitive		± 3%
Smart Air	Ozone	Serial Data Interface at 1200 baud	Detection threshold 0,02 ppm		
Smart Air	Fine particle	Electric Voltage	Sensor by laser scattering	-20°C to 50°C	0,0 to 999,9 mg/m3
Smart Building	Door opening	Electric Voltage	Magnetic aperture detector	-20°C to 70°C	
Smart Water	pH	Serial Data Interface at 1200 baud	Combined electrode (pH / reference) with special glass - reference Ag/AgCl, gel electrolyte (KCl) -		Measuring range (0-14 pH)
Smart Water	RedOx	Serial Data Interface at 1200 baud	Combined electrode (RedOx / reference), platinium tip / reference Ag/AgCl, gel electrolyte (KCl)		Resoluion 0,1 MV ; accuracy ± 2 mV
Smart Water	Dissolved oxygen	Serial Data Interface at 1200 baud	Optical measurement by luminescence	-10°C to 60°C	± 0,1 mg/L - ± 0,1 ppm ± 1%
Smart Weather	Pyranometer	Electric Voltage		-40°C to 70°C	Spectral range 360nm to 11200nm
Smart Weather	Raingauge	Counter		-20°C to 60°C	
Smart Weather	Wind (force and direction)	Counter			Wind speen accuracy ± 5% ans wind direction ± 7%
Smart Weather / Smart Building	Relative humidity	Numerical	Antiradiation shelter	-40°C to 70°C	± 2 to 4%
Smart Weather / Smart Building	Temperature	Numerical	Antiradiation shelter	-20°C to 60°C	(25°C) : ± 0,3°C / (5°C to 40°C) : ± 0,4°C / (-40°C to 70°C) : ± 0,9°C
Smart Weather / Smart Building	Pressure	Electric Voltage	0,15 to 1,15 Bar / Max Value : 4 Bar / Sensibility : 45 mV/Kpa	0°C to 85°C	0,2 Vcc

Figure 5. WSN deployment (water, agriculture, water quality, weather, buildings)

This system is complemented by dedicated tools for smart farming with a LoRa GPS tracker.

B. *Tracking system*

One of the rural activities of this Corsican area is free-range pigs farming. We developed a GPS tracker called AMBLoRa, illustrated in Figure 6. Based on LoRa communication, the system will help the farmers to know the position of the animals [22] and we apply this on a pigs farming, as showed in Figure 7. These trackers are energy consumption optimized to have a lifetime battery of one year. This tool aims to limit the farmer's movements and allows him to rethink his farm organization with new services, such as the real-time monitoring.

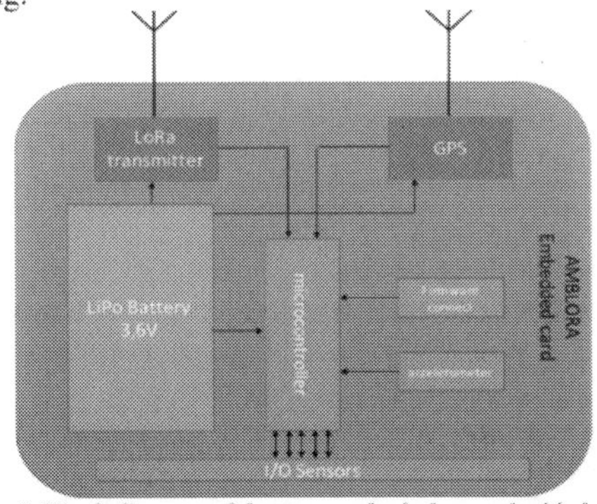

Figure 6. Block diagram of the proposed wireless embedded card

All pigs positions are sent to the gateway and stored in the database. These data are used to create real-time dashboard, which is presented in the following section.

Figure 7. Pig with AMBLoRa GPS Tracker

C. *Discussions on WSN and LoRa gateway deployment*

The development of the LoRa network revealed some difficulties. Indeed, power outages are common in a rural area and we had data loss because of the unpowered antenna. We tried to limit these problems by using a second antenna with solar panel (weather dependent). This was enough to increase the resilience of a system, but it did not make the system 100% reliable.

For the signal range, theoretically, it should cover tens of kilometers. However, this does not take into account the topography and the vegetation cover which very strongly reduces to just a few kilometers.

D. *Visualization system*

To display in real-time the collected data from database, we developed an information system with Web interface for the visualization. This architecture is built on an indexed database. All the data collected are stored and indexed to allows a dynamic visualization.

This architecture is based on Elasticsearch [23], a real-time distributed search and analytics engine. It is built on a full-text search-engine library called Apache Lucene. To visualize the data, we use the Kibana tool [23]. Kibana is a data visualization software on top of the ElasticSearch engine. It provides a number of tools to display information, like dashboards, queries, filters and time ranges. Information stored in an ElasticSearch cluster can be visualized as interactive plots such as pie charts, histograms, text, maps, etc. We develop different dashboards according to the different activities such as: weather, air quality, smart water, smart agriculture, smart building and smart farm. In Figure 8, we can see an example of a dashboard built with Kibana, with different information for the farmer and a heat map with last pigs positions. We can also have the signal quality from the LoRa devices using a Received Signal Strenght Indication (RSSI).

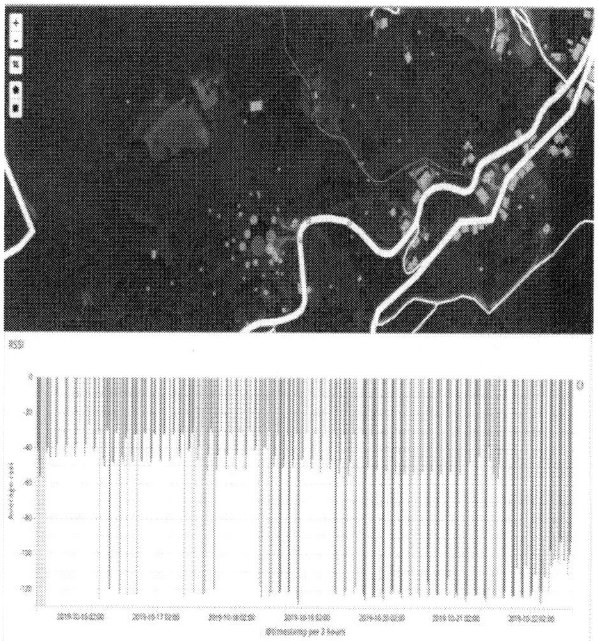

Figure 8. First Kibana tracking visualization based on Elasticsearch engine

We have presented the LoRa architecture, the deployment of WSN and the dashboards for the real-time visualization of the data collected using our architecture. However, to become a smart system, our approach needs to predict the behavior of the observed system to help in the resources and activities management.

V. Machine learning system called Smart entity

To reach our objective of a real smart system, we developed a model to predict behaviors evolution of observed systems using popular Machine Learning (ML) Libraries. The prediction must help to manage the village environment and to provide decision support for the municipality. Our ML system is based on a model called Smart Entity Model (SEM). This model must be generic and be able to treat all kinds of data collected on the Smart Village.

The SEM [24] is a generic model based on modeling approach using Discrete Event System Specification (DEVS) Formalism. DEVS is a modelling and simulation formalism proposed by B. P. Zeigler [25] in the 70s. The main DEVS objective is to provide an explicit separation between modeling description and simulation core. The formalism is based on two mains concepts: Atomic Model (AM) and Coupled Model (CM). AM describes the system behavior in a modular way and CM describes the system structure by abstraction levels and model encapsulations. This genericity of model description provides a reusable abstract simulator independent of the studied systems. The model is defined with a fixed number of inputs and outputs ports in order to maintain a high level of interoperability.

As represented in Figure 9, the collected data are stored in the database. These data become the SEM AM inputs (XE) and they are used as dataset to select the best ML algorithms for the prediction of the observed system according to the most popular libraries [26]-[29]. The XE dataset is divided in two parts: 80% for the training process of ML algorithms and 20% for the prediction comparison test. SEM defines a ratio between the predicted data and the actual data and gives a score for each ML algorithm. The best algorithm is chosen to build the prediction model. This selection is made every thousand new data entries.

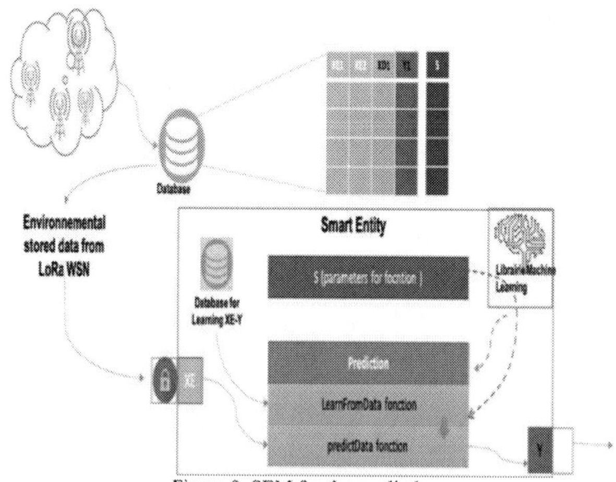

Figure 9. SEM for the prediction

Figure 10 and Figure 11 show the first results of prediction according to the collected by the WSN on the Smart Village project. We can see in Figure 10, the prediction of air temperature by hour. The diagram in Figure 11 shows the prediction of air temperature by day.

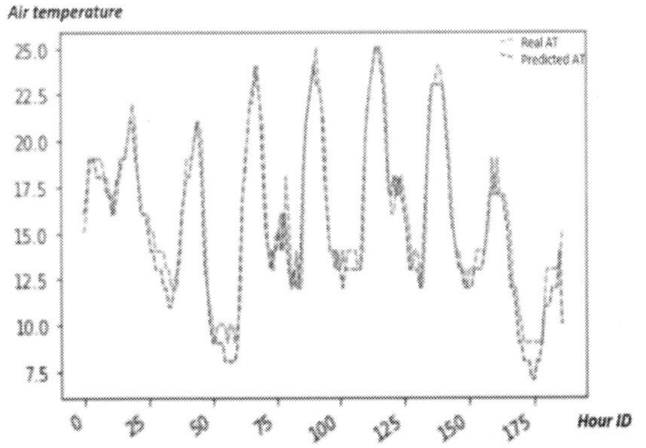

Figure 10. Hourly Prediction outputs on Smart Village Air temperature

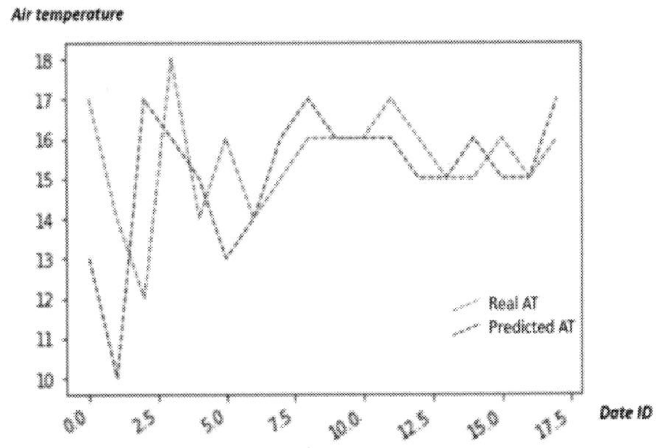

Figure 11. Daily Prediction outputs on Smart Village Air temperature

VI. Conclusion

This paper introduces the first research and development (R&D) steps of a scientific program called Smart Village - Smart Paesi, emergence of Smart Territories. We propose a definition of a Smart Village and our global architecture according to 4 parts: (1) a WSN built around a LoRa Gateway, (2) a database, (3) a data displays interface and a (4) prediction system to anticipate the evolution of the observed systems: water, air, weather, building, agriculture and farm.

We deployed a WSN based on LoRa communication to observe different systems in the village (weather, water quality, agriculture, air quality, buildings, farm). All the collected data are stored in a dynamic database using the Elasticsearch engine. The data are also used to supply a ML/DL model called Smart Entity Model to predict the evolution of observed systems. We also built dashboards to display the data according to the different observed applications.

This first step of R&D is quite conclusive for many reasons:

- The network architecture is robust enough to collect regularly the data without major communication problems and to obtain a resilient network architecture to provide a real Quality of Service (QoS) on the Smart Village;
- LoRa Technology capacities (coverage, long range, low power consumption) allow us to develop different applications for the Smart Village;
- The first results of SEM are sufficient to validate the first step of our smart approach.

The future objectives in the project are as follows:

- New deployment of WSN based on LoRaWAN communication technology to observe other Smart Village systems (public lighting, waste) and improvement of network architecture;
- Integrate and develop several SEM (for all observed systems) as a Web service directly connected to the database.
- Reduce energy consumption to improve battery lifetime of LoRa devices;
- Develop dashboards for all activities;
- Cozzano's municipality supports this project by providing access to its infrastructures, its building for researchers and organizing events in the field of sustainable development.

Citizen are involved in the research program and they are proactive through different events. During regular meetings, field surveys, or interviews realized by the students of the University of Corsica, people expose the impacts of the project on their living environment, their needs or their wishes. We also included the school in a project through a school journal for the project information dissemination.

Acknowledgment

This project is financed by an European fund and supported by the Regional Council of Corsica during the period 2017 - 2020.

References

[1] P. Raj and A. C. Raman, *Intelligent Cities: Enabling Tools and Technology*, CRC Press. 2015.

[2] R. Du, P. Santi, M. Xiao, A. V. Vasilakos, and C. Fischione, "The sensable city: A survey on the deployment and management for smart city monitoring," *IEEE Commun. Surv. Tutor.*, pp. 1–1, Nov. 2018.

[3] A. Zanella, N. Bui, A. Castellani, L. Vangelista, and M. Zorzi, "Internet of Things for Smart Cities," *IEEE Internet Things J.*, vol. 1, no. 1, pp. 22–32, Feb. 2014.

[4] European Commission, "Consultation on the working definition of 'Smart Villages,'" 2018.

[5] M. Dener and C. Bostancıoğlu, "Smart Technologies with Wireless Sensor Networks," *Procedia - Soc. Behav. Sci.*, vol. 195, pp. 1915–1921, Jul. 2015.

[6] S. Tang, Q. Zhu, X. Zhou, S. Liu, and M. Wu, "A conception of digital agriculture," in *IEEE International Geoscience and Remote Sensing Symposium*, Toronto, Ont., Canada, 2002, vol. 5, pp. 3026–3028.

[7] A. Tzounis, N. Katsoulas, T. Bartzanas, and C. Kittas, "Internet of Things in agriculture, recent advances and future challenges," *Biosyst. Eng.*, vol. 164, pp. 31–48, Dec. 2017.

[8] A. Nayyar and V. Puri, "Smart farming: IoT based smart sensors agriculture stick for live temperature and moisture monitoring using Arduino, cloud computing & solar technology," in *Communication and Computing Systems*, Dronacharya College of Engineering, Gurgaon, India, 2016, pp. 673–680.

[9] F. Ferrández-Pastor, J. García-Chamizo, M. Nieto-Hidalgo, and J. Mora-Martínez, "Precision Agriculture Design Method Using a Distributed Computing Architecture on Internet of Things Context," *Sensors*, vol. 18, no. 6, p. 1731, May 2018.

[10] F. Balducci, D. Impedovo, and G. Pirlo, "Machine Learning Applications on Agricultural Datasets for Smart Farm Enhancement," *Machines*, vol. 6, no. 3, p. 38, Sep. 2018.

[11] T. Truong, A. Dinh, and K. Wahid, "An IoT environmental data collection system for fungal detection in crop fields," in *2017 IEEE 30th Canadian Conference on Electrical and Computer Engineering (CCECE)*, Windsor, ON, 2017, pp. 1–4.

[12] J. Duarte-Carvajalino, D. Alzate, A. Ramirez, J. Santa-Sepulveda, A. Fajardo-Rojas, and M. Soto-Suárez, "Evaluating Late Blight Severity in Potato Crops Using Unmanned Aerial Vehicles and Machine Learning Algorithms," *Remote Sens.*, vol. 10, no. 10, p. 1513, Sep. 2018.

[13] R. Kays, M. C. Crofoot, W. Jetz, and M. Wikelski, "Terrestrial animal tracking as an eye on life and planet," *Science*, vol. 348, no. 6240, pp. 2478–2478, Jun. 2015.

[14] R. Zviedris, A. Elsts, G. Strazdins, A. Mednis, and L. Selavo, "LynxNet: Wild Animal Monitoring Using Sensor Networks," in *Real-World Wireless Sensor Networks*, vol. 6511, P. J. Marron, T. Voigt, P. Corke, and L. Mottola, Eds. Berlin, Heidelberg: Springer Berlin Heidelberg, 2010, pp. 170–173.

[15] V. R. Jain, R. Bagree, A. Kumar, and P. Ranjan, "wildCENSE: GPS based animal tracking system," in *2008 International Conference on Intelligent Sensors, Sensor Networks and Information Processing*, Sydney, Australia, 2008, pp. 617–622.

[16] B. O'Flynn *et al.*, "Smart Coast: A Wireless Sensor Network for Water Quality Monitoring," in *32nd IEEE Conference on Local Computer Networks (LCN 2007)*, Dublin, Ireland, 2007, pp. 815–816.

[17] Z. Rasin and M. R. Abdullah, "Water Quality Monitoring System Using Zigbee Based Wireless Sensor Network," *Int. J. Eng.*, vol. 9, no. 10, p. 6.

[18] T. Sugapriyaa, S. Rakshaya, K. Ramyadevi, M. Ramya, and P. G. Rashmi, "Smart water quality monitoring system for real time applications," in International Journal of Pure and applied Mathematics, volume 118, p 1363-1369,2018.

[19] K. Khedo, R. Perseedoss, and A. Mungur, "A Wireless Sensor Network Air Pollution Monitoring System," *Int. J. Wirel. Mob. Netw.*, vol. 2, no. 2, pp. 31–45, May 2010.

[20] W. Yi, K. Lo, T. Mak, K. Leung, Y. Leung, and M. Meng, "A Survey of Wireless Sensor Network Based Air Pollution Monitoring Systems," *Sensors*, vol. 15, no. 12, pp. 31392–31427, Dec. 2015.

[21] J. de Carvalho Silva, J. J. P. C. Rodrigues, A. M. Alberti, P. Solic, and A. L. L. Aquino, "LoRaWAN — A low power WAN protocol for Internet of Things: A review and opportunities," in *2017 2nd International Multidisciplinary Conference on Computer and Energy Science (SpliTech)*, 2017, pp. 1–6.

[22] T. Antoine-Santoni, J.-S. Gualtieri, F.-M. Manicacci, and A. Aiello, "AMBLoRa: a Wireless Tracking and Sensor System Using Long Range Communication to Monitor Animal Behavior," pp. 35–40, 2018.

[23] M. Bajer, "Building an IoT Data Hub with Elasticsearch, Logstash and Kibana," in *2017 5th International Conference on Future Internet of Things and Cloud Workshops (FiCloudW)*, Prague, 2017, pp. 63–68.

[24] T. Antoine-Santoni, B. Poggi, E. Vittori, H. V. Hieux, M. Delhom, and A. Aiello, "Smart Entity – How to build DEVS models from large amount of data and small amount of knowledge ?," in *Proceedings of 11th EAI International Conference on Simulation Tools and Techniques (SIMUtools 2019)*, Chengdu, People's Republic of China, 2019.

[25] B. P. Zeigler, G. Kim, and H. Praehofer, *Theory of Modeling and Simulation 2nd edition*, Academic Press. 2000.

[26] M. Abadi *et al.*, "TensorFlow: Large-Scale Machine Learning on Heterogeneous Distributed Systems," Software available from tensorflow.org.

[27] "https://pytorch.org/." (March 2019)

[28] "https://keras.io/." (March 2019)

[29] F. Pedregosa *et al.*, "Scikit-learn: Machine Learning in Python," *Mach. Learn. PYTHON*, p. 6.

Wearable Fall Detection System Using Barometric Pressure Sensors and Machine Learning

Yingnan Sun
The Hamlyn Center
Imperial College London
London, UK
e-mail:ys4315@ic.ac.uk

Frank P.-W. Lo
The Hamlyn Center
Imperial College London
London, UK
e-mail:pwl15@ic.ac.uk

Surapa Thiemjarus
National Science and
Technology Department Agency
Thailand
e-mail:surapa.thiemjarus@nectec.or.th

Benny Lo
The Hamlyn Center
Imperial College London
London, UK
e-mail:benny.lo@imperial.ac.uk

Abstract—**As the global population is aging, healthcare systems in developed countries are facing many new challenges, such as insufficient human resources for quality patient monitoring and elderly care. One of the major health threats to elderly patients is falling, which could cause severe injuries and the associated complications can lead to mortality. To reduce the potential damage caused by falling, there are many wearable-based monitoring systems commercially available, but they often suffer from high false alarm rates and high costs. Most of the available solutions are based on embedded Inertial Measurement Units (IMUs), which can easily detect a sudden slip fall or a sudden trip fall from standing, but often fail to detect short falls, such as falling from a bed or a chair when an elderly is trying to get up. In this paper, a wearable fall detection system using barometric pressure sensors is proposed. The system is capable of detecting falls from high and low positions with high accuracy, and it was tested using a dataset collected from 10 healthy subjects and validated using a 5-fold inter-subject cross-validation.**

Keywords-Fall detection; Body Sensor Network; Healthcare; Barometric pressure sensor.

I. INTRODUCTION

Due to declining fertility rates and rising life expectancy in many countries, the world elderly population is expected to continue to increase rapidly. According to the World Health Organization (WHO), the proportion of the world population who is over 60 years old will rise from 12% in 2015 to 22% by the end of 2050 [1]. Elderly population is often at risks of falling, which is one of the most consequential events leading to severe injuries. According to the Centers for Disease Control and Prevention (CDC), one in every four elderly people living in the United States report one or several falls each year [2]. When elderly people fall down, they are often immobilized due to joint dislocations, bone fractures or head trauma. Therefore, fall detection systems are of vital importance for elderly people who live alone, as a study of 125 elderly people who fell shows that half of the elderly fallers who remain laying on the ground for more than an hour after falls died within 6 months after the incidents [3]. If the injuries caused by falls are not fatal, it still leads to a significant burden to the public healthcare service, as elderly fallers require longer time to heal, and they often have a higher chance of falling again. In 2012, 30.3 billion dollars were spent in medical treatments related to non-fatal falls in the U.S. [4].

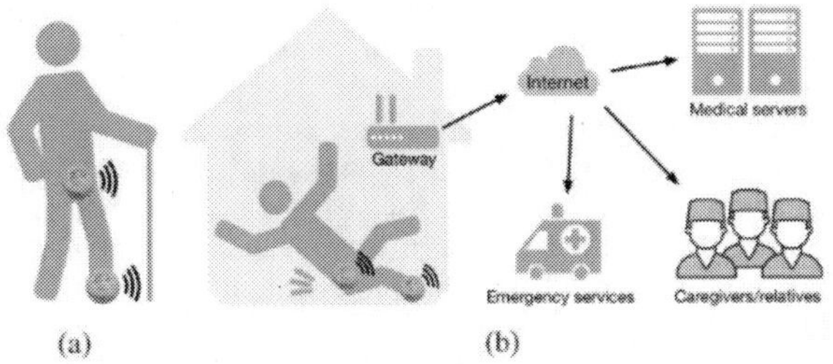

Figure 1. (a) Sensor positions and (b) System architecture

Although it is difficult to prevent elderly people from falling, fall detection systems can significantly reduce the time between falls and medical treatments by informing emergency services automatically and promptly after the incidents [5]. Extensive research has been proposed for fall detection, which can be categorized into two basic types of systems: vision-based and wearable sensor-based. Vision-based systems, such as [6], are less intrusive and can detect multiple fall events simultaneously [7]. However, such systems have very limited range of usage, as fall events will not be detected outside the sight of cameras or are occluded by other people or objects. On the other hand, wearable fall detection systems are effective almost anywhere, and less expensive than vision-based systems. With recent advancement in sensing technologies, many wearable sensors have been developed for fall detection, such as those based on Inertial Measurement Units (IMUs). IMUs often consist of accelerometers, gyroscopes, and magnetometers, and they can measure the acceleration, angular velocity, direction, and tilt of a device in three dimensions [8].

The research on IMU-based fall detection systems is mature, and the majority of such systems are based on the algorithms that can detect sudden sharp changes in the magnitude of acceleration signals, such as [9][10]. To avoid false alarms on other activities, such as squat and sit on a chair, the threshold value for detecting falls of these algorithms must be set very accurately for different individuals, as they might have different muscle reflection and strength, causing difference in acceleration signals [11]. Another disadvantage of using IMUs for fall detection is that the IMUs must have very high sampling rates to detect sudden changes in magnitude. As fall detection devices are ought to be worn by elderly people 24/7, the battery of the devices will drain very quickly. In addition, if the fall detection is not processed on node, the data collected by IMUs needs to be transmitted over wireless channels constantly, which can cause congestions of the wireless network. Instead of measuring the sudden changes in magnitude of acceleration signals, barometric pressure sensors can measure actual drop in altitude of the body mass of the elderly people. It has three advantages over IMUs, first, pressure sensors can operate at much lower sampling rates than IMUs; second, elderly people's initial falling positions, such as standing and sitting, can be determined by air pressure signals, which is useful for assessing the severity of the falls; third, the orientation of devices will not affect the fall detection algorithms using air pressure signals.

In this paper, we propose a wearable fall detection system using only barometric pressure sensors and machine learning algorithms, to detect the actual drop in altitude of the body using air pressure signals. The proposed wearable fall detection system has low power consumption, and it can be worn in any orientation in the waist or just be attached to the top of the trousers. The rest of the paper is organized as follows. Detailed experimental setup, feature extraction, and fall detection algorithms are presented in Section II. The experimental results on the performance of the proposed system are shown in Section III, and the conclusion is presented in the final section.

TABLE I. FALL DETECTION PROTOCOL

	Incidents	Fall	Initial Positions	Final Positions
1	Fall forward slowly	Y	Standing	Lying
2	Fall forward fast	Y	Standing	Lying
3	Fall backward slowly	Y	Standing	Lying
4	Fall from a chair slowly	Y	Sitting	Lying
5	Fall from a bed slowly	Y	Lying	Lying
6	Walking	N	Standing	Standing
7	Standing	N	Standing	Standing
8	Sitting on a chair	N	Sitting	Sitting
9	Lying on a bed	N	Lying	Lying
10	Pick up an item on the floor	N	Standing	Standing

II. METHDOLOGY

Figure 1 shows the system architecture of our proposed solution. The pressure signal captured by the sensors is transmitted to the gateway, where the fall detection algorithms are executed. If a fall occurs, the gateway will inform caregivers and relatives.

A. Experimental Setup

The barometric pressure sensors used in the study were Infineon DPS310 Pressure Shield2Go [12], which has a relative accuracy of ±0.06Pa, a sampling rate of 128Hz, and a precision of ±0.005hPa (or ±5cm in altitude). The pressure sensors were used with an Infineon XMC2go development board during data collection, then integrated with a Body Sensor Network (BSN) wireless sensor node [13], as shown in Figure 2. 10 healthy subjects (8 males and 2 females) were recruited in the experiments, and the participants were asked to perform the incidents as listed in Table I for 3 times per incident in one session. The participants simulated falls from standing, sitting, and lying positions onto a mattress, and also performed non-fall incidents, such as walking and standing. There were two pressure sensors used in the experiments, the first sensor was attached to participants' trousers at waist positions or on the belts, and the second sensor was attached to the shoes of the participants. The second pressure sensor is used as a reference, and it can also be fixed on a wall or placed on the floor in a room. The proposed system can potentially work without a reference sensor, but the accuracy will drop and could lead to higher false alarm rates.

(a) DPS310 sensor (b) Case

Figure 2. The proposed fall detection sensor node, which consists of a a BSN node, a battery, and a casing of the sensor (with a quarter US dollar coin on the side)

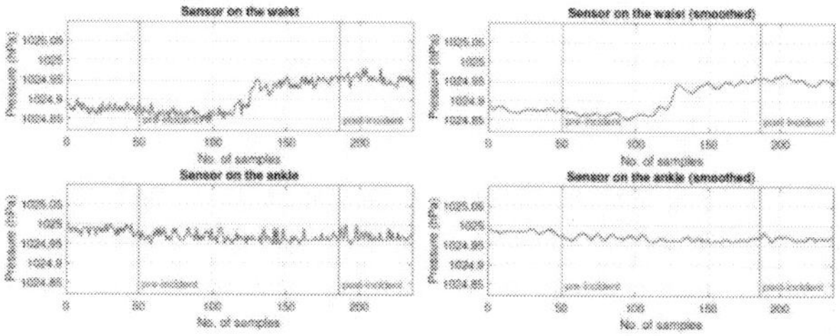

(a) Raw signals (b) Smoothed signals

Figure 3. Raw and smoothed air pressure sensor signals

B. Feature Extraction

The feature extraction process can be done either on the sensor node or on the network gateway. Before feature extraction, the barometric pressure signals with high frequency noises are smoothed, as shown in Figure 3, using a moving average algorithm, which can be generalized as.

$$\overline{x}_i = \frac{1}{2K+1} \sum_{n=i-K}^{i+K} x_n \qquad (1)$$

where x_i is the moving averaged signal at time instant i, which is also at the center of moving window with a window size of $2K+1$. Then, the entire sample S, which contains only one repetition of an incident, is normalized by subtracting its mean, which ensures the overall signal energy of the sample is zero for different incidents. Then, the sample is partitioned equally into M parts and feature extraction is conducted for each part individually. This is to extract features for different stages of incidents. For example, if M is set to 3, the sample will roughly be divided into 3 parts: pre-incident, incident, and post-incident. For each part of the sample, 6 features are extracted for each sensor. Therefore, if M is set to 3 and 2 sensors are used, there will be 36 features per sample. Assuming there are N data points in the mth part of the sample S, the first feature is the standard deviation, which can be expressed as

$$\sigma_m = \sqrt{\frac{\sum_{n=1}^{N}(x_{mn} - \bar{x}_m)^2}{N-1}} \qquad (2)$$

where x_{mn} is the mn^{th} moving averaged signal point $\bar{x}_i$, and $\bar{x}_m$ is the mean of the mth part of the sample. Then, the minimum and maximum of the mth part of the sample are extracted using $min(x_{mn})$ and $max(x_{mn})$ where $mn = m_1, m_2, \ldots, m_N$. The root mean square deviation r_m is also calculated using

$$r_m = \sqrt{\frac{1}{N}(\sum_{n=1}^{N} x_{mn}^2)} \qquad (3)$$

and Shannon entropy E_m is calculated as

$$E_m = -\sum_{n=1}^{N} x_{mn}^2 log(x_{mn}^2) \qquad (4)$$

These features are selected as they can present the status of the pressure signals. Finally, all the features R_m extracted for different parts of the sample are concatenated together to form a final feature maps for the sample, which can be expressed as

$$\mathbb{R} = [R_1, R_2, \ldots, R_M] \qquad (5)$$

Algorithm 1 Pseudo code for fall detection with k-fold inter-subject cross validation

```
Require:
    dataset ← Samples from 10 subjects
    label ← Label of incidents
    M ← 3 (3 parts per sample) K ← 5 (5-fold)
    learner ← supervised machine learning algorithms
function CROSSVALIDATION(learner,dataset,label,M,K)
    results ← empty array
    for k=1 to K do
        feature ← FEATUREEXTRACTION(dataset)
        trainSet,testSet ← PARTITION(feature,label,M)
        model ← TRAINMODEL(learner,trainSet)
        performance ← TESTMODEL(model,testSet)
        results[k] ← performance
    end for
    return results
end function
```

Figure 4. Pseudo code for the fall detection algorithm

C. Experiments

To evaluate the performance of the proposed fall detection system, a series of experiments were conducted to classify fall and non-fall incidents under various conditions. The performance evaluation followed pseudo codes presented in Figure 4, where a k-fold inter-subject cross validation is presented to demonstrate the robustness and effectiveness of the proposed fall detection system. The cross validation function requires 5 inputs: the dataset which contains barometric pressure readings from participants while emulating different incidents, the labels of these incidents, which are in numeral orders listed in Table I, M, which is set from 2 to 5, K, which represents the number of partitions for cross validation and is set to 5, and learner, which is the type of classifier used for the machine learning process. There are 4 types of classifiers used in the experiments: Decision Tree, k-Nearest Neighbor (kNN), linear Support Vector Machine (SVM), and medium Gaussian SVM.

The algorithm will iterate K times and will return a metric called *results*, which contains matrices, such as True Positive (TP) rates and True Negative (TN) rates. In each iteration, first of all, feature maps $\mathbb{R}$ are extracted from the dataset using the equations presented in feature extraction subsection, which are then partitioned into training and testing sets with a ratio of $(1-\frac{1}{K})/\frac{1}{K}$. The training set is then fed to the model training function with one of the 4 classifiers to produce the trained model, which is then tested using the testing set and compared with testing labels to produce classification metrics, which are stored in results and returned when all K iterations are completed.

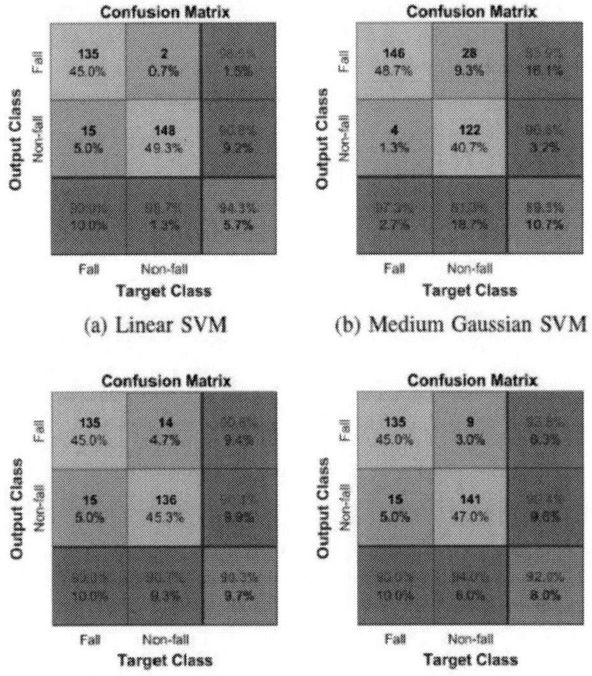

(a) Linear SVM (b) Medium Gaussian SVM (c) Decision Tree (d) kNN

Figure 5. Confusion matrices of the proposed system (M=4) when using linear SVM (a), medium Gaussian SVM (b), decision tree (c), and kNN (d) of 300 samples

III. Experimental Results

The first experiment is fall detection, which contains only two classes: fall and non-fall. Figure 5 shows the confusion matrices of the proposed system using 4 different machine learning classifiers, and Table II presents the performance of the proposed fall detection system using different machine learning classifiers. There are totally 300 samples and all of them were tested using 5-fold inter-subject cross validations with M set to 4. Among these classifiers, linear SVM has the best accuracy of 94.3% and medium Gaussian SVM performs the worst in terms of overall accuracy. However, medium Gaussian SVM has an accuracy of 97.3% when detecting falls, but also has the worst false alarm rate at 18.7%. Decision tree and kNN have similar performance on detecting falls, but both have slightly worse false alarm rates than linear SVM. Similarly, linear SVM has the best fall detection performance in terms of accuracy, specificity, and F1 score at 94.3%, 98.7% and 93.5% respectively, whereas medium Gaussian SVM has the best sensitivity of 97.3% for detecting falls. In addition, Figure 6 shows Receiver Operating Characteristic (ROC) curves of the proposed fall detection systems when M was set to 3 and 4, respectively.

TABLE II. PERFORMANCE OF THE PROPOSED SYSTEM ON CLASSIFYING FALL AND NON-FALL INCIDENTS

	Accuracy	Sensitivity	Specificity	F1 score
Linear SVM	**0.943±0.064**	0.900±0.135	**0.987±0.016**	**0.935±0.080**
Gaussian SVM	0.893±0.056	**0.973±0.025**	0.813±0.107	0.903±0.050
Decision Tree	0.903±0.031	0.900±0.106	0.907±0.057	0.900±0.041
kNN	0.920±0.053	0.900±0.092	0.940±0.044	0.916±0.059

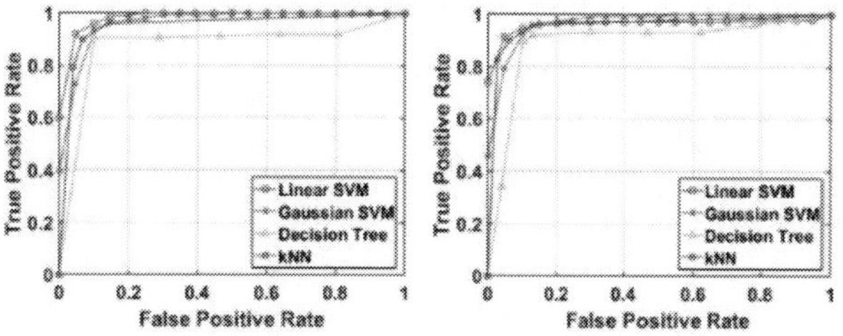

(a) $M = 3$ (b) $M = 4$

Figure 6. ROC curves of the proposed system using different machine learning classifiers when (a) $M = 3$ and (b) $M = 4$

In the second experiment, initial falling positions were also taken into consideration. As indicated in the confusion matrix in Figure 7, there are 6 classes instead of only fall and non-fall. Experiment participants are falling from standing (F_{stand}), which includes action 1, 2, and 3 in the fall detection protocol in Table I, falling from sitting ($F_{sitting}$), falling from lying (F_{lying}), walking (Walk), staying still (Still), which correspond to actions 7, 8, and 9 in Table, and pick up items on the floor (Pickup). The proposed system has an averaged accuracy of 81.7% for all classes. The system distinguishes falling from standing at sensitivity of 93.3%, but can only distinguish falling from sitting and lying at 63.3% and 66.7% respectively. This is because, as presented in Figure 7, many falling from sitting and lying samples were detected as falling from standing by the proposed system.

IV. CONCLUSIONS

In this paper, a novel wearable fall detection system using only barometric pressure sensors and machine learning algorithms is proposed. This paper demonstrates the feasibility and accuracy of using only barometric pressure for fall detection, especially for slow fall situations. In addition, this study shows that the barometer can complement IMU sensors in a wearable fall detector to provide better accuracy in detecting different types of falls and optimize the energy consumption. Future work can include more types of incidents of falling, analyze the power consumption and the processing time of the system, conduct an in-depth comparative study with IMU-based fall detection systems, recruit more subjects for the experiments, and test the system in more practical and natural settings, such as in nursing home and hospitals.

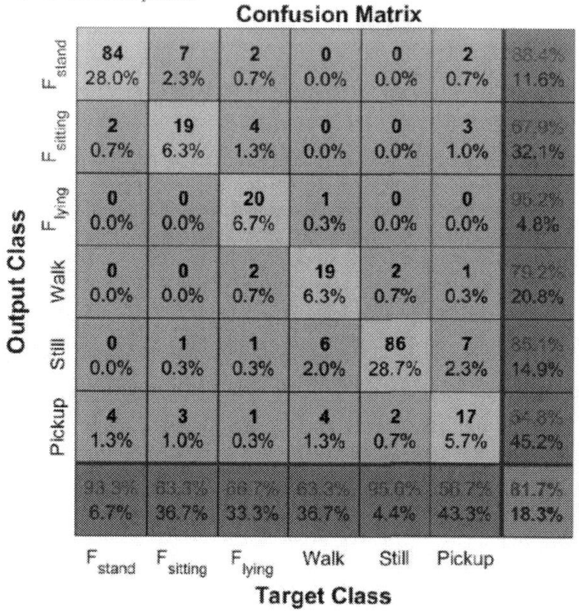

Figure 7. Confusion matrix for classifying initial falling positions and non-fall events $M = 4$), F=Fall

ACKNOWLEDGMENT

This research is supported by Newton Fund Institutional Links grant ID: 330760239, under the Newton-Thailand Research Fund (TRF) partnership. The grant is funded by the UK Department of Business, Energy and Industrial Strategy (BEIS) and TRF and delivered by the British Council.

REFERENCES

[1] World Health Organization, "Ageing and health," 2018, URL: https://www.who.int/news-room/fact-sheets/detail/ageing-and-health [retrieved: Oct, 2019].

[2] B. Elizabeth and R. Kakara, "Deaths from falls among persons aged over 65 years - United States, 2007-2016", 2018, URL: https://www.cdc.gov/mmwr/volumes/67/wr/mm6718a1.htm [retrieved: Oct, 2019].

[3] D. Wild, U. S. Nayak, and B. Isaacs, 2018, "How dangerous are falls in old people at home?" British medical journal (Clinical research ed.), vol. 282(6260), Jan. 1981, pp. 266-268, doi: 10.1136/bmj.282.6260.266.

[4] E. R. Burns, J. A. Stevens, and R. Lee, "The direct costs of fatal and nonfatal falls among older adults-united states,"

Journal of safety research, vol. 58, May. 2016, pp. 99-103, doi: 10.1016/j.jsr.2016.05.001.

[5] B. Wolfe, "How to set up and use fall detection on apple watch series 4," 2018, URL: https://www.imore.com/how-set-and-use-fall-detection-apple-watch-series-4 [retrieved: Oct, 2019].

[6] L. Shen, Q. Zhang, G. Cao, and H. Xu, "Fall detection system based on deep learning and image processing in cloud environment," in Conference on Complex, Intelligent, and Software Intensive Systems, Springer, Jun. 2018, pp. 590-598, doi: 10.1007/978-3-319-93659-8_53.

[7] M. Mubashir, L. Shao, and L. Seed, "A survey on fall detection: Principles and approaches," Neurocomputing, vol. 100, 2013, pp. 144-152, doi: 10.1016/j.neucom.2011.09.037.

[8] F. Wu, H. Zhao, Y. Zhao, and H. Zhong, "Development of a wearable sensor-based fall detection system," International journal of telemedicine and applications, 2015, p. 2, doi: 10.1155/2015/576364

[9] T. N. Gia, V. K. Sarker, I. Tcarenko, A. M. Rahmani, T. Westerlund, P. Liljeberg, and H. Tenhunen, "Energy efficient wearable sensor node for iot-based fall detection systems," Microprocessors and Microsystems, vol. 56, Feb. 2018, pp. 34-46, doi: 10.1016/j.micpro.2017.10.014

[10] P. Pierleoni, A. Belli, L. Palma, M. Pellegrini, L. Pernini, and S. Valenti, "A high reliability wearable device for elderly fall detection," IEEE Sensors Journal, vol. 15, no. 8, Aug. 2015, pp. 4544-4553, doi: 10.1109/JSEN.2015.2423562

[11] W. Saadeh, S. A. Butt, and M. A. B. Altaf, "A patient-specific single sensor iot-based wearable fall prediction and detection system," IEEE transactions on neural systems and rehabilitation engineering, vol. 27, no. 5, Apr. 2019, pp. 995-1003, doi: 10.1109/TNSRE.2019.2911602

[12] Infineon Technologies AG, "Dps310 Digital XENSIV™ Barometric Pressure Sensor for Portable Devices," 2019, URL: https://www.infineon.com/dgdl/Infineon-DPS310-DataSheet-v01_01-EN.pdf?fileId=5546d462576f34750157750826c42242 [retrieved: Oct, 2019].

[13] B. P. Lo, H. Ip, and G.-Z. Yang, "Transforming health care: Body sensor networks, wearables, and the internet of things," IEEE Pulse, vol. 7, no. 1, Jan. 2016, pp. 4-8, doi: 10.1109/MPUL.2015.2498474

Design, Development and Field Deployment of a Low-cost Distributed Wireless Sensor Network System for Real-time Hydraulic Fracturing Monitoring in Mines

Amirali Soroush, Wen Shen (Vincent) Mow
Onshore Gas Program, Energy
Commonwealth Scientific and Industrial Research Organisation (CSIRO)
Melbourne, Australia
e-mails: amirali.soroush@csiro.au, vincent.mow@csiro.au

Abstract **— A low-cost Distributed Wireless Sensor Network (DWSN) system designed and developed for real-time monitoring and diagnostics of hydraulic fracturing activities applicable to mine preconditioning operations is introduced in this paper. Built on open-source electronics platforms, as well as XBee wireless transceiver modules, and powered by solar energy, the system was deployed during the preconditioning operation in Whitehaven's Narrabri mine (New South Wales (NSW), Australia) and Luossavaara-Kiirunavaara Aktiebolag's (LKAB) Malmberget iron ore mine (Norrbotten County, Sweden). Over a period of two years, the system successfully monitored the placement of more than 2000 hydraulically-induced fractures in real-time, while providing an average packet delivery success rate of more than 99.995%.**

Keywords - Tiltmeter Monitoring; Surface Deformation Monitoring; Mine Preconditioning; Hydraulic Fracturing Monitoring and Diagnostics; Distributed Wireless Sensor Network Systems.

I. INTRODUCTION

DWSN systems are growing rapidly and being used extensively in various domains, such as environmental monitoring [1][2], agriculture [3][4], urban monitoring [5] and structural health monitoring [6] as a viable solution for monitoring various parameters of interest, such as pressure, temperature, humidity, strain, and acceleration in real-time and for long periods. The evolution of open source platforms for hardware and software development, along with the commercialization of modular low-cost and low-power electronics for data logging, processing, and wireless communication has provided developers with the opportunity for rapid prototyping and implementation of DWSNs for scientific, industrial and commercial applications.

Hydraulic fracturing refers to the process of injecting pressurized fluid into a wellbore with the intention to create new fractures in the deep rock formations and/or increase the size, extent, and connectivity of existing fractures. The process can be applied in the mining industry, particularly to the underground long-wall and block-cave mines, to induce predictable rock caving within excavation cavities. Hydraulic fracturing treatments are usually applied to the undisturbed rock or ore-body in advance of the mining operation as a method to pre-weaken or pre-condition the rock for improved operation productivity and safety during resource extraction [7]–[9].

To ensure the effectiveness of a hydraulic fracturing treatment, an array of high-resolution tiltmeters is placed beneath the ground in concentric circles surrounding the injection hole to measure the displacement gradient induced by the injected fluid and hence, map the fracture propagation process [10]. Flowmeters can also be used at the observation boreholes around the injection hole to determine any fracture connectivity between the injection hole and monitoring holes by measuring and confirming potential fluid return. The data recorded by tiltmeters and flowmeters provide helpful guidance for the operators to control the injection fluid, thus optimizing the fracturing treatment and ensuring its effectiveness where required, therefore reducing the operational costs [11].

In this paper, we introduce a novel DWSN system as a low-cost and flexible solution for real-time monitoring of hydraulic fracturing activities during the preconditioning operation on mine sites. The system, built on the Arduino open-source platform and XBee wireless transceiver modules, aims at providing sensory information for the operators in real-time while allowing for remote management and control of the sensor array over the Internet.

This paper is organized as follows. The overall architecture of the system is introduced in Section II. The design and development of various hardware and software components of the DWSN system is then detailed in Section III. Section IV elaborates the system optimizations in terms of total power consumption. Finally, the results of the field deployment of the system are illustrated in Section V, before drawing the conclusion and providing the outline for future work.

II. SYSTEM ARCHITECTURE

The overall architecture of a DWSN system designed and developed for monitoring preconditioning operations is illustrated in Figure 1. The system comprises a number of surface nodes interfaced with a sensor of interest (tiltmeter and/or flowmeter). The sensor array is usually scattered across a 1000 [m] × 1000 [m] area, and the average distance between sensor nodes is typically 50 to 100 meters. The ground surface is covered by vegetation and tall trees, so line of sight is not necessarily available between sensor nodes for wireless communication.

Each sensor node is equipped with an XBee radio transceiver, as well as a microcontroller unit interfacing various modules, such as Global Positioning System (GPS), micro Secure Digital (microSD) card, voltage scaler and serial-to-TTL (transistor-transistor logic) converter for integrating multiple sensors with analog or digital output to the system. The base station also consists of an XBee transceiver, connected to a laptop using an XBee Universal Serial Bus (USB) shield. The XBee transceivers (sensor nodes and the base station) form a mesh network using DigiMesh communication protocol. DigiMesh is a proprietary wireless mesh networking topology which allows for time synchronized sleeping nodes and low-power operation [12].

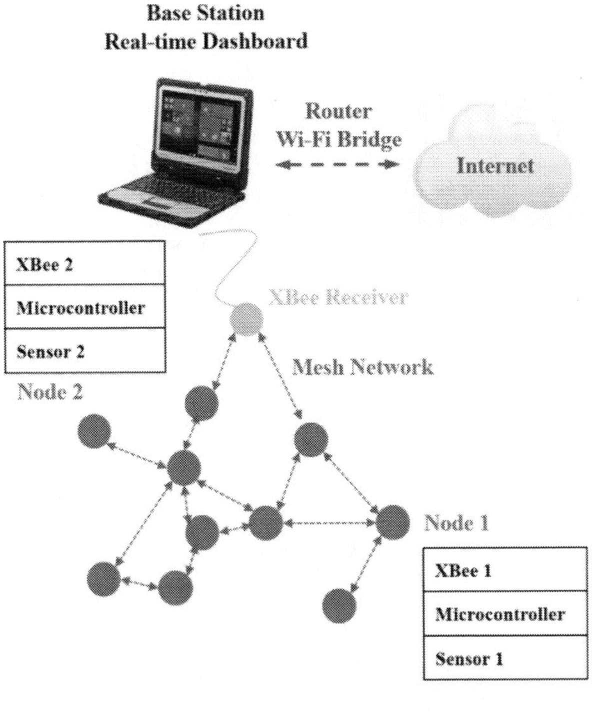

Figure 1. Overall system architecture.

The main advantage of the DigiMesh protocol is that all devices on a network are configured the same. Therefore, no complex architecture is required to define different nodes on the network as end-nodes, routers, coordinators, border routers, etc. Every device is the same, and capable of routing, sleeping for power optimization, and communicating via a mesh network [12].

The base station is connected to the Internet via a Wi-Fi bridge allowing for direct access to the nearest mobile tower. The real-time dashboard on the base station laptop serves as an interface to control the DWSN system, monitor sensor health, record sensor data, and synchronize data with CSIRO's online cloud servers in real-time. The dashboard can be accessed by authorized staff both on-site and off-site using third-party remote desktop connection software.

III. Design and Development

A. Sensor Node

The sensor node is developed around the Atmel SAM3X8E 32-bit Advanced RISC Machine (ARM) core microcontroller on the Arduino Due framework. Arduino is an open-source electronics platform integrating commonly-used flexible and low-cost hardware and software for rapid-prototyping of science and engineering projects [13]. The Arduino Due prototyping board offers 54 digital input/output pins, 12 analog inputs, 4 Universal Asynchronous Receiver-Transmitter (UART) ports, an 84 MHz clock, a 12-bit analog-to-digital converter (ADC), and a Serial Peripheral Interface (SPI).

The Lily self-leveling borehole tiltmeter is the instrument used for surface deformation monitoring. The dual-axis tiltmeter senses the displacement gradient induced by the underground fluid injection in two orthogonal vertical axes using precision electrolytic tilt sensors with nano-radian resolution. The instrument's on-board electronics samples the analog tilt signal and then, outputs a data string containing the X and Y tilts, azimuth (sensor heading with respect to magnetic north), temperature, power supply voltage and the instrument's serial number over RS-232 or RS-485 serial communication protocol [14]. This output is interfaced with the Arduino microcontroller using a MAX485 chip on a UART-to-RS485 converter module and a MAX3232 on a transceiver breakout module.

A u-blox NEO-M8M Global Navigation Satellite System (GNSS) module interfaced to each sensor node facilitates global geo-spatial positioning and time synchronization, provided antenna reception to sufficient satellites. Major GNSS, such as GPS, Galileo, and Globalnaya Navigazionnaya Sputnikovaya Sistema (GLONASS) are supported, and data is outputted in standard National Marine Electronics Association (NMEA) string format [15]. The tilt-sensing application involves immobile assets, so geospatial data is not time-critical and only require a single update in most cases. The location and time data are used as a redundancy in tiltmeter installation information and also clock synchronization of data between various sensors. On-site operators can access these visualized data via the real-time dashboard.

The wireless network is designed and developed based on a mesh topology using XBee-PRO 900HP embedded modules from Digi International. This radio transceiver utilizes the Australian Industrial, Scientific and Medical (ISM) 918-926 MHz frequency band and offers up to 200 Kbps data transfer rate at maximum transmit power. It is capable of outdoor communication of up to 6.5 kilometers line of sight range using 2.1 dBi dipole antennas, and up to 28 kilometers line of sight range using high gain antennas [12]. XBee-PRO 900HP modules utilize DigiMesh networking protocol, an innovative mesh protocol developed by Digi International specifically for power-sensitive applications relying solely on batteries. DigiMesh is built on the Institute of Electrical and Electronics Engineers (IEEE) 802.15.4 technical standard, which specifies the Physical (Binary Phase Shift Keying (BPSK) modulation at the 900MHz band) and Media Access Control

TABLE I. HEXADECIMAL BYTE OUTLINE OF AN EXAMPLE FRAME TO BE PASSED TO THE XBEE TRANSCEIVER VIA UART FOR RADIO TRANSMISSION OF THE DATA PAYLOAD.

Start Delimiter	Frame Length	Frame Type	Frame ID	64-bit Dest. Address	16-bit Dest. Address	Broadcast Radius	Options	Payload (shown in ASCII text)		Checksum
								Tilt-data	GNSS-data	
7E	00 7C	10	00	01 3A A2 00 41 5B 7E 79	FF FE	00	00	$ 13.232, -25.221,239.83, 21.71,10/12/18 16:32:49,13.07,N7928	,12/10/2018,06:33:46,-30.5055199,+149.85530093	87

(MAC) layer protocols. DigiMesh offers a wide range of advantages, such as added network stability through self-healing, self-discovering, and dense network operation. At the user-level, only the destination module serial address, preamble ID, and network ID are required for one-to-one transmission. Data transmitted are packed into frames in the XBee API2 format [16]. Reserved characters for frame formatting and an integrated checksum byte improve the reliability of the received data, at the cost of using more bandwidth. The current average size of the frames per transfer is approximately 127 total bytes (example shown in Table I). Data acknowledgments and failure retries are disabled to decrease network bandwidth, reduce energy consumption, and enforce sleep mode. Data encryption is also an available feature, but is currently disabled.

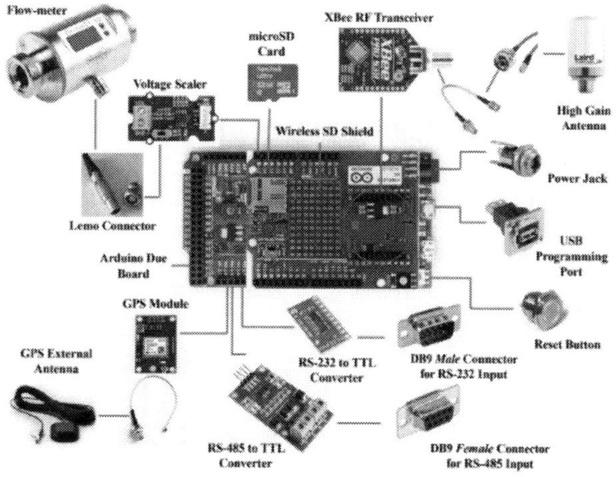

Figure 2. Electronics layout for the sensor node.

An Arduino Wireless SD shield is used to interface the XBee transceivers with the Arduino Due board. Communication between the microcontroller and the XBee, as well as microSD card is via UART and SPI, respectively. Each XBee transceiver is equipped with a Laird 3 dBi outdoor omni-directional antenna to enhance the communication range. The microcontroller firmware is developed in C/C++ and has the primary function of relaying the tiltmeter output data-string to the XBee module for wireless data transfer to the base station. Secondarily, it integrates all other additional peripherals, such as the microSD card and GPS module. Lastly, it performs additional housekeeping, including implementing a watchdog for potential software hang-ups, node health reporting, GNSS data refresh, and modification of communication parameters. Other features of the firmware are over-the-radio firmware updates and reset. The set-up and calibration commands designated for the tiltmeter are relayed across to the instrument, and node-specific commands are intercepted by the firmware.

Over-the-radio firmware updating is achieved without the need for any additional electronics due to the dual partition memory capability of the Atmel SAM3X8E microcontroller. The binary file of the firmware update is transmitted, checksum verified, and flashed into the adjacent memory bank before a software reset into the correct memory boot location. The sensing instrument and the sensor node are powered indefinitely using solar power and an Absorbent Glass Mat (AGM) battery. The electronics layout for the sensor node is well illustrated in Figure 2.

B. *Base Station*

The base station consists of an XBee transceiver interfaced with a Panasonic Toughbook via an XBee Explorer USB module (USB to UART). The XBee module baud-rate at the base station is set to 230,400 bps to take advantage of the maximum bandwidth allowed by the XBee-PRO 900HP transceiver. The XBee receiver is equipped with an omni-directional antenna. The electronics layout for the XBee receiver at the base station is shown in Figure 3.

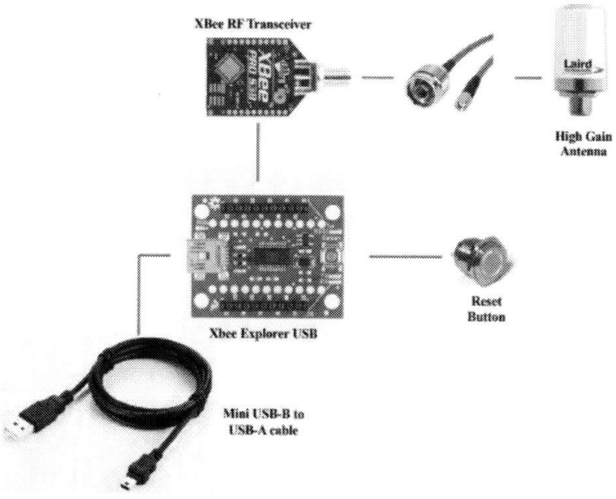

Figure 3. Electronics layout for the XBee receiver at the base station.

A real-time dashboard developed in the LabVIEW environment is used for recording and visualizing the measurements. The application is hosted on a Windows-based laptop at the base station on-site, and receives the data from the XBee receiver via a USB port. The objective of the software is to consolidate the data collection process, the diagnostics needed by the on-site operators to maintain system health, and interaction with the instruments' core firmware into a single intuitive platform. High-level functionalities, such as data quality control, preliminary processing, data visualization, command generation, issue reporting, and alarms are examples of the features implemented in the dashboard. The recorded data are instantly synced with CSIRO's online cloud service, so off-site engineers and scientists have real-time access to the data as required. An example of the application interface is shown in Figure 4.

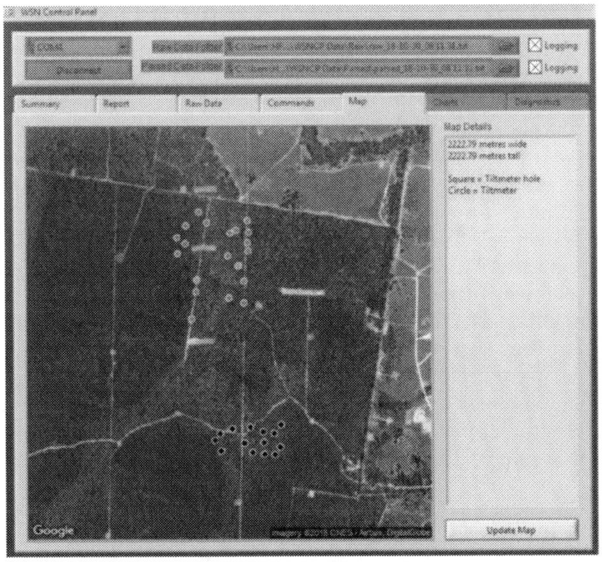

Figure 4. Real-time Dashboard for monitoring the tiltmeter array during preconditioning Long Wall 108 at Narrabri mine, NSW, Australia.

Data arriving into the dashboard is checksum verified for quality control, before being sorted and logged according to date-time and the instrument's serial number. Charted tiltmeter data, mapped locations, color-coded alarms, and tabulated tiltmeter health allow for quick system health verification at a glance. Operators can use the commands' panel to access the tiltmeter core utilities, such as instrument calibration, by sending the commands over the radio. Command transfer can be instrument specific or broadcasted to the entire array. Some special commands are reserved to be intercepted by the sensor node microcontrollers for radio module functionality, such as firmware reset and radio communication parameter changes.

IV. Power Optimization

As a preliminary prototype, the sensor node components were selected based on high-level compatibility and availability. Upon successful field demonstration, the sensor node firmware was revised to reduce average power consumption, with the hardware remaining mostly unchanged. Improvements to the microcontroller firmware include putting the SAM3X8E microcontroller into 'Backup' (i.e., deep sleep) mode between the sampling intervals. In this state, the microcontroller's internal core voltage regulator and memory peripherals are powered down. The still-running internal real-time timer is synced to the tiltmeter output rate and provides the trigger to restart the microcontroller, effectively implementing a 20% duty cycle on-time. A relatively-large buffer period (approximately 15% duty cycle) is used due to slow startup, non-constant XBee transmission time, and for a command reception window. The GNSS is configured to run on low-power, which involves a slower satellite scanning rate. The microcontroller disables the GNSS upon the registry of valid geo-location and time data. The XBee module is placed in sleep mode at the same duty cycle as the microcontroller.

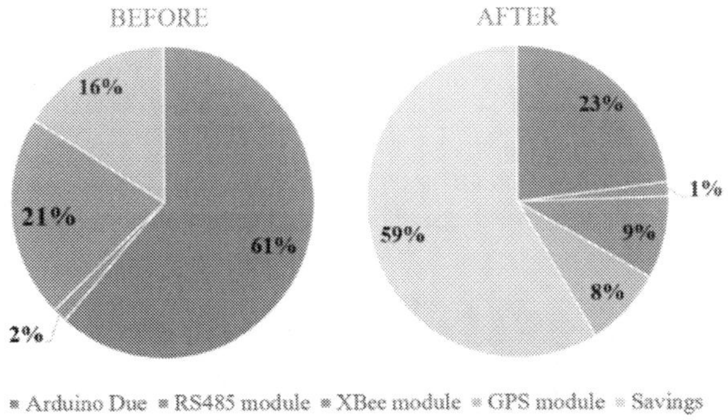

Figure 5. Sensor node power consumption before and after optimization.

The power consumption of the sensor node before and after the firmware revision is shown in Figure 5. The revised firmware includes algorithms that disable unused peripherals and enable periodic system sleep in-between sensor data sample. The average power consumption of the sensor node (at 0.1 Hz sample transmission) was reduced by 58.5% to approximately 500 mW through firmware optimization. At the moment, the majority of power is consumed to transmit the radio signal and store the data into the microSD card.

V. Field Deployment

A total of fifty sensor nodes (radio modules) and six receivers were developed as part of the DWSN system introduced in this paper. The total cost of each sensor node was approximately A$250, which is low relative to similar products currently available on the market. An example of the developed sensor node is shown in Figure 6.

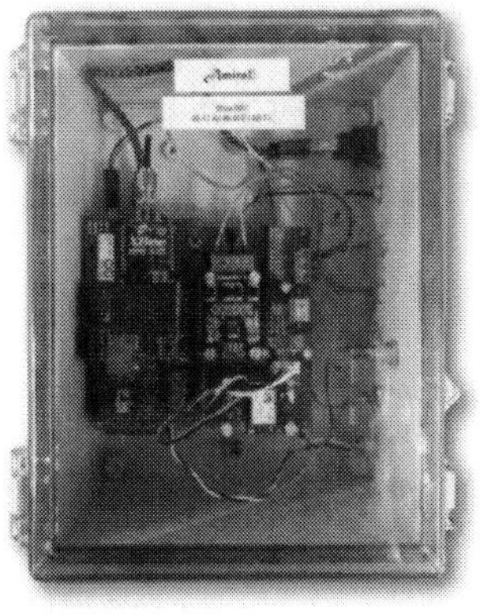

Figure 6. Example of developed radio module enclosure or sensor node.

The DWSN system was first deployed in April 2017 during the preconditioning operation of Long Wall 107 in Narrabri mine located in NSW, Australia. Up to 34 tiltmeters were used throughout the preconditioning operation, and the real-time dashboard was deployed on-site in 2018. The DWSN system introduced in this paper has been operating in Narrabri mine 24/7 ever since, and has successfully monitored the propagation of more than 2000 hydraulically induced fractures placed in ~500 boreholes during the preconditioning operation of three long-walls (LW107, LW108 and LW109) from April 2017 to June 2019.

In 2017, the DWSN system was also deployed at the Malmberget iron ore mine in Sweden for the purpose of monitoring the preconditioning operation for mitigating the seismic hazards in the underground mine [17]–[19]. The deployment included 15 tiltmeters buried underground, each connected to a sensor node on the surface and a base station with a receiver for logging the data in real-time, as shown in Figure 7.

Figure 7. DWSN system sensor node surface setup. Monitoring preconditioning in LKAB's Malmberget iron ore mine, Sweden, July 2017.

Overall, the DWSN system improved the quality of the recorded tilt data significantly by minimizing data loss across the network and removing data access latency problems by supplying the recorded data to the CSIRO's cloud service in real-time. The system proved robust and reliable by providing an average packet delivery success rate of more than 99.995%.

VI. Conclusion and Future Work

In this paper, the design, development, and deployment of a low-cost DWSN system for real-time monitoring of the hydraulic fracturing operations in mines is introduced. The system is built on the Arduino open-source platform and XBee wireless transceiver modules. The sensor nodes are scattered around the injection borehole in a 1000 [m] × 1000 [m] area with ~50-100 meters spacing, and interfaced with tiltmeters buried underground.

Over the course of two years, the DWSN system deployed in Narrabri (Australia) and Malmberget (Sweden) mines successfully monitored the preconditioning operation with real-time data delivery success rate of more than 99.995%. The system deployment showed great potential in automating the tilt monitoring operation for the purpose of fracture monitoring, system diagnostics, and reducing the time required for sensor calibration from days to minutes. The system has also improved the quality of the recorded tilt data significantly by minimizing data loss across the network and removing data access latency limitations by pushing the recorded data to the CSIRO's cloud service in real-time.

The successful deployment of the DWSN system demonstrates the advantage of developing in-house low-cost and low-power data collection system using open-source electronics platforms with modular components as compared to commercially available solutions which are often limited in offering long term reliability, flexibility, and scalability across various scenarios. The system has proven easy to implement, cheap to maintain, and simple to modify when future adjustments and upgrades were required.

Future works include reducing the system bandwidth (a potential 70% reduction) by replacing the system data encoding format with binary. This, along with the second revision of hardware and electronics, will drastically reduce system power consumption, as well as physical dimensions of the radio module unit. Transitioning the final product away from the prototyping platform to fully-integrated printed circuit boards and electronics at scale can reduce the per-unit cost to below A$100. Furthermore, the implementation of the lower-power Long Range (LoRa) radio technology to replace the existing radio system can unlock the capability for the DWSN system to be deployed in no-recharge scenarios, such as in underground mines.

Acknowledgment

The authors would like to thank CSIRO Energy for granting permission to publish this work.

References

[1] P. Corke, T. Wark, R. Jurdak, W. Hu, P. Valencia, and D. Moore, "Environmental Wireless Sensor Networks," *Proc. IEEE*, vol. 98, no. 11, pp. 1903–1917, 2010.

[2] S. Ferdoush and X. Li, "Wireless Sensor Network System Design Using Raspberry Pi and Arduino for Environmental Monitoring Applications," *Procedia Comput. Sci.*, vol. 34, pp. 103–110, 2014.

[3] J. Gutiérrez, J. F. Villa-Medina, A. Nieto-Garibay, and M. Á.

Porta-Gándara, "Automated Irrigation System Using a Wireless Sensor Network and GPRS Module," *IEEE Trans. Instrum. Meas.*, vol. 63, no. 1, pp. 166–176, 2014.

[4] J. Polo, G. Hornero, C. Duijneveld, A. García, and O. Casas, "Design of a low-cost Wireless Sensor Network with UAV mobile node for agricultural applications," *Comput. Electron. Agric.*, vol. 119, pp. 19–32, 2015.

[5] J. Lee, Z. Zhong, B. Du, S. Gutesa, and K. Kim, "Low-Cost and Energy-Saving Wireless Sensor Network for Real-Time Urban Mobility Monitoring System," *J. Sensors*, vol. 2015, p. 8, 2015.

[6] T. Torfs *et al.*, "Low Power Wireless Sensor Network for Building Monitoring," *IEEE Sens. J.*, vol. 13, no. 3, pp. 909–915, 2013.

[7] A. van As and R. G. Jeffrey, "Caving Induced by Hydraulic Fracturing at Northparkes Mines," *4th North American Rock Mechanics Symposium*. American Rock Mechanics Association, Seattle, Washington, p. 8, 2000.

[8] R. G. Jeffrey and K. W. Mills, "Hydraulic Fracturing Applied to Inducing Longwall Coal Mine Goaf Falls," *4th North American Rock Mechanics Symposium*. American Rock Mechanics Association, Seattle, Washington, p. 8, 2000.

[9] R. G. Jeffrey, X. Zhang, A. Settari, K. W. Mills, and E. Detournay, "Hydraulic fracturing to induce caving: fracture model development and comparison to field data," *DC Rocks 2001, The 38th U.S. Symposium on Rock Mechanics (USRMS)*. American Rock Mechanics Association, Washington, D.C., p. 10, 2001.

[10] R. G. Jeffrey, Z. Chen, K. W. Mills, and S. Pegg, "Monitoring and Measuring Hydraulic Fracturing Growth During Preconditioning of a Roof Rock over a Coal Longwall Panel," *ISRM International Conference for Effective and Sustainable Hydraulic Fracturing*. International Society for Rock Mechanics and Rock Engineering, Brisbane, Australia, p. 22, 2013.

[11] V. Pandurangan, Z. Chen, and R. G. Jeffrey, "Mapping hydraulic fractures from tiltmeter data using the ensemble Kalman filter," *Int. J. Numer. Anal. Methods Geomech.*, vol. 40, no. 4, pp. 546–567, 2016.

[12] "XBee-PRO 900 DigiMesh RF Module User Guide." [Online]. Available: https://www.digi.com. [Accessed: 23-Sep-2019].

[13] "Arduino Due." [Online]. Available: https://www.arduino.cc/en/Guide/ArduinoDue. [Accessed: 23-Sep-2019].

[14] "LILY Self-Leveling Borehole Tiltmeter User Manual." [Online]. Available: http://www.jewellinstruments.com. [Accessed: 23-Sep-2019].

[15] "ublox NEO-M8 series." [Online]. Available: https://www.u-blox.com/en/product/neo-m8-series. [Accessed: 23-Sep-2019].

[16] "API Mode for XBee Modules." [Online]. Available: https://www.digi.com/resources/documentation/Digidocs/90001942-13/concepts/c_api_escaped_operating_mode.htm?TocPath=XBee API mode%7COperating mode configuration%7C_____1. [Accessed: 23-Sep-2019].

[17] R. Jeffrey, D. Kasperczyk, K. Quinlan, R. Pandurangan, and A. Soroush, "Hydraulic fracturing trial in Malmberget Printzsköld crown pillar." Confidential Report, 2017.

[18] P. K. Boeg-Jensen, K. Jonsson, and R. G. Jeffrey, "Hydraulic Fracturing Trial Layout and Approach to Mitigate the Seismic Hazard at LKAB ' s Mines in Kiruna and Malmberget," *9th International Symposium on Rockburts and Seismicity in Mines*. Santiago, Chile, pp. 1–6, 2017.

[19] K. Jonsson and J. Martinsson, "Evaluating the effect on seismicity of a hydraulic fracturing trial using Bayesian data analysis," *Fourth International Symposium on Block and Sublevel Caving*. Australian Centre for Geomechanics PP - Perth, Perth, pp. 451–658, 2018.

Theoretical Models for Underwater RFID

Caroline Peres, John Buckley, Nadeem Rather, Brendan O'Flynn
Tyndall National Institute
University College Cork
Cork, Ireland
email: caroline.peres@tyndall.ie, john.buckley@tyndall.ie, nadeem.rather@tyndall.ie, brendan.oflynn@tyndall.ie

Abstract—**Underwater wireless communications pose challenges due to the characteristics of water as a propagation channel medium. Regardless, it is needed for a range of systems that operate underwater. Commonly used technologies for these use cases (radio-frequency, acoustic and optical communications) are lacking, as they usually suffer from strong attenuation, multipath and propagation delays. In this context, we explore Radio Frequency Identification (RFID) systems underwater and the feasibility of their application. This paper aims to discuss the theoretical transmission models for RFID systems underwater, separating them into near-field systems - which use Magnetic Induction (MI) to communicate - and far-field systems - that transfer data via Radio Frequency (RF). We determine the path loss for each case, explore its value for different system configurations and present preliminary measurements of magnetic field strength.**

Keywords–RFID; underwater wireless communications; underwater RFID; near-field communication; magnetic induction.

I. Introduction

Underwater wireless communications present some challenges due to the channel medium. The underwater environment has different characteristics and phenomena compared to the terrestrial radio propagation channel [1]. Despite these difficulties, underwater wireless communications are needed for underwater systems. Practical applications include seismic activity monitoring, equipment monitoring and control, underwater wireless sensor networks, underwater robots and Underwater Autonomous Vehicles (UAVs), aquaculture and underwater environment monitoring [2][3].

There are three commonly used technologies for underwater communications [1][4][5]. Radio-frequency (RF) communication consists of propagating electromagnetic waves, and it has high data rates at short ranges but suffers from multipath propagation, strong attenuation and Doppler effect [1]. Due to the increasing attenuation for higher frequencies, it requires that systems operate at lower frequencies for longer ranges, which demands large antennas. Acoustic communication makes use of propagating sound waves, which have low attenuation underwater, achieving the longest range. However, this type of communication exhibits high propagation delay due to the speed of sound underwater, suffers from multipath propagation, and is affected by a large delay spread that leads to intersymbol interference. Temperature gradients and ambient noise are also problems for acoustic communications. Another technology is optical communication, that leverages electromagnetic waves in the visible spectrum to transmit data. They have large data rates with low propagation delay. However, they suffer severe absorption in water and strong backscatter due to suspended particles.

Underwater Radio-Frequency Identification (RFID) is not an extensively explored topic due to the problems outlined above. However, some RFID systems communicate via Magnetic Induction (MI), which could provide an alternative for the existing technologies. In this paper, we want to explore this possibility. We examine the different methods of communication that different RFID systems employ, separating them into two categories: near-field communication and far-field communication. Theoretical mathematical models exist for terrestrial RFID systems, from which the system functionality, communication properties and link budged can be derived. This paper aims to derive similar models for underwater RFID communications, by describing the underwater channel physical properties for near-field and far-field electromagnetic fields by presenting the path loss for each. This can then be used to predict communication range, link budget and channel capacity.

This paper is organised as follows. Section II discusses the related work. In Section III, we give a brief overview of an RFID system and its components. Section IV then presents the model for underwater RFID for near-field and far-field communications. In Section V, we present preliminary results of measurements done of magnetic field strength in free-space and freshwater. Section VI discusses underwater RFID in light of the theory presented and the measurement results. We conclude the paper in Section VII.

II. Related Work

Underwater RFID is not a common topic due to the challenges that the underwater environment poses to RF communications. However, some preliminary work has been done. For example, [6] explores the use of Near-Field Communication (NFC) underwater. Using smartphones and smart cards operating at 13.56 MHz, they tested the read range achieved and the influence of dissolved salts in water in the read range. Another group used Low-Frequency (LF) RFID to track the sediment movements in a beach [7]. Transponders were coupled to pebbles, creating "smart" pebbles that could be detected at up to 50 cm underwater. They were then released into the beach and tracked to map the sediment movement. Systems that use LF RFID underwater can be found in Passive Integrated Transponder (PIT) tags used to uniquely identify fish in fisheries and research [8][9].

The authors in [10] summarised the current understanding of underwater RFID, examining the penetration depth in freshwater and seawater. However, the model presented is simplified and accounts only for the far-field operation. They also showcase other uses of RFID underwater, such as underwater pipeline monitoring. Other authors have explored MI communications underwater, where the system communicates via induction coupling. [11] provides an overview of the current research findings and challenges for MI. Models for MI can be found in [12]–[16].

III. RFID System

RFID uses electromagnetic fields to identify, track and communicate with electronic data carrying devices (usually called tags) [17]. An RFID system is comprised of a *transponder or tag* that is the object to be identified and a *reader* that reads/writes data from/to the transponder. The tag consists of a coupling element (antenna or coil) and a microchip that stores the data, while the reader has an antenna, a control unit and a radio frequency module.

For data transfer, the reader generates an electromagnetic field to query any transponders in its range. The tag receives the signal via its coupling element, and the energy captured from the electromagnetic field is used to power up the transponder's chip. This chip then sends back the data to the reader via load modulation or backscatter. In general, the transponder is passive (does not contain a power source), and it is powered by the field generated by the reader. There are also semi-active and active devices that have power sources that can power up additional circuitry and extend the range of communication.

IV. RFID Channel Physical Characteristics

The antenna or coil of the RFID reader generates an electromagnetic field. These fields can be described as time-harmonic fields in a lossy medium [18]:

$$\nabla^2 \mathbf{E} = \gamma \mathbf{E} \tag{1}$$
$$\nabla^2 \mathbf{H} = \gamma \mathbf{H} \tag{2}$$

where γ is the propagation constant, with α as the attenuation and β as the phase constants. The wavelength λ is $\lambda = 2\pi/\beta$.

$$\gamma = \alpha + j\beta = \sqrt{j\omega\mu(\sigma + j\omega\varepsilon)} \tag{3}$$

$$\alpha = \omega\sqrt{\mu\varepsilon}\left[\frac{1}{2}\left(\sqrt{1+\left(\frac{\sigma}{\omega\varepsilon}\right)^2} - 1\right)\right]^{1/2} \quad \left(\frac{Np}{m}\right) \tag{4}$$

$$\beta = \omega\sqrt{\mu\varepsilon}\left[\frac{1}{2}\left(\sqrt{1+\left(\frac{\sigma}{\omega\varepsilon}\right)^2} + 1\right)\right]^{1/2} \quad \left(\frac{rad}{m}\right) \tag{5}$$

The dielectric permittivity of the medium ε is further defined by $\varepsilon = \varepsilon_r\varepsilon_0$, $\varepsilon_0 = 8.854 \cdot 10^{-12} F/m$ being the permittivity in air and ε_r the relative permittivity of the medium (also known as dielectric constant) that is 81 for water. $\mu = \mu_0 = 4\pi \cdot 10^{-7} H/m$ is the magnetic permeability of the medium, that does not change for non-magnetic media.

The salinity of the water is proportional to the concentration of dissolved salts (chloride, sodium, sulphate, etc.). The conductivity σ is dependent on temperature, pressure and salinity. In marine water, the conductivity ranges from 2 S/m to 6 S/m, being considered constant 4 S/m in most cases [10]. In freshwater, the considerations are the same. However, the salinity is lower, which means that the conductivity is lower (typically ranging from 30 to 2000 μS/cm) [10]. Due to this high conductivity, Eddy currents are induced within the water, caused by the propagating magnetic field. These Eddy currents are a source of attenuation of the magnetic field.

For the Transverse Electromagnetic Mode to the positive z direction in lossy medium (in this case, water), $\mathbf{E}$ and $\mathbf{H}$ can be derived as [18]:

$$\mathbf{E}(\mathbf{z}) = \hat{\mathbf{a}}_x E_0 e^{-\gamma z} \tag{6}$$
$$\mathbf{H}(\mathbf{z}) = \hat{\mathbf{a}}_y \frac{\gamma}{j\omega\mu} E_0 e^{-\gamma z} \tag{7}$$

For a given antenna, the space that surrounds it can be separated into three regions: (a) a reactive near-field, (b) a radiating near-field and (c) the far-field. There are no abrupt changes at their boundaries [19]. A representation of these regions can be seen in Figure 1.

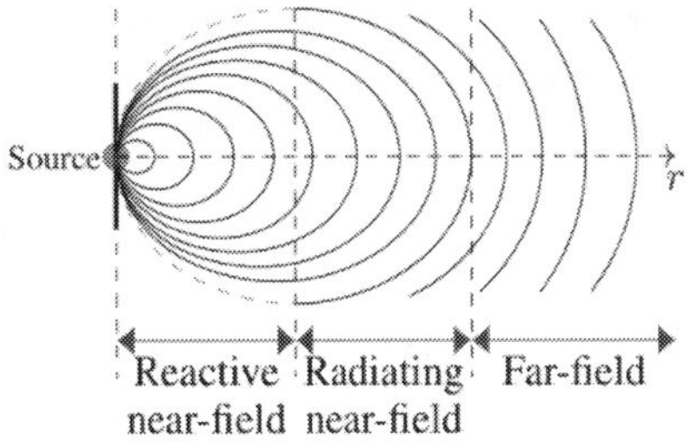

Figure 1. Field regions.

The *Reactive Near-Field* is the space immediately near the antenna where the reactive field predominates (magnetic field). For most antennas, the limit of this region is at $0.62\sqrt{D^3/\lambda}$ [19], where D is the biggest dimension of the antenna. The *Radiating Near-Field* is located between the reactive near-field and the far-field and is the space wherein radiation fields are dominant. The angular field distribution is determined by the distance from the antenna. This field existence depends on the ratio between antenna size D and the wavelength λ: if $D/\lambda \ll 1$ then this region does not exist. The *Far-Field* is the region wherein the electrical and magnetic components of the field become orthogonal to each other as they separate from the antenna and propagate as an electromagnetic wave. The lower boundary of this region is located at $2D^2/\lambda$ for any antenna [18], also considered to be $\lambda/2\pi$ for dipole antennas. According to [17], a good rule of thumb for RFID systems is to place the beginning of the far-field at $\lambda/2\pi$.

The field boundary distance is different for each medium due to the difference in wavelength. Tables I and II show the values for the attenuation coefficient, wavelength and far-field boundary for freshwater and seawater respectively.

Current RFID systems can be separated into two categories: near-field systems that work with inductive coupling due to the dominance of the magnetic field in the near-region, and far-field systems that receive power from the propagating

TABLE I. VALUES OF ATTENUATION COEFFICIENT α, WAVELENGTH λ AND FAR-FIELD BOUNDARY $z_F = \lambda/2\pi$ FOR FRESHWATER ($\sigma = 2 \cdot 10^{-3}$ S/M).

Frequency	α (Np/m)	λ (m)	z_F (m)
134.2 kHz	$2.81 \cdot 10^{-2}$	$1.66 \cdot 10^{2}$	26.5
13.56 MHz	$4.19 \cdot 10^{-2}$	2.46	0.391
433.92 MHz	$4.19 \cdot 10^{-2}$	$7.68 \cdot 10^{-2}$	$1.22 \cdot 10^{-2}$
915 MHz	$4.19 \cdot 10^{-2}$	$3.64 \cdot 10^{-2}$	$5.79 \cdot 10^{-3}$
2.4 GHz	$4.19 \cdot 10^{-2}$	$1.39 \cdot 10^{-2}$	$2.21 \cdot 10^{-3}$

TABLE II. VALUES OF ATTENUATION COEFFICIENT α, WAVELENGTH λ AND FAR-FIELD BOUNDARY $z_F = \lambda/2\pi$ FOR SEAWATER ($\sigma = 4$ S/M).

Frequency	α (Np/m)	λ (m)	z_F (m)
134.2 kHz	1.46	4.32	0.687
13.56 MHz	14.5	0.426	$6.78 \cdot 10^{-2}$
433.92 MHz	65.4	$6.00 \cdot 10^{-2}$	$9.55 \cdot 10^{-3}$
915 MHz	76.5	$3.33 \cdot 10^{-2}$	$5.30 \cdot 10^{-3}$
2.4 GHz	82.4	$1.37 \cdot 10^{-2}$	$2.17 \cdot 10^{-3}$

electromagnetic waves in the far-field [20]. The frequencies used in each region are different. Since the lower frequencies – such as Low Frequency (LF) at around 134.2kHz and High Frequency (HF) at 13.56MHz – have a far-field boundary that is further away, they are mainly used in inductive coupling systems. Higher frequencies are then used mostly in far-field systems.

A. Near-field

In the near-field, the magnetic field created by the reader's antenna induces a voltage in the transponder immersed in this field. This is called *inductive coupling* and the interaction between reader and transponder can be considered as coupled inductors. This method of communication can also be called *Magnetic Induction (MI)*.

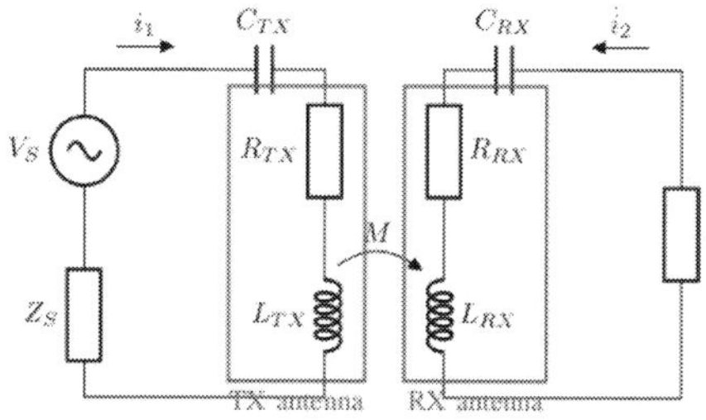

Figure 2. Inductive coupling between reader and transponder.

Consider the equivalent circuit for the inductively coupled system shown in Figure 2. The transmitter antenna is fed by a source with internal impedance Z_S and the receiver antenna is terminated by a load impedance Z_L. The transmitter coil antenna has a impedance of $Z_{TX} = R_{TX} + j\omega L_{TX} + 1/(j\omega C_{TX})$ and the receiver coil antenna is $Z_{RX} = R_{RX} + j\omega L_{RX} + 1/(j\omega C_{RX})$.

Using the two-port network equivalent (Figure 3) and considering an ideal source for V_S, $Z_{11} = Z_{TX}$ and $Z_{22} = Z_{RX}$ are the self-impedances of the coils and $Z_{12} = Z_{21} = j\omega M$ are the mutual impedances due to the coupling.

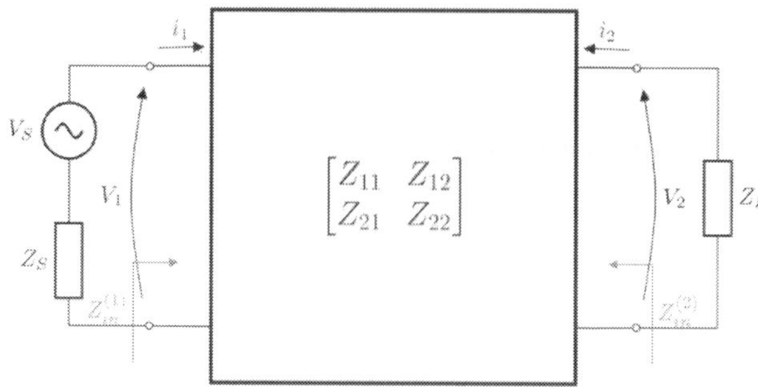

Figure 3. Two-port network equivalent of the system.

$$\begin{pmatrix} V_1 \\ -Z_L I_2 \end{pmatrix} = \begin{bmatrix} Z_{11} & Z_{12} \\ Z_{21} & Z_{22} \end{bmatrix} \cdot \begin{pmatrix} I_1 \\ I_2 \end{pmatrix} \tag{8}$$

The resistance of a coil is $R = N \cdot 2\pi a \cdot R_0$, where N is the number of turns of the coil, a is the diameter of the coil and R_0 is the resistance of a unit of length of the wire used to fabricate the coil. The self-inductance is

$$L = \frac{\mu \pi^2 N^2 a}{l} \tag{9}$$

where l is the length of the coil. In the free space, the magnetic field strength generated by a coil antenna in the near field is [17]:

$$H_0 = \frac{N a^2 I}{2(a^2 + z^2)^{3/2}} \tag{10}$$

The magnetic field magnitude for a lossy medium is then $H = H_0 exp(-\alpha z)$ according to (7). This magnetic field induces a voltage in the tag's coil antenna, given by:

$$U_2 = -N_2 \frac{d\Phi_{21}}{dt} = -M \frac{di_1}{dt} \tag{11}$$

where $\Phi_{21} = \int \mathbf{B} \cdot d\mathbf{S}$ is the magnetic flux through each turn, $\mathbf{B} = \mu \mathbf{H}$ the magnetic field and $\mathbf{S}$ the surface area of the coil. Considering that the reader's and tag's coils are aligned, and using (10):

$$B_z = \left(\frac{\mu N a_1^2 I}{2(a_1^2 + z^2)^{2/3}} \right) e^{-\alpha z} \tag{12}$$

Therefore, the mutual inductance $M = k\sqrt{L_1 L_2}$ is:

$$M = \left(\frac{\mu \cdot \pi \cdot N_1 \cdot a_1^2 \cdot N_2 \cdot a_2^2}{2 \cdot (a_1^2 + z^2)^{3/2}} \right) \cdot e^{-\alpha z} \tag{13}$$

where α is the attenuation constant of the medium.

The transmission power can be defined as the power consumed by the radiation resistance in the reader (transmitter) antenna:

$$P_{TX} = \frac{1}{2} Re(Z_{11}) \cdot |I_1|^2 \quad (14)$$

The received power is defined as the power consumed in the load:

$$P_{RX}(z) = \frac{1}{2} Re(Z_L) \cdot |I_2|^2 \quad (15)$$

Using (8) and considering $Z_S \approx 0$, the received power can be written as:

$$P_{RX}(z) = P_{TX} \frac{Re(Z_L)\omega^2 M^2}{Re(Z_{TX})|Z_L + Z_{RX}|^2} \quad (16)$$

Path loss in decibels (dB) can be defined as:

$$PL = -10\log_{10}\left(\frac{P_{RX}}{P_{TX}}\right)(dB) \quad (17)$$

The path loss is a function of the number of turns and radius of both coils and the impedances of the system, as well as the frequency and the distance between reader and tag. The highest amount of power is transferred to the load when its impedance is matched with the impedance of the antenna.

For an example system with a transmitter antenna with 100 turns and 1 m of radius paired with a receiver antenna with 100 turns and 10 cm of radius, both resonant at 134.2 kHz, the path loss in terms of range is shown in Figure 4. The path loss as a function of frequency is shown in Figure 5.

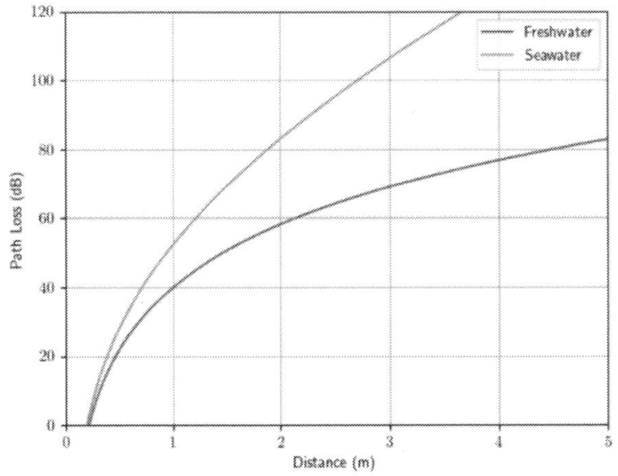

Figure 4. Path loss for an inductively coupled system operating at $f = 134.2$kHz.

The path loss for the MI system increases with the increasing distance between reader and tag. Also, the path loss is higher for seawater due to the higher conductivity of the medium. In freshwater, an increase in frequency decreases the path loss. However, as the frequency increases, the distance from the reader where the border between the near and the far-field is located decreases. This implies that the maximum theoretical range decreases with frequency. We can then conclude that there is an optimal combination of frequency and distance for each application. The decrease in path loss for

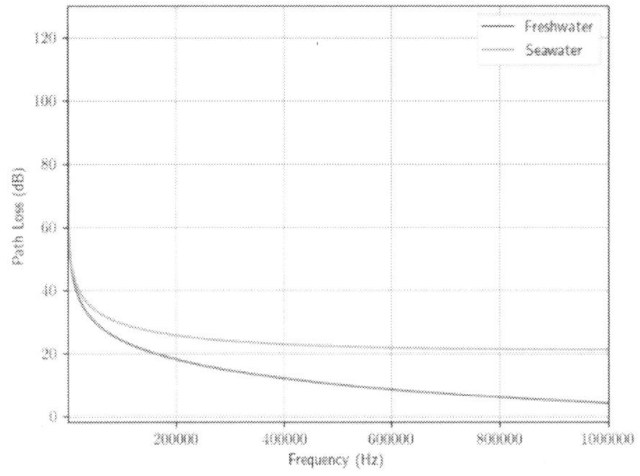

Figure 5. Path loss for an inductively coupled system at range $z = 50$ cm.

higher frequencies is not as significant in seawater. This is due to the higher conductivity, where the attenuation factor is stronger for higher frequencies.

The influence of the number of turns of the transmitter or the receiver coil in the mutual inductance M is linear. Therefore the power received would increase quadratically with the increase in the number of turns. The relationship between the power and radius of the coil is not so straightforward. Figure 6 shows this relationship for a system operating at 134.2kHz with a transmitter antenna with 100 turns and variable radius, with a receiver antenna with 100 turns and 10 cm of radius, at 50 cm of distance between reader and tag.

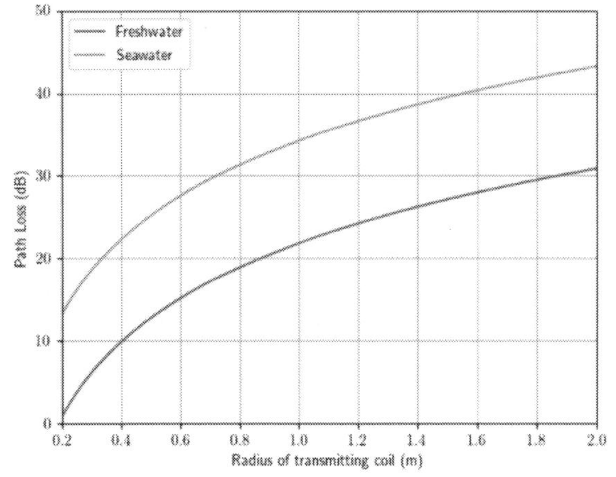

Figure 6. Path loss for an inductively coupled system at range $z = 50$ cm and frequency $f = 134.2$kHz.

A more in-depth model of underwater magnetic induction communication can be found in [13]. The model shown here assumes that the reader and tag coils are oriented in the same direction, with the field strength reaching zero if the angle between coils is 90°. To remove this limitation, the authors in [21] present a model of the Underwater MI channel for a tri-directional coil. To increase the achievable range of MI systems, waveguides can be used [12][22].

Data transmission from tag: When a transponder is located in the magnetic alternating field generated by the reader, the reader 'sees' the transponder as the secondary wing of the transformer. This means that the transponder's impedance is reflected back to the reader as the *transformer impedance* Z_T.

If the transponder antenna impedance changes, this is reflected back to the reader's coil via the reflected impedance Z_T. Therefore, a data stream can be transmitted via modulation of the voltage U_L in the reader's coil (called *Load Modulation*); this can be demodulated by the reader via rectification of the voltage [17]. This is only feasible in the near-field as if the transponder leaves the coupling is lost and the transmission link is not operational anymore.

For an amplitude modulating system, due to the weak coupling between reader and transponder antennas, the voltage fluctuation is orders of magnitude smaller than the voltage provided by the reader. As a direct result, the reader has to integrate a complex circuitry to separate noise from the signal and detect the data stream. On the other hand, if the transponder modulates the signal at a frequency f_S, smaller than the frequency of the magnetic field (f_0), two spectral lines $\pm f_S$ are created and they can be filtered with a band-pass filter and demodulated more easily [20].

B. Far-field

In the far-field, the electromagnetic fields separate completely from the reader's antenna and become propagating waves, no longer retroacting upon the reader's antenna. These waves are captured by the antenna on the transponder. The energy on the antenna is rectified and used to power up the IC. The frequency range commonly used for this type of transmission is the Ultra-High Frequency (UHF) and Microwave.

A linearly polarized plane EM wave propagating in lossy media in the z-direction can be described by the electric field strength E_x:

$$E_x = E_0 e^{j\omega t - \gamma z} \tag{18}$$

With $\gamma = \alpha + j\omega\beta$ as the propagating constant according to (4) and (5).

In [23], the authors propose a review of this model to account for the difference between the theoretical model and the empirical data of attenuation of the radio waves underwater. The experiments show that the signal attenuation at higher distances ($\gg 10m$) is not as strong as predicted. Therefore, they redefine the attenuation constant α as a corrected absorption factor $\alpha\prime$ that matches experimental results closely:

$$\alpha\prime = \left(\frac{\lambda}{\lambda + r}\right) \cdot \alpha \tag{19}$$

Figure 7 shows the difference in the path loss for both models in freshwater and seawater for a system operating at 13.56 MHz.

The radiation power density S is the instantaneous value of the Poynting vector $\mathbf{S} = \mathbf{E} \times \mathbf{H}$. From [18] and considering (7):

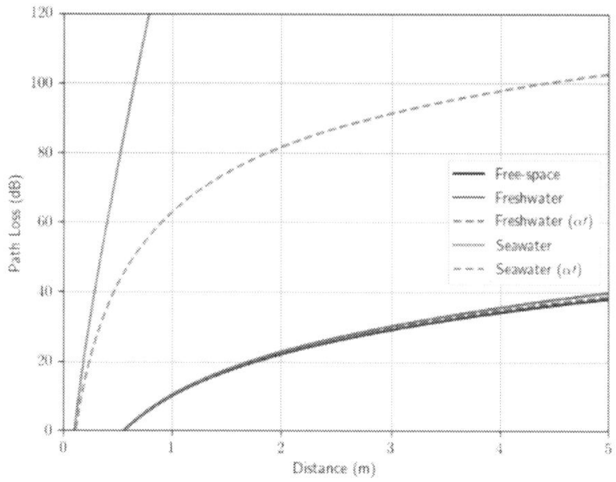

Figure 7. Comparison of path loss for two dipole antennas operating at $f = 13.56$MHz using α and $\alpha\prime$.

$$\mathbf{S} = \frac{1}{2} Re(\mathbf{E} \times \mathbf{H}) = \hat{\mathbf{a}}_z \frac{|E_0|}{2} e^{-2\alpha z} Re\left(\frac{1}{\eta_c^*}\right) \tag{20}$$

where η_C is the intrinsic impedance of the medium:

$$\eta_C = \sqrt{\frac{j\omega\mu}{\sigma + j\omega\varepsilon}} \tag{21}$$

For the transmitting antenna in the free-space, S_0 is the power supplied to it over the area of the spread surface:

$$S_0 = \frac{P_{EIRP}}{4\pi z^2} = \frac{P_{TX} G_{TX}}{4\pi z^2} \tag{22}$$

Whereas the radiation power density in a lossy medium is then:

$$S = S_0 e^{-2\alpha z} \tag{23}$$

For the receiving antenna, the average power received is the radiation power density times its effective receiving area A_e [23]:

$$P_{RX} = S \cdot A_e = S \cdot \frac{G_{RX} \lambda^2}{4\pi} \tag{24}$$

The transmission equation then can be written as:

$$P_{RX} = P_{TX} \left(\frac{G_{TX} G_{RX} \lambda^2}{(4\pi z^2)^2}\right) e^{-2\alpha z} \tag{25}$$

where G_{TX} and G_{RX} are the antenna gains for transmitter and receiver respectively, $\lambda = (2\pi)/\beta$ is the wavelength and z is the distance between antennas. This equation assumes that the antennas are aligned and have the same polarization. The path loss PL_{EM} in decibels is then defined as $PL_{EM} = -10\log_{10}(P_{RX}/P_{TX})$.

Figures 8 and 9 show the path loss of different operating frequencies for a dipole transmitting antenna (reader) and

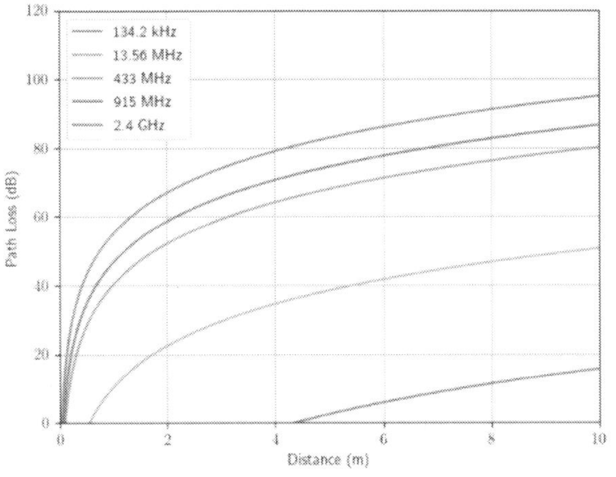

Figure 8. Path loss for RF as a function of distance for two dipole antennas in freshwater using $\alpha\prime$.

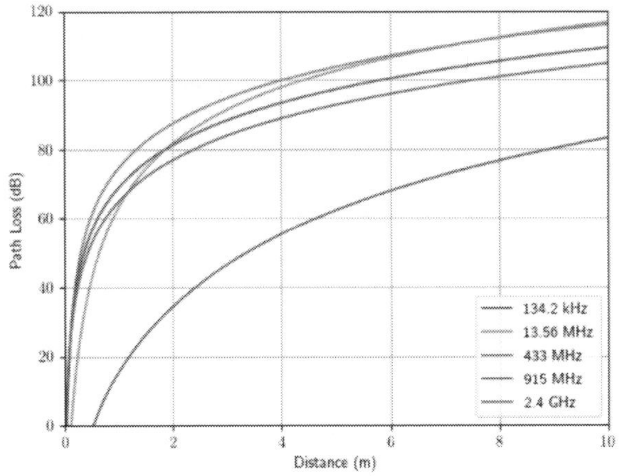

Figure 9. Path loss for RF as a function of distance for two dipole antennas in seawater using $\alpha\prime$.

a dipole receiving antenna (tag), both with gain 1.63. For freshwater, it is clear that the higher frequencies suffer more from attenuation than lower frequencies. However, in Figure 9, the path loss increases with the frequency for 134.2 kHz, 13.52 MHz and 433 MHz, after which the path loss starts to stabilise around a region. This happens due to the difference in the behaviour of the propagating medium for different frequencies: the medium can be classified as a good dielectric (insulator) if $(\sigma/\omega\varepsilon)^2 \ll 1$ and – contrastingly – as a good conductor if $(\sigma/\omega\varepsilon)^2 \gg 1$. The frequency at which this behaviour change is around 666 Hz for freshwater ($\sigma = 0.002$ S/m) and 888 MHz for seawater ($\sigma = 4$ S/m). This behaviour can be seen in Figure 10, in which the path loss for a reader and a tag with dipole antennas separated by 50 cm is plotted as a function of the frequency of transmission. In this figure, the path loss for seawater peaks at around 888 MHz.

Data transmission from tag: For passive RFID, the method of transmitting back to the reader is via *Backscatter*. Electromagnetic waves are reflected by objects that are larger than half the wavelength ($\frac{\lambda}{2}$). The efficiency of this reflection depends

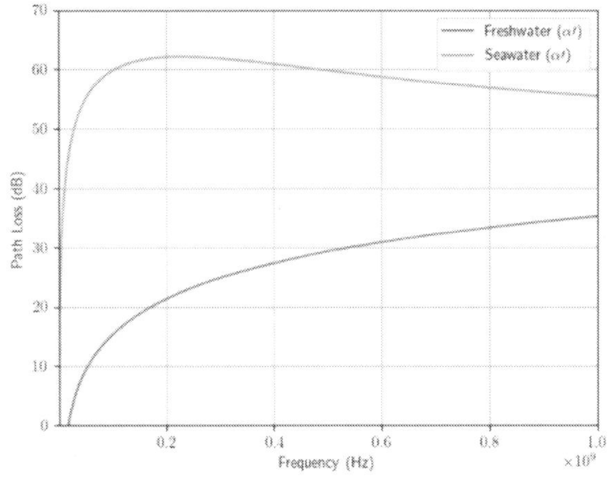

Figure 10. Path loss for RF as a function of frequency for two dipole antennas in freshwater and seawater using $\alpha\prime$.

on the reflection cross-section of the object: antennas that are resonant with the waves have a larger reflection cross-section. The reflection characteristics can be altered by changing the load that is connected to the antenna. For example, if a load R_L is switched on and off while connected to the antenna, this changes the reflection characteristics of the antenna, generating a modulated backscatter signal [17]. The range is limited by the amount of energy that reaches the tag (path loss) and the sensitivity of the reader's receiver to the reflected signal (reflected signal strength $\propto 1/x^4$) [24]. The authors in [25] present a method for measuring the backscatter of an RFID tag and for calculating its radar cross-section. They utilise a network analyzer connected to an anechoic chamber.

V. MEASUREMENTS

To explore the difference in magnetic field strength between free-space and water in the near-field region, a preliminary experiment was designed. The Anritsu MS2038C VNA Master [26] vector network analyser and the probe 100C from Beehive Electronics, USA [27] were used to measure the magnetic field strength at the system's resonant frequency. Two Evaluation Kit RFID readers were used: *MRD2EVM* from Texas Instruments, USA that operates at 134.2 kHz [28] and *Pepper Wireless C1 USB* from Eccel Technology Ltd, UK that operates at 13.56 MHz [29]. Both have square loop antennae embedded on the printed circuit board, with sides of length 3.0 cm and 4.5 cm, and number of turns 5 and 1, respectively.

For a square loop antenna with N-turns, the magnetic field strength in free-space can be written as [30]:

$$H_0 = \frac{NI}{2\pi\left(\frac{z^2}{l^2}+\frac{1}{4}\right)\sqrt{z^2+\frac{l^2}{2}}} \quad (26)$$

Where z is the distance from the centre of the antenna and l is the length of the side of the antenna. Using 7, for a lossy medium (in this case freshwater), the magnetic field strength is then $H = H_0 exp(-\alpha z)$. Using α from I we can then calculate the theoretical values for the magnetic field strength for any distance and compare this with the measurements made with the probe.

For both systems, the setup for the experiments was the same, as seen in Figure 11. The probe was placed in different distances z from the centre of the embedded antenna of the reader. The free-space tests were done without the water container, while the freshwater measurements were done using a plastic container bigger than the antenna filled with tap water. The plastic container was then placed touching the antenna, and the probe was submerged in the water to get the measured field strength.

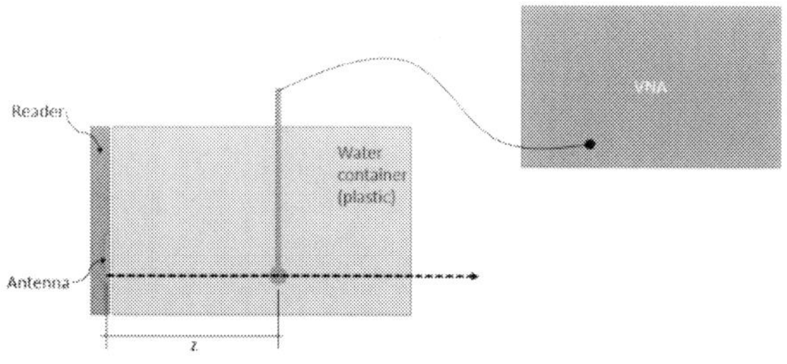

Figure 11. Experiment setup for measuring the magnetic field strength in water.

Figure 12 shows the theoretical and measured values for the 134.2kHz system, while Figure 13 shows the values for the 13.56MHz system. We can see that for both cases the measured values agree with the calculated theoretical ones. The difference between free-space and freshwater for the theoretical values is very small due to the small α for freshwater. However, we can see that the difference between measured field strength in freshwater and free-space is greater. This is could be due to the interfaces of water and plastic and water and air that could introduce losses to the system. For the 13.56MHz system, the attenuation underwater is bigger than the attenuation for the 134.2kHz. This is due to the higher attenuation coefficient α for higher frequencies.

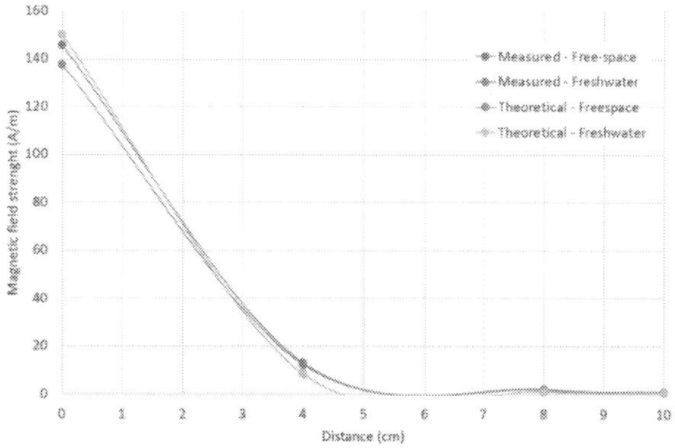

Figure 12. Theoretical and measured field strength values for the Texas Instruments MRD2EVM evaluation kit ($f = 134.2$kHz).

VI. Discussions

The most common method of wireless transmission underwater is acoustic communication. This is due to the long range that can be accomplished with this technology. However, some applications do not need such long range and are deeply affected by acoustic noise and refractions, reflections and multipath due to the proximity to the water surface, such as coastal environments. In these cases, wireless communication can be better served by other methods that do not suffer from these problems. We explore the possibility of using RFID technology to better serve these environments.

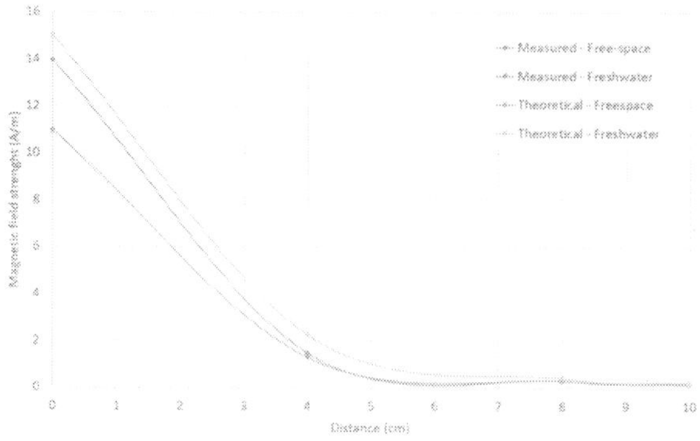

Figure 13. Theoretical and measured field strength values for the Eccel Technology Pepper C1 USB evaluation kit ($f = 13.56$MHz).

In the near-field region, the magnetic component of the electromagnetic field dominates. The method of communication for RFID in this region is MI. Compared to other methods of underwater communications, MI has several advantages. It is not affected by multipath propagation or fading and the magnetic field can cross the water to air boundary with low attenuation [12]. The signal propagation delay is negligible if compared to acoustic waves. The channel response is predictable, and a sufficiently large range can be achieved with modest data rates [11].

For the far-field, the electromagnetic field propagates as a wave, and the communication is realised through radio-frequency. Due to the high attenuation, there is a severe constraint on data rates and propagation distances for this method [1]. Lower frequency signals have lower attenuation (due to conductivity of the water) but require larger antennas. This also limits the bandwidth of the system due to the lower frequency of operation. Higher frequency systems would then require more power to reach the same ranges. Shallow water environments, in particular, pose a problem to wave propagation due to the proximity to the water to air upper boundary and to the river/sea bed, which causes multipath propagation [5].

Both technologies do not require line-of-sight and are unaffected by light and acoustic ambient noise. Moreover, the channel response is independent of water quality conditions, such as turbidity. The achievable range for a given transmission power is not great for both methods, as long-range transmissions underwater are best served by acoustic communication. However, the numerical results show that MI has lower attenuation than RF for freshwater, and similar results for seawater, which agrees with other studies such as [12]. Combined with its immunity to multipath and fading, MI is a great alternative for wireless communications underwater.

Added to that, the achievable range of MI communications can be greatly extended by deploying waveguides that do not require power – simple passive relay coils that guide the magnetic field – such as demonstrated in [12][22]. For example, [12] uses an MI waveguide and achieves a range 26 times higher than a normal MI system. Another development that improves MI communications underwater is to use omnidirectional coils that remove the requirement of the transmitting and receiving coils being aligned [11][21].

However, to design an underwater RFID system is to balance a trade-off between range, transmission power and frequency (and therefore data rate and channel capacity). Nonetheless, the RFID system can always be engineered to achieve the best range given its power budget. For an MI system, the size and number of turns of the transmitting and receiving coils has an impact on the path loss. In the far-field category, the antenna can be carefully designed to provide the best radar cross-section, and therefore antenna gain, for the desired application.

An example application that would benefit from MI communication over acoustic would be sensors deployed in coastal areas and fish farms. In these environments, the acoustic noise – from waves, animal life and vessels – and the proximity with the water surface negatively impact acoustic underwater communications. In these cases, MI underwater communication would better fulfil the needs of the system.

VII. Conclusions and Future Work

Given the existing challenges in wireless underwater communications, it is worth exploring alternatives, such as RFID. However, underwater RFID is not a well-explored topic. In this paper, we expanded on the existing theoretical model for RFID channel characteristics to account for the attenuation that the electromagnetic field suffers underwater. The RFID operation was separated into two categories: near-field and far-field. For both cases, the physical characteristics of the transmission were presented and from this, the equation for path loss was obtained and the values for different system configurations were explored.

In both technologies, the water salinity is a problem, as it increases its conductivity and, therefore, its attenuation. However, MI communication has advantages that RF does not have: immunity to multipath propagation and fading. Added to that, the magnetic field can cross the air/water boundary, which is required for some applications. Therefore, near-field RFID communication is a promising alternative for underwater wireless communications.

The model presented in this paper considers that both the transmitting and receiving antennas are located underwater with no transition borders and other losses. This model could be expanded to account for transition borders such as the air-water interface located at the water surface or the interface with the waterproofing material of the reader and tag. In this paper, we also presented some preliminary measurements for magnetic field strength in free-space and freshwater. For future work, we plan to include underwater measurements with water of different salinity values and refine the measurement procedure.

VIII. Acknowledgement

This work is part of IMPAQT (https://impaqtproject.eu/) – This project has received funding from the European Union's Horizon 2020 research and innovation programme under Grant Agreement No 774109.

References

[1] C. M. G. Gussen, P. S. R. Diniz, M. L. R. Campos, W. A. Martins, F. M. Costa, and J. N. Gois, "A Survey of Underwater Wireless Communication Technologies," *Journal of Communication and Information Systems*, vol. 31, no. 1, pp. 242–255, 2016, 00018.

[2] J. Heidemann, Wei Ye, J. Wills, A. Syed, and Yuan Li, "Research challenges and applications for underwater sensor networking," in *IEEE Wireless Communications and Networking Conference, 2006. WCNC 2006.* Las Vegas, NV, USA: IEEE, 2006, pp. 228–235, 00974.

[3] M. C. Domingo, "An overview of the internet of underwater things," *Journal of Network and Computer Applications*, vol. 35, no. 6, pp. 1879–1890, Nov. 2012.

[4] L. Lambo, Z. Shengli, and C. Jun-Hong, "Prospects and problems of wireless communication for underwater sensor networks," *Wireless Communications and Mobile Computing*, vol. 8, no. 8, pp. 977–994, Oct. 2008.

[5] X. Che, I. Wells, G. Dickers, P. Kear, and X. Gong, "Re-evaluation of RF electromagnetic communication in underwater sensor networks," *IEEE Communications Magazine*, vol. 48, no. 12, pp. 143–151, Dec. 2010.

[6] A. Pozzebon, "Bringing near field communication under water: Short range data exchange in fresh and salt water," in *2015 International EURASIP Workshop on RFID Technology (EURFID)*, Oct. 2015, pp. 152–156, 00003.

[7] D. Bertoni, G. Sarti, G. Benelli, A. Pozzebon, and G. Raguseo, "Radio Frequency Identification (RFID) technology applied to the definition of underwater and subaerial coarse sediment movement," *Sedimentary Geology*, vol. 228, no. 3, pp. 140–150, Jul. 2010.

[8] E. B. Thorstad, A. H. Rikardsen, A. Alp, and F. Økland, "The Use of Electronic Tags in Fish Research – An Overview of Fish Telemetry Methods," *Turkish Journal of Fisheries and Aquatic Sciences*, vol. 13, no. 5, pp. 881–896, 2013.

[9] S. J. Cooke, S. G. Hinch, M. C. Lucas, and M. Lutcavage, "Biotelemetry and Biologging," in *Fisheries Techniques*, 3rd ed. American Fisheries Society, 2012, pp. 819–860.

[10] G. Benelli and A. Pozzebo, "RFID Under Water: Technical Issues and Applications," in *Radio Frequency Identification from System to Applications*, M. I. B. Reaz, Ed. InTech, Jun. 2013.

[11] I. F. Akyildiz, P. Wang, and Z. Sun, "Realizing underwater communication through magnetic induction," *IEEE Communications Magazine*, vol. 53, no. 11, pp. 42–48, Nov. 2015, 00054.

[12] M. C. Domingo, "Magnetic Induction for Underwater Wireless Communication Networks," *IEEE Transactions on Antennas and Propagation*, vol. 60, no. 6, pp. 2929–2939, Jun. 2012.

[13] B. Gulbahar and O. B. Akan, "A Communication Theoretical Modeling and Analysis of Underwater Magneto-Inductive Wireless Channels," *IEEE Transactions on Wireless Communications*, vol. 11, no. 9, pp. 3326–3334, Sep. 2012, 00080.

[14] Z. Sun and I. F. Akyildiz, "Magnetic Induction Communications for Wireless Underground Sensor Networks," *IEEE Transactions on Antennas and Propagation*, vol. 58, no. 7, pp. 2426–2435, Jul. 2010, 00376.

[15] U. Azad, H. C. Jing, and Y. E. Wang, "Link Budget and Capacity Performance of Inductively Coupled Resonant Loops," *IEEE Transactions on Antennas and Propagation*, vol. 60, no. 5, pp. 2453–2461, May 2012, 00058.

[16] H. Nguyen, J. I. Agbinya, and J. Devlin, "Channel Characterisation and Link Budget of MIMO Configuration in Near Field Magnetic Communication," *International Journal of Electronics and Telecommunications*, vol. 59, no. 3, pp. 255–262, Sep. 2013, 00013.

[17] K. Finkenzeller, *RFID Handbook: Fundamentals and Applications in Contactless Smart Cards, Radio Frequency Identification and near-Field Communication*. Hoboken, N.J.: Wiley, 2014, oCLC: 883259929.

[18] C. A. Balanis, *Advanced Engineering Electromagnetics*, 2nd ed. Hoboken, N.J: John Wiley & Sons, 2012, 08263.

[19] ——, *Antenna Theory: Analysis and Design*, 3rd ed. Hoboken, NJ: John Wiley, 2005, 26986.

[20] H. Lehpamer, *RFID Design Principles*, 2nd ed. Boston: Artech House, 2012.

[21] H. Guo, Z. Sun, and P. Wang, "Channel Modeling of MI Underwater Communication Using Tri-Directional Coil Antenna," in *2015 IEEE Global Communications Conference (GLOBECOM)*, Dec. 2015, pp. 1–6, 00023.

[22] Z. Sun, I. F. Akyildiz, S. Kisseleff, and W. Gerstacker, "Increasing the Capacity of Magnetic Induction Communications in RF-Challenged Environments," *IEEE Transactions on Communications*, vol. 61, no. 9, pp. 3943–3952, Sep. 2013, 00048.

[23] C. Uribe and W. Grote, "Radio Communication Model for Underwater WSN," in *2009 3rd International Conference on New Technologies, Mobility and Security*, Dec. 2009, pp. 1–5, 00039.

[24] R. Want, "RFID Explained: A Primer on Radio Frequency Identification Technologies," *Synthesis Lectures on Mobile and Pervasive Computing*, vol. 1, no. 1, pp. 1–94, Jan. 2006.

[25] K. V. S. Rao and P. V. Nikitin, "Theory and measurement of backscattering from RFID tags," *IEEE Antennas and Propagation Magazine*, vol. 48, no. 6, pp. 212–218, Dec. 2006, 00484.

[26] *VNA Master MS20xxC Technical Data Sheet*, Anritsu, Aug. 2019, version AE.

[27] *100 Series EMC Probes*, Beehive Electronics, 2005, rev. 2.2.

[28] *HDX RFID Reader System – Microreader RI-STU-MRD2*, Texas Instruments, Aug. 2012.

[29] *Pepper C1 User Manual*, Eccel Technology Ltd, Sep. 2019, rev. 1.4.

[30] G. D. Durgin, *ECE 3065 Notes*, TESSAL - Georgia Institute of Technology, Notes on Inductive RFID.

A Battery-Less NFC Sensor Transponder for Museum Artefact Monitoring

A Review of NFC Sensor Technology and a Proposed Solution

Dinesh R. Gawade[1], John Buckley[1], Nadeem Rather[1], Steffen Ziemann[2], Alex Zabeo[3], John Barton[1], Daniela Iacopino[1], Katharina Schuhmann[2], Manfred Anders[2], Micheal Burke[1], Aidan Quinn[1], Brendan O'Flynn[1]
[1]Tyndall National Institute, University College Cork, Cork, Ireland,
[2]ZFB Zentrum für Bucherhaltung GmbH, Bücherstraße 1, 04347 Leipzig, Germany,
[3]Ca 'Foscari University of Venice, Dorsoduro 3246, 30123, Venice, Italy
E-mail: [1]dinesh.gawade@tyndall.ie, [2]ziemann@zfb.com, [3]alex.zabeo@unive.it

Abstract— **This paper presents a novel, low-cost, battery-less Near-Field Communication (NFC) sensor transponder for museum artefact monitoring of Cultural Heritage objects. The proposed solution combines a unique combination of packaging materials and NFC technology to enable a low-cost preventive conservation solution that is practical to implement, something that is not possible at present. Cultural Heritage objects and artefacts are valuable objects housed by museums and are often stored in uncontrolled climatic conditions, which may lead to degradation of these objects. Preventive conservation is a new strategy that aims to avoid future degradation of these types of valuable objects. Recently, NFC sensor transponders have shown an increased use in food and pharmaceutical cold supply chains for monitoring, but these commercial solutions are expensive to implement and cannot be easily adapted for museum artefact monitoring. In this work, we present a battery-less, long shelf life, low-cost sensor transponder for monitoring the temperature and humidity conditions inside cardboard artefact storage boxes. In developing the proposed solution, the state of the art NFC sensor technology is first reviewed in detail, and a battery-less NFC sensor transponder is proposed with a cost of less than €5 in quantities of 10k. In addition to this, early-stage prototype results are also presented.**

Keywords- Artefacts; Battery-less; Cultural Heritage; Energy Harvesting; High-Frequency RFID; Internet of Things; Museum; NFC; Preventive conservation; Sensor Technology.

I. INTRODUCTION

Degradation of movable tangible Cultural Heritage (CH) objects can significantly increase by unfavorable and unstable climatic conditions, environmental pollutants, pollutants emitted from artefacts and their packaging materials. An effective and affordable Preventive Conservation (PC) strategy is highly necessary to minimize the ageing and degradation of such artefacts. In small and medium-sized museums, only a very small percentage of all museum objects are on display; the vast majority are in storage. The stored artefacts are often exposed to daily and seasonal temperature and humidity fluctuation. Currently used Passive Sampling Devices (PSDs) and monitoring systems are expensive and cumbersome to calibrate and also fail to deliver the correct sensing in a timely manner [1]. One critical disadvantage of monitoring the storage conditions by PSDs is the necessity of opening the box for analysis.

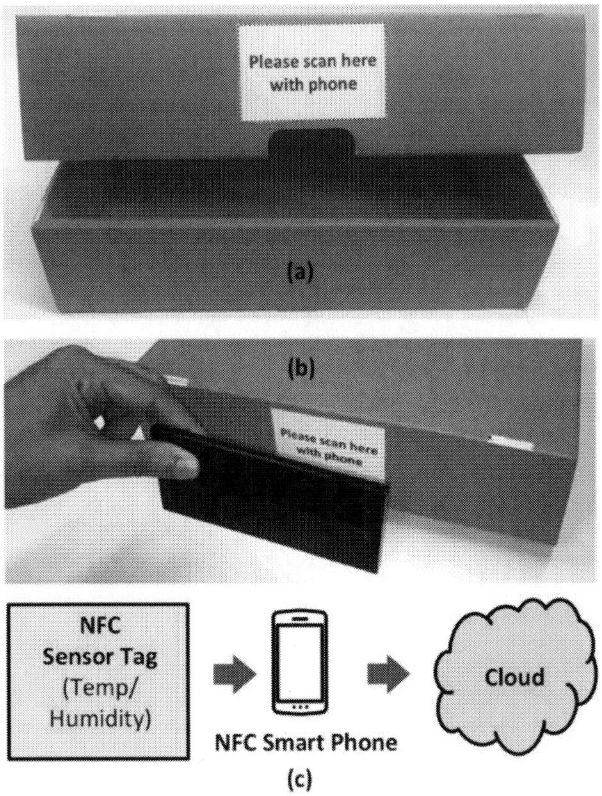

Figure 1. Depiction of proposed NFC temperature/humidity sensor solution. (a) Cardboard artefact storage box with proposed NFC sensor attached, (b) NFC sensor scan using a Smartphone, (c) Depiction of NFC sensor-to-cloud data flow.

This can lead to a loss of the desired microclimate, and reading the sampled results would be time-consuming. The values obtained by PSDs further do not represent the current Volatile Organic Compounds (VOC) concentrations inside the box but show an accumulation during the measurement time, which can not be related to a current concentration at a specific moment. For making rapid decisions, such as whether an absorbent must be replaced or if any further adjustment is required, these values have to be as reliable as possible.

The APACHE (Active & intelligent Packaging materials and display cases as a tool for preventive conservation of

Cultural Heritage) project is a Horizon 2020 project focused on the reduction of costs for maintaining and controlling constant climate conditions for CH artefacts. This project also focuses on 'long-term storage' as a tool of preventive conservation for a wide range of tangible CH artefacts [2]. The proposed solution is shown in Figure 1. The cardboard box contains the cultural artefact, along with a smart NFC temperature and humidity sensing label as shown in Figure 1(a). The transponder will be read using an NFC Type 5 (NFC-V) enabled smartphone and the data will be uploaded to the cloud for storage and analysis, as shown in Figure 1(b) and 1(c).

A key motivation for this work stems from the fact that the diversity of the objects themselves, as well as their degradation mechanisms, are quite large and mainly influenced by Temperature (T) and Relative Humidity (RH). For these reasons, specific strategies for their preventive conservation during storage in appropriate containers have to be established. Each material, like cellulose-based paper or wood objects, photographs, leather, or contemporary art out of plastics, require a different specific climate for optimized long-term storage conditions [3]. In collections with different materials, all these specific requirements cannot be met, even if air conditioning and climate control are available for the room. However, as the latter is not affordable by the majority of small and medium-sized museums, the APACHE project aims to create specific optimized climate conditions in each storage item. This strategy allows collectors to build up a climate control system for their collection step by step in accordance with their financial resources.

Furthermore, within this project, the developed storage boxes and containers shall enhance the buffering of temperature and humidity fluctuations and therefore reduce their accelerating effect on the material degradation process. Already small temperature fluctuations can cause significant changes in relative humidity conditions, which, in turn, can cause mechanical stress in art objects by elongation and shrinkage processes. For example, if an art object is packed under standard climate conditions (23°C, 50% RH) and the temperature decreases by about 10 degrees during transport or day/night change, which is not unusual, the relative humidity in an airtight enclosure would increase to 90% [4] [5]. At colder temperatures, condensation on the artefact surface could lead to mould growth, and hence, catastrophic damage. Moreover, air pollutants and VOCs like plasticizers or organic acids lead to further destruction, especially of cellulose-based materials [6][7]. As a consequence, a remarkable effort is made in the development and application of novel temperature regulating, humidity, and pollutants absorbing materials to exclude damaging impacts as far as possible [8]. For the definition of thresholds, which allow expressing if humidity or VOC concentrations are in a critical range, materials modeling simulations, and the development of damage functions as a decision-making tool are included. In the end, a possible acquirement of sensed temperature and RH data will ensure the preservation of microclimates found in archive boxes. In this method, the archive boxes can remain closed permanently.

Wireless Sensor Technologies (WST) such as Near-field communication (NFC) technology are essential to monitor the inside microclimatic conditions of a closed archive box. NFC is a short-range wireless communication technology that has evolved from existing contactless identification technologies [9]. Additional NFC standards ensure the interoperability of NFC-enabled devices and enable communication between them. The NFC standard defines the data rate (26.48 to 424 kbit/s), data frame formats such as NFC Data Exchange Format (NDEF), modulation, initialization, and collision control during initialization [10]. NFC uses magnetic coupling between two loop antennas located within each other's proximity or vicinity. It follows the ISO/IEC 18092 communication mode and ISO/IEC 18000-3 mode 1 protocol and operates at 13.56 MHz Industrial, Scientific, and Medical (ISM) band [11][12]. NFC has shown increased growth in the past few years due to the incorporation of NFC readers into smartphones and increasing significance of the Internet of Things (IoT). NFC technology not only enables consumers to perform payments, access stored data, and connect electronic devices, but also helps to sense various parameters. The decisive advantage of NFC against PSDs is that the data can be remotely read and analyzed without direct physical contact or the need to open the storage box. The resources and costs required to use, maintain, and read the sensors are thus significantly reduced compared to traditional monitoring systems. STMicroelectronics have recently introduced NFC sensor integrated circuits that are suitable for this application [11]. With this interdisciplinary approach, APACHE will lead to an active and intelligent solution for storage and archive boxes, where NFC sensing acts as an intelligent tool to replace currently used PSDs. An NFC sensor transponder represents a fast, convenient, sustainable, and precise alternative to check actual concentrations, temperatures, and humidity in archive boxes. An atomized sensing would give further information about the inside conditions during e.g. heating periods or an institution's closure times, which can be very useful for management decisions.

In this paper, the technical requirements of this application are first defined in Section II. A detailed review of the literature is described in Section III to survey the existence of prior work (both academic and commercial works) in the area of NFC sensor technology. Section IV describes the proposed solution architecture where a low-cost, battery-less NFC temperature and humidity sensor transponder is outlined for a museum artefact monitoring application. Early prototype results are described in Section V.

II. TECHNICAL REQUIREMENTS

Early detection of temperature and humidity fluctuations is of crucial importance to successful PC in museums. The technical requirements of every component related to this are described in the following subsections.

A. Storage Box

Corrugated board material represents an environmentally friendly, recyclable, and inexpensive material, which exhibits tremendous stability, needed for stackable boxes and the storage of heavier artefacts. Corrugated board in aging resistant archive quality (following DIN ISO 16245) furthermore provides the opportunity to enable an alkaline reserve, which acts primarily as an absorbent for acidic emissions, arisen from paper degradation [13]. The production of archive boxes out of corrugated board allows the design of individually sized boxes, which provides the significant advantages of a space-saving storage solution combined with the best possible protection of the objects by a reduced volume of "packed air." To detect microclimate fluctuations, the sensor transponder needs to be located at the inner surface of the box, such as in the fore-edge area of a storage box: The surface of potentially degrading material should be maximal at this point, which gives the most representative critical Temperature and Relative Humidity values.

B. NFC Radio and sensor

The implementation of sensors transponder into storage boxes requires the development of low cost, (typically less than €5 per piece), and high durability and stability of typically greater than 5 years. The sensor transponder should be able to sense and transmit the surrounding temperature and humidity of packed artefacts with metadata such as storage boxes unique ID, artefacts type and location using NFC technology. Thus, to transmit this small payload rapidly, a low bit rate is expected, typically less than 25kbit/s. As this application does not encounter a sudden fluctuation in temperature and humidity, no data logging is required. The sensor transponder must be battery-less and capable of harvesting up to 10mW power from a reader (NFC Enabled smartphone) magnetic field.

Furthermore, harvested power will be utilized to power up the sensor and microcontroller. The sensor transponder should be able to communicate, without any collision with adjacent sensor transponders. The NFC radio should have at least 4 Kbit memory and should support dual access (RF and I^2C). A communication distance of typically 4 cm is also required. The size of the sensor transponder must comply with ISO/IEC 7810, ID-1 card size standard (85.60 mm×53.90 mm). It should be assembled on a flexible PCB substrate and must be flat with a self-adhesive layer, hence, making it easy to be attached inside and on the front of storage boxes. The NFC sensor transponder must be compliant to NFC-V specification and should also comply with the ISO/IEC 15693 air interface. Therefore, it operates in the vicinity of the reader and provides the desired data rate, communication distance, and interoperability with NFC-V enabled smartphone. Transponders based on the ISO/IEC 14443 air interface have a shorter read range (typically, 3 cm) and thus unsuitable for this application.

The implementation of sensor transponders into storage boxes requires low cost, high durability, long shelf-life, and high sensitive temperature and humidity sensors. The readable temperature range should be -10°C to 60°C with a sensitivity of 0.5°C. The readable humidity range should be 0 to 100% RH with a sensitivity of 0.5 %.

C. Smartphone Application

In order to allow small to medium collections with low available resources and still have a chance to monitor the status of their artefacts, a widely available cheap solution resides in the use of NFC readers embedded in everyday smartphones. Raw data received from sensors should be managed by a specific smartphone app compatible with different smartphone brands and operative systems. Data should initially be stored in the smartphone's internal memory and displayed to the user for an immediate consultation. This allows performing of readings in conditions where reduced or absent external connections are available in the artefacts storing facility. Once the smartphone comes back to sufficient connectivity conditions, the internally stored data is automatically sent to the cloud server for storage and further processing. The smartphone app should be able to tag each reading properly with the timestamp and distinctive details about the analyzed artefact. The app should also be able to receive information from the cloud about status and previous readings related to artefacts to allow a fast check from the operator.

D. Cloud Processing

The remote server, receiving data gathered through the smartphone app, might be located inside an intranet (local cloud) or on the Internet (cloud). In both cases, the same infrastructure is needed, which should be composed of a web server, an application server, and database storage. The web server waits for incoming data through a specially designed API software interface. The smartphone app establishes a secure connection with the server through the API and then utilizes the channel to funnel the gathered raw data to the server. On reception, the webserver passes information to the application server, which immediately stores the raw data in the database and successively processes it to generate all requested information for decision support. Finally, the processed information is correctly displayed to users through dynamic charts and tables, while alarm messages are broadcasted as soon as danger thresholds are reached for any of the assessed artefacts.

III. Technology Review

A thorough review of the literature is described in the following subsections to survey the existence of academic and commercial prior work in the area of NFC and Radio Frequency Identification (RFID) sensor technology.

A. Literature Review of NFC sensor Technology

In 2013, an early review of NFC technology, related academic studies, white papers, and innovative issues was reported in [14]. In [15], a detailed survey on NFC sensor transponders for IoT, cold supply chain and wearable applications is presented. This paper also presents a brief summary of NFC sensor integrated circuits and their main specifications. Later in [16], a review of recent progress in NFC sensor technology has been reported. In this paper, NFC sensor transponder antenna design, manufacturing techniques and development of new material along with their application in wearable devices and food safety has been discussed. Likewise in [17], RFID sensing techniques, innovative application, fabrication techniques, commercial solutions and technical challenges have been reported.

In [18], an NFC sensor transponder design and a six-month pilot result for long term preventive care of fine art objects have been reported. The developed transponder evaluates inside and outside temperature and humidity buffering performance of microclimatic enclosure constructed to protect a late 16th Century panel painting. It is based on the ISO/IEC 15693 standard and compliant NFC forum NFC-V specification. This study explicitly explains the critical role of object-specific sensor transponders in improving long term preventive care of fine art objects. In [19], the authors presented the design and implementation of RFID and sensor web-based cultural relics management system. In this, RFID has been used for cultural relic identification and life cycle management during storage and circulation. Video and sensing parameters such as temperature, humidity, vibration, and displacement are transmitted using both wired and wireless communications. For preventing theft, a camera is deployed in collaboration with RFID and a vibration sensor. This system has been installed in a museum in Yongding District, Fujian Province, China. Furthermore, in [20], an RFID based museum environmental monitoring system is reported. Here, a flexible RFID platform is presented, which enables operation specific direct plugging of sensors into monitoring station. The pilot trials of this system under various environmental conditions has taken place in the Hong Kong film archive and Hong Kong Museum of history and was finally installed in the Hong Kong Science museum in 2015.

Several papers report the design and performance of NFC/RFID sensor transponders, specifically for cold supply chain (food, pharmaceutical, beverage etc.) and environmental parameters monitoring. In [21], a flexible RFID sensor transponder for temperature monitoring is reported. The proposed transponder is based on the ISO/IEC 15693 standard and is compliant to NFC-V specification. The transponder prototype was realized by hybrid technology combining a printed antenna, surface mount RFID integrated circuit and flexible battery assembled with the help of Ag-based conductive epoxy adhesive. The size (85.60 mm×53.90 mm) of the designed transponder complies with ISO/IEC 7810, ID-1 card size standard. Smartphone and Web applications have similarly been developed for reading sensor data. Escopedo et al, [22] present a flexible NFC sensor transponder for Oxygen, Carbon Dioxide, Ammonia, and Relative Humidity monitoring. It is based on the ISO/IEC 15693 standard and compliant NFC forum NFC-V specification and includes a smartphone application. Likewise, in [23], an RFID based critical temperature indicator for the food supply chain has been reported. In [24], a low cost, passive NFC sensor transponder for pH monitoring based on a colorimetric sensor and smartphone application has been developed. In [25], Eldebiky et al, implemented an environmental monitoring system with the help of Hybrid System-in-Foil (HySiF) components, such as microcontroller, on-chip temperature, on-foil humidity sensors and NFC radio. In [26], an RFID patch for food spoiling monitoring with the help of a temperature sensor has been reported.

Recently, battery-less NFC sensor transponders and their various applications have been reported in the literature. In [27][28], battery-less sensor transponders for volumetric water content (soil moisture), temperature and relative humidity monitoring has been presented. Also, this work has shown that the magnetic field generated by NFC enabled smartphones is enough to supply energy for the transponder. Further, in [29], a battery-less chronic wound monitoring system has been presented. In order to monitor the chronic wound, the proposed solution acquires temperature and pH information of the wound, and consumes 5 mW of power. In [30], a battery-less NFC transponder for classifying fruit ripeness grade based on color measurement has been presented. Likewise, in [31], a battery-less diaper has been reported where diaper moisture is detected by capacitance variation.

B. Commercial solutions based on 13.56 MHZ NFC/ HF RFID

Table I shows NFC and High-Frequency (HF) RFID-based commercial sensor transponders. Various organizations have developed and marketed such a solution, particularly for cold supply chain or temperature-sensitive product monitoring. Gosense Wireless Ltd, UK developed and demonstrated TH-Stat ID for fine art preventive care [18][32]. Reviewed commercial solutions have a limited shelf life of a maximum of 3 years [33][34] and only a few of them are battery-less [32][35]. However, all these solutions are quite costly and, therefore, cannot be easily adapted for low cost museum artefacts monitoring.

TABLE I. NFC / HF RFID BASED SOLUTION

Manufacturer	Cost €	Life (Years)	Passive	Sensor	Ref.
Monarch Instrument, USA	71	3	No	T, RH	[33]
Microsensys, Germany	48	3	No	T, RH	[35]
	24	NA	Yes	RH	[34]
GoSense, UK	23	NA	Yes	T, RH	[32]
UID, USA	18	1	No	T	[36]
Intellilog, Germany	17	1	No	T	[37]
Avery Dennison, USA	15	1	No	T	[38]
Identiv, USA	8	1	No	T	[39]
This work	**5**	**5**	**Yes**	**T, RH**	**[2]**

TABLE II. UHF RFID BASED SOLUTION

Manufacturer	Cost €	Life (Years)	Passive	Sensor	Ref.
Powercast, USA	73	NA	Yes	T, RH	[40]
	73	NA	No	T, RH	[41]
Datalogic, USA	22	5	No	T	[42]
Farsens, Spain	17	1	No	T	[43]

C. Commercial solutions based on 860-960MHZ UHF RFID

Table II shows the Ultra High-Frequency (UHF) RFID based commercial sensor transponders, developed mainly for cold supply chain monitoring. The UHF RFID transponders can provide read range less than 10m [41] [40], but the cost of the UHF reader is too high [44]. Thus, UHF RFID is not suitable for low-cost museum artefacts monitoring.

IV. PROPOSED SYSTEM-LEVEL SOLUTION

The proposed system-level architecture of NFC temperature and humidity sensor transponder is described in the following subsections.

A. Near field Communication and Hardware

The proposed solution block diagram and system architecture are shown in Figure 2. The NFC radio Analog Front End (AFE) consists of an RF interface and the energy harvesting circuitry, which will connect to the loop antenna. The energy harvester will harvest energy from the magnetic field (H-field) of an NFC-V enabled smartphone with the help of an internal rectifier and capacitor. The harvested voltage will further be regulated using a low dropout regulator and will be used to power up an ultra-low-power Microcontroller Unit (MCU), as well as a temperature and humidity sensor. The NFC radio ASK demodulator will demodulate the messages from the reader and responds to the reader with the help of load modulation. The load modulation is achieved by varying the impedance of the loop antenna [45]. When the magnetic field strength from the reader is sufficient, the harvested energy will be available to power up the MCU, NFC radio, temperature, and humidity sensor. The NFC radio, temperature and humidity sensor will be interfaced with MCU using the Inter-Integrated Circuit (I^2C) Protocol. Having powered up, the NFC radio sends RF events signal to the MCU. The sensor will start sensing temperature and humidity and its raw value will transmit to the MCU through the I^2C. The MCU will determine temperature, relative humidity and generate an NDEF message. The generated message will contain payload such as sensed data, artefacts type, box UID and their location. The MCU will write the NDEF message in the user memory area of the NFC radio [46] [11], and the NFC-V Smartphone will read this memory with the help of a dedicated read message command. In this way, the smartphone will read the data from the NFC sensor transponder at a 26kbit/s bit rate. The hardware will be implanted on a flexible PCB substrate, such as polyimide (130μm thickness) with a self-adhesive layer. The size of proposed sensor transponder will be 85.60 mm×53.90 mm. The system architecture of the proposed transponder is shown in Figure 2b. After analysing technical information and several experiments with different NFC sensor evaluation boards, the ST25DV04K NFC radio from STMicroelectronics was chosen [11]. This radio is capable of harvesting up to 10mW power from NFC-V enabled smartphone magnetic fields.

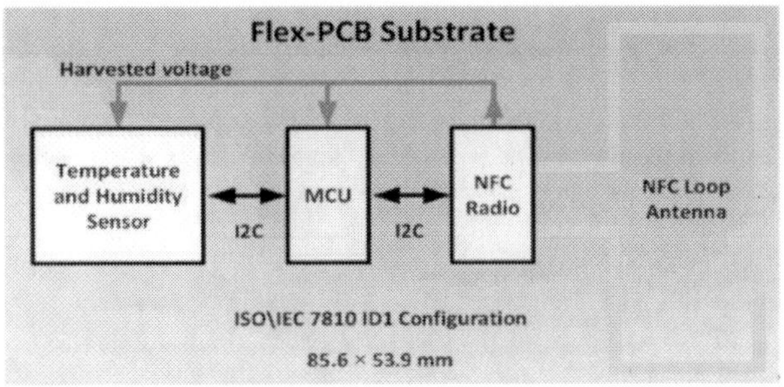

(a)

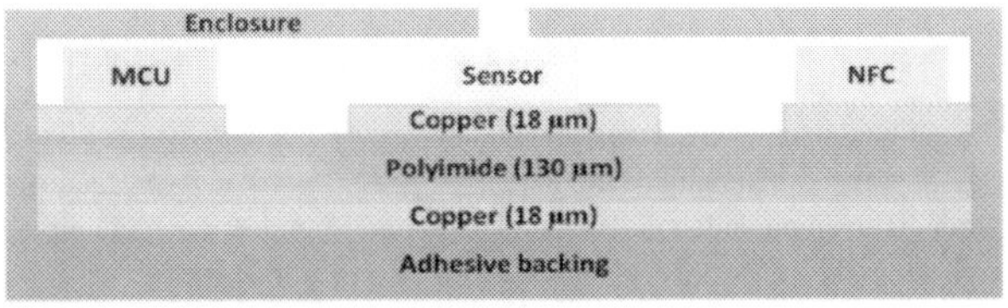

(b)

Figure 2. (a) Block diagram, (b) System architecture of the proposed NFC temperature/humidity sensor.

The unit cost of ST25DV04K is €0.43 and aggregated cost of other selected tag electronics such as MCU (€1.05), voltage regulator (€0.26) and passive components (€1) are €2.31 per device for 10k quantity. Also, the 2-layer flexible PCB manufacturing and components assembly cost will be less than €0.90 per device for the same quantity.

B. Smartphone Application

The smartphone application will rely on specific libraries for NFC data gathering as well as for storage and communication of retrieved information for both the Android and iOS smartphone operative systems. Data will check for consistency to avoid false or incomplete readings; right after this check, a timestamp will be attached to the retrieved data. Information about the ID of the artefact and all specific readings will come from the NFC sensor transponder. The smartphone application starts up automatically when approaching a suitable NFC sensor transponder, and autonomously performs the first reading and displays the raw contents of the reading. The app user can decide through a setting whether to automatically upload each reading instead of having to send out the currently displayed reading manually. Once the app is activated, the user will decide to perform (and upload) several successive readings by clicking the corresponding user interface button.

C. Cloud Processing

Data uploaded by the smartphone app to the cloud Linux web server will immediately be stored in a relational MySQL database, which will regularly be backed up. The connection and data transfer occurs thanks to a specific RESTful web API implementing all required rules for a proper service endpoint [47]. The gathered information is elaborated by the server immediately after being stored, and results obtained by the application of the mathematical models embedded in the application server will also store and back up in the same database as the readings. User interface dashboard, dynamic charts and tables will also update live with the new upcoming readings, and a routine, which checks whether the alert thresholds are met is run and automatically sends alert signals (emails, phone notifications, etc.) to the registered users. The server role will be completely transparent to the source of information as the smartphone app hides the lack of direct connection with the NFC sensors. Thanks to timestamps related to each reading coming from sensors with different sampling frequencies, the application server will be able to integrate heterogeneous information in a single coherent interface and decision support framework.

V. Early Stage Result And Discussion

The early evaluation kit based working prototype shown in Figure 3. This working prototype is a proof of concept, and experimental results show that the harvested power from NFC-V enabled the smartphone's magnetic field is enough to run the transponder without a battery. A graph of power consumption for the device is shown in Figure 4. In order to measure temperature and relative humidity, the prototype transponder requires a peak power of 2.37 mW.

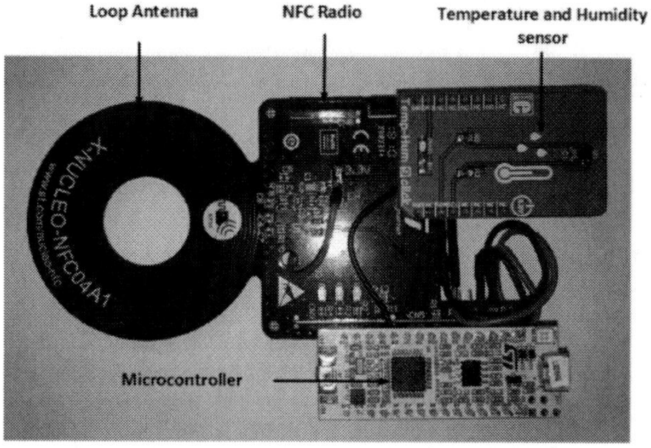

Figure 3. Early NFC sensor transponder prototype (Evaluation kit based)

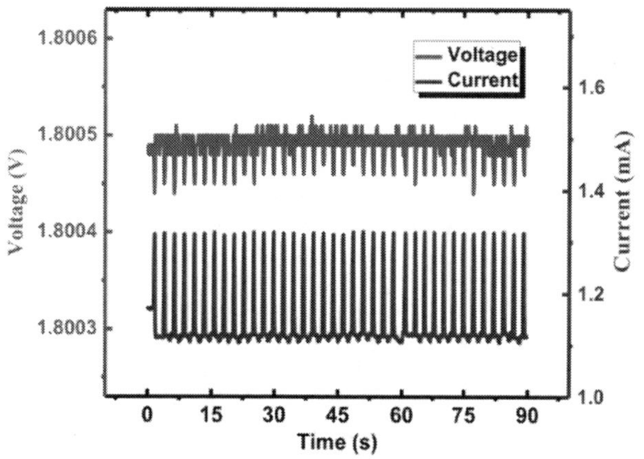

Figure 4. Prototype NFC sensor transponder power consumption graph

Also, the experimental communication distance obtained for the prototype transponder is up to 28 mm with a Vodafone X9 smartphone and up to 37 mm with the iPhone XR. The battery-less NFC sensor transponder signifies a sustainable and specific alternative to measure actual concentrations, microclimatic parameters inside closed artefacts storage boxes. These solutions could be beneficial, especially for small and middle-size museums, which cannot afford air conditioning systems and those in countries that have very humid climates. To exclude mould growth on paper, for example, the maintaining of adjusted relative humidity values is crucial and can be monitored in this way. Also, the deterioration of plastic composed artefacts emitted VOC's during this process could lead to health detriment if accumulated and even affect surrounding paper-based objects which are prevented if those VOC's are chemically immobilized at the source.

VI. Conclusions And Future Work

This paper has presented the architecture and early prototype (Evaluation kit based) result of a novel battery-less, low-cost, and long shelf-life NFC sensor transponder for museum artefact monitoring. The proposed transponder total cost is less than €5 per device for 10k quantities. The prototype transponder consumes 2.37 mW peak power to read temperature and relative humidity along with metadata. The experimental read range obtained for the prototype transponder is up to 28 mm with a Vodafone X9 smartphone and up to 37 mm with the iPhone XR. In order to improve communication range, future work will focus on the development of low power embedded hardware, loop antenna and optimization of the firmware. In the next phase, a smartphone application and cloud platform will be developed, and system-level testing and calibration will be performed. A new low-cost temperature and humidity sensor will be developed using Laser Induced Graphene (LIG) electrodes to overcome conventional sensor limitations such as accuracy, size, power consumption, shelf-life and cost. In another development, chemical modification of the above electrodes will be performed targeting the electrochemical detection of VOCs. New artefacts storage boxes using RF friendly material will also be developed during the project. The first hardware prototype will be available in Q1 2020.

Acknowledgement

We would like to acknowledge funding support from the European Union's Horizon 2020 research and innovation program for APACHE project under the grant agreement number 814496. We also acknowledge support from Science Foundation Ireland under grant 13/RC/2077 (CONNECT) as well as the support of Andrew Wallace and the team from National Instruments for their continued support with the AWR toolset.

References

[1] C. M. Grzywacz, Monitoring for gaseous pollutants in museum environments. Getty Publications, 2006.

[2] APACHE, "APACHE Project Objective " 2019, Available: http://www.apacheproject.eu/objectives/, Accessed on: 2019.09.15.

[3] A. Schieweck and T. Salthammer, "Pollutants in museums, libraries and archives, Room air – building materials – exhibits," Aufl. Wolfram Schmidt, Braunschweig, 2014.

[4] T. Padfield, "Fundamental microclimate concepts," 2009, Available: https://www.conservationphysics.org/intro/fundamentals.html, Accessed on: 2019.09.20.

[5] M. K. Kumaran, Air and Moisture Transfer Through New and Retrofitted Insulated Envelope Parts. International Energy Agency IEA Annex 24, 1996.

[6] A.-L. Dupont and J. Tétreault, "Cellulose degradation in an acetic acid environment," Studies in conservation, vol. 45, no. 3, pp. 201-210, 2000.

[7] K. Curran et al., "Cross-infection effect of polymers of historic and heritage significance on the degradation of a cellulose reference test material," Polymer degradation and stability, vol. 107, pp. 294-306, 2014.

[8] K. Ziani, I. Fernández-Pan, M. Royo, and J. I. Maté, "Antifungal activity of films and solutions based on chitosan against typical seed fungi," Food Hydrocolloids, vol. 23, no. 8, pp. 2309-2314, 2009.

[9] R. Minihold, "Near field communication (nfc) technology and measurements," White Paper, vol. 6, 2011.

[10] ECMA-340 Near Field Communication - Interface and Protocol (NFCIP-1), 2013.

[11] STMicroelectronics, "ST25DV04K- Datasheet," 2018, Available: https://www.st.com/resource/en/datasheet/st25dv04k.pdf, Accessed on: 2019.09.15.

[12] NFC_Forum, "New NFC Forum Technical Specifications Broaden Tag Support and Enhance Interoperability," in New and Candidate Specifications Bring Additional Flexibility and Range of Communications to NFC Interactions, ed, 2015.

[13] M. A. Hubbe et al., "Deacidification of acidic books and paper by means of non-aqueous dispersions of alkaline particles: A review focusing on completeness of the reaction," BioResources, vol. 12, no. 2, pp. 4410-4477, 2017.

[14] V. Coskun, B. Ozdenizci, and K. Ok, "A survey on near field communication (NFC) technology," Wireless personal communications, vol. 71, no. 3, pp. 2259-2294, 2013.

[15] A. Lazaro, R. Villarino, and D. Girbau, "A survey of NFC sensors based on energy harvesting for IoT applications," Sensors, vol. 18, no. 11, p. 3746, 2018.

[16] Z. Cao et al., "Near-Field Communication Sensors," Sensors, vol. 19, no. 18, p. 3947, 2019.

[17] L. Cui, Z. Zhang, N. Gao, Z. Meng, and Z. Li, "Radio Frequency Identification and Sensing Techniques and Their Applications—A Review of the State-of-the-Art," Sensors, vol. 19, no. 18, p. 4012, 2019.

[18] M. D. Steinberg, C. S. Kimbriel, and L. S. d'Hont, "Autonomous near-field communication (NFC) sensors for long-term preventive care of fine art objects," Sensors and Actuators A: Physical, vol. 285, pp. 456-467, 2019.

[19] C. Xiao, N. Chen, D. Li, Y. Lv, and J. Gong, "SCRMS: An RFID and sensor web-enabled smart cultural relics management system," Sensors, vol. 17, no. 1, p. 60, 2017.

[20] J. Tse, "Development of a new environmental monitoring system for museums and galleries using RFID-enabled technology," Studies in Conservation, vol. 61, no. sup2, pp. 334-336, 2016.

[21] K. Sima et al., "Flexible smart tag for cold chain temperature monitoring," in 2017 40th International Spring Seminar on Electronics Technology (ISSE), 2017, pp. 1-5.

[22] P. Escobedo et al., "Flexible passive near field communication tag for multigas sensing," Analytical chemistry, vol. 89, no. 3, pp. 1697-1703, 2017.

[23] G. S. Lorite et al., "Novel, smart and RFID assisted critical temperature indicator for supply chain monitoring," Journal of Food Engineering, vol. 193, pp. 20-28, 2017.

[24] M. Boada, A. Lazaro, R. Villarino, and D. Girbau, "Battery-less NFC sensor for PH monitoring," IEEE Access, 2019.

[25] A. Eldebiky, M. Elsobky, H. Richter, and J. N. Burghartz, "Humidity and temperature sensor system demonstrator with NFC tag for HySiF applications," Advances in Radio Science, vol. 16, no. D., pp. 109-116, 2018.

[26] M. Yuan, R. Ghannam, P. Karadimas, and H. Heidari, "Flexible RFID Patch for Food Spoilage Monitoring," in 2018 IEEE Asia Pacific Conference on Postgraduate Research in Microelectronics and Electronics (PrimeAsia), 2018, pp. 68-71.

[27] M. Boada, A. Lazaro, R. Villarino, and D. Girbau, "Battery-less soil moisture measurement system based on a NFC device with energy harvesting capability," IEEE Sensors Journal, vol. 18, no. 13, pp. 5541-5549, 2018.

[28] M. Boada, A. Lazaro, R. Villarino, E. Gil, and D. Girbau, "Near-field soil moisture sensor with energy harvesting capability," in 2018 48th European Microwave Conference (EuMC), 2018, pp. 235-238.

[29] H.-W. Cho, J. H. Yoon, S.-S. Yoo, B. G. Choi, and H.-J. Yoo, "A Batteryless Chronic Wound Monitoring System with NFC," in 2019 IEEE Eurasia Conference on Biomedical Engineering, Healthcare and Sustainability (ECBIOS), 2019, pp. 31-34.

[30] A. Lazaro, M. Boada, R. Villarino, and D. Girbau, "Color Measurement and Analysis of Fruit with a Battery-Less NFC Sensor," Sensors, vol. 19, no. 7, p. 1741, 2019.

[31] A. Lazaro, M. Boada, R. Villarino, and D. Girbau, "Battery-less Smart Diaper based on NFC Technology," IEEE Sensors Journal, 2019.

[32] Gosense, "Gosense wireless ltd Product Index- NFC and RFID Mobile Sensors ", Available: http://www.gosense-wireless.com/GoSense%20TH-StatID%20DS%20Rev1.pdf, Accessed on: 2019.09.17.

[33] Monarch_Instrument, "Track-It RFID Temp or Temp/Humidity Data Logger," Available: https://monarchinstrument.com/products/track-it-rfid-temp-temp-humidity-data-logger?variant=30756070984, Accessed on: 2019.09.18.

[34] Microsensys, "product datasheet- TELID 232.nfc ", Available: https://www.microsensys.de/fileadmin/user_upload/pdf-dateien/datasheets/TELID232nfc-01.pdf, Accessed on: 2019.09.15.

[35] Microsensys, "TELID 332-th product datasheet," Available: https://www.microsensys.de/fileadmin/user_upload/pdf-dateien/ds_sensor-transpond/TELID332-05.pdf, Accessed on: 2019.09.15.

[36] Unified_Information_Devices, "Tempevent Temperature Data Logger," Available: https://www.uidevices.com/product/tempevent-temperature-data-logger/, Accessed on: September 2019.

[37] Intellilog, "End-to-End Cold Chain Monitoring," Available: https://intellilog.io/, Accessed on: 2019.09.18.

[38] Avery_Dennison, "TT Sensor Plus Product Datasheet ", Available:

https://label.averydennison.com/content/dam/averydennison/lpm-responsive/europe/english/documents/data-sheet/product/intelligent-labels/time-and-temp-tracking/ds-eu-tt-sensor-plus-en.pdf, Accessed on: 2019.09.15.

[39] Identiv, "uTrust Sense Temperature Tracker," Available: https://www.identiv.com/products/rfid-nfc-inlays/sensors/, Accessed on: 2019.09.17.

[40] Powercast, "PCT200 Powercast High-Function RFID Sensor Datalogger- Datasheet ", Available: http://www.powercastco.com/wp-content/uploads/2017/06/PCT200-Datasheet-Rev-1.pdf, Accessed on: 2019.09.20.

[41] Powercast, "PCT100 Powercast High-Function RFID Sensor Tag," Available: https://www.powercastco.com/wp-content/uploads/2019/02/PCT100-Datasheet-Rev-4.pdf, Accessed on: 2019.09.20.

[42] Datalogic, "DLR-TL001", Available: https://www.datalogic.com/eng/transportation-logistics/rfid-systems/dlr-tl001-pd-706.html, Accessed on: 2019.09.16.

[43] Farsens, "Logos-T battery assisted passive temperature sensor," Available: http://www.farsens.com/en/products/logos-t/, Accessed on: 2019.09.16.

[44] Zebra-logiscenter, "Zebra RFD8500 RFID READERS," Available: https://www.logiscenter.ie/rfd8500-5000100-eu-zebra-rfd8500-rfid-readers, Accessed on: 2019.09.19.

[45] K. Finkenzeller, RFID handbook: fundamentals and applications in contactless smart cards, radio frequency identification and near-field communication. John Wiley & Sons, 2010.

[46] STMicroelectronics, "TN1216 Technical note ST25 NFC guide," 2016, Available: https://www.stmicroelectronics.com.cn/content/ccc/resource/technical/document/technical_note/f9/a8/5a/0f/61/bf/42/29/DM00190233.pdf/files/DM00190233.pdf/jcr:content/translations/en.DM00190233.pdf, Accessed on: 2019.09.15.

[47] E. W. Cesare Pautasso, "RESTful Web Services: Principles, Patterns, Emerging Technologies," WWW '10 Proceedings of the 19th international conference on World wide web Raleigh, North Carolina, USA pp. 1359-1360 April 26 - 30, 2010.

An OPC UA PubSub MQTT Configuration Tool

Zepeng Liu

LTCI, Télécom Paris
Institut Polytechnique de Paris, France
Email: zepeng.liu@telecom-paris.fr

Patrick Bellot

LTCI, Télécom Paris
Institut Polytechnique de Paris, France
Email: patrick.bellot@imt.fr

Abstract—**With the ongoing progression of incorporating massive emerging technologies into industrial systems, Information and Communication Technology (ICT) based systems face increasing difficulties of vertical and horizontal integration. One main objective of industrial system integration is to use flexible and scalable communication technology to fulfill requirements on the different levels of an automation pyramid. With the Client/Server model being the de facto standard in industrial automation at upper levels, Open Platform Communication Unified Architecture (OPC UA) is extended by adding a new communication architecture, called Publish Subscribe, to provide asynchronous information exchange capabilities. An OPC UA PubSub and Message Queuing Telemetry Transport (MQTT) based configuration tool is introduced in this paper. It can be easily added to any C/C++ OPC UA Server/Client implementation.**

Keywords–IoT; OPC UA; MQTT.

I. Introduction

Major advances in ICT have contributed to significant changes in the manufacturing domain, from the office to the field level. The massive ICT integrated industrial systems were deployed not only following the success of the Internet, which has broadly spread the idea of ubiquitous connectivity, but also because of increasing global competition [1].

In retrospective, the progress of the network of "things" in the manufacturing field has encountered different stages. From the beginning of the 1970s, Computer Integrated Manufacturing (CIM) was first introduced into manufacturing systems and designed for field-level engineering process management. This was followed by Product Data Management (PDM), networks within engineering departments that were responsible for product data and connection. Since the 1990s, the emerged Product Lifecycle Management (PLM) concept adopted services and interfaces provided by PDM to manage all product-related information, from product design, production, maintenance to retirement, essentially, the entire product life cycle. The Digital Factory concept was proposed at the turn of the century, and aims to simulate a real factory by integrating data, models, and the engineering process [2]. Enterprise Resource Planning (ERP) was derived from its Manufacturing Resource Planning (MRP) predecessor rather than tailored to particular market sectors. ERP aims at being a framework for integration of all business-related information including material and production management, human resource management, financial accounting, etc. Below the ERP, the Manufacturing Execution System (MES) accomplishes the short-term planning task and acts the role of bridge between strategic level and control level [3].

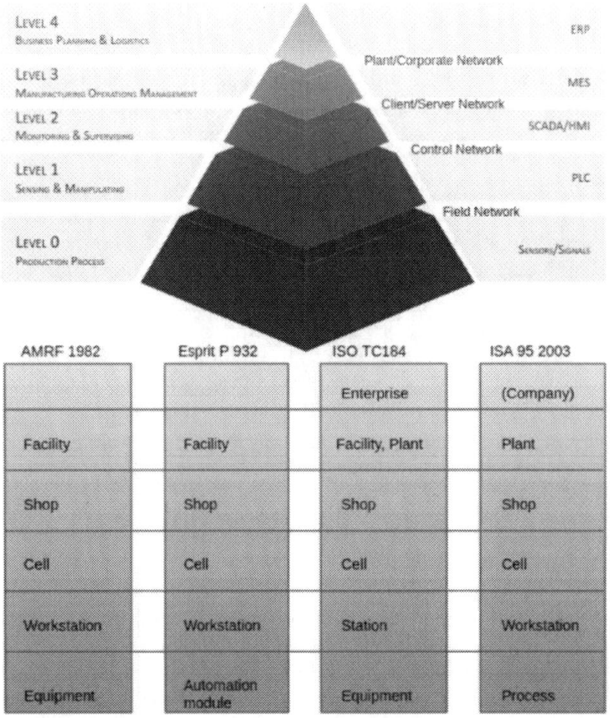

Figure 1. ISA 95 Automation Pyramid and development

Though it was difficult to convey the idea of ubiquitous connectivity during the fledgling IT and communication technologies of the 1980s, even data exchange on a broad scale within the factory was almost impossible to implement; CIM, PDM, and PLM were consequently unheard of at that time. Fortunately, the automation pyramid was established and is still evolving up to present day, as depicted in Figure 1. Eventually, the idea of product data as a basis for meaningful communication became a prerequisite for Industrial Internet of Things (IIoT) [4].

While PLM and the Digital Factory established a data backbone of IIoT, hardware for manufacturing, the evolution of mechatronics, and Cyber-Physical System (CPS) consider communication between subsystems and networked nodes as a necessary part of future mass customization manufacturing [5]. The systems described by multi-disciplined theories need to be integrated for manufacturing, which means various pieces of the system need to be implemented: networks, interfaces, databases, and various specific functions for manufacturing [4].

Overall, the trend of industrial automation is continuously evolving from local functionality to complex and systematic architecture. However, at least one area of industrial automation that deserves one's attention is how to use appropriate technologies to exchange and share information among various industrial components. For example, the Germany Industrie 4.0 [6] focuses on improving the vertical and horizontal integration of manufacturing system components. Solutions should be characterized by necessary technical, syntactic and semantic interoperability, and provide interaction-based information exchange and data communication capabilities. Among the solutions, OPC UA is one of the most up-to-date standards satisfying these requirements.

The main contribution of this paper is to present: 1) our implementation of the new extension of OPC UA, the OPC UA specification part 14 [7], and 2) an OPC UA PubSub MQTT configuration tool. The implementation includes necessary PubSub related entities, communication parameters and configuration steps. In order to facilitate the configuration of OPC UA Publisher and Subscriber, and reduce local configuration work, the OPC UA PubSub MQTT configuration tool is able to provide flexible configurations to OPC UA Publisher and Subscriber. Both the OPC UA PubSub component and the configuration tool are programmed in C and C++, so that the implementation could be easily integrated into other C/C++ projects.

This paper is organized as follows. Section II provides an overview of OPC UA and its latest specifications; part 14 OPC UA PubSub and MQTT will be introduced. Section III describes a configuration tool for parameters of MQTT and OPC UA PubSub. Finally, in Section IV, we conclude the paper and discuss future studies.

II. OPC UA AND MQTT

A. *OPC UA and OPC UA PubSub*

Classic Object Linking & Embedding for process control (OPC) is a series of specifications developed by an industrial automation task force in 1996 for providing real-time communication capabilities to the Component Object Model(COM) or the Distributed Component Object Model (DCOM) based industrial equipment. Its successor, OPC UA, was released in 2006 and integrated classic standards (e.g., OPC Data Access, OPC Historical Data Access, etc.) into a single standard. Nowadays, OPC UA is a widely recognized standard in industrial automation and is known for its interoperability, platform independence, securing communication, and scalability [8].

The latest specification of OPC UA Part 14 PubSub introduces PubSub logical components for Publisher and Subscriber, defines necessary communication parameters, and provides configuration procedures. In this section, we will present the OPC UA's interoperability, its communication capabilities, and the new added specification, PubSub.

1) Interoperability: Manufacturing companies face increasing global competition and market pressures which inversely drive them to adopt emerging and competitive technologies. However, manufacturing plants are often forced to invest a great deal of time on the installation, setup, and maintenance of such systems along with the difficulties of transferring existing automation systems to new ones and the adaptability to different suppliers' products. Therefore, more flexibility and adaptability within the automation system are required for future industrial automation.

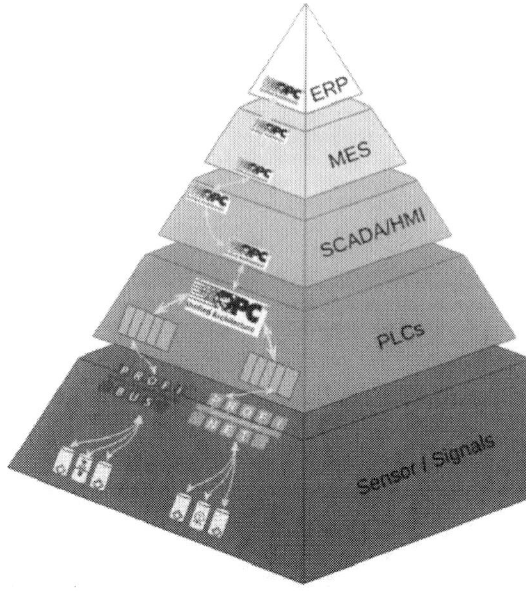

Figure 2. Automation Pyramid with OPC UA vertical and horizontal integration

Industrial automation systems based on Service-Oriented Architecture (SOA) emerged as a promising solution thanks to its advantages, such as integration capabilities and flexibility. Services provided by such components, machines, and systems are flexible and not tied to production tasks, but rather are a part of the service set, and invokable for other equipment [9].

Numerous technologies and specifications are created by following the SOA principle. For example, OPC UA, Devices Profile for Web Services (DPWS), EXI, CoAP, RESTful, Distributed Service Bus, Complex Event Processing (CEP), etc. European projects Service Infrastructure for Real-time Embedded Networked Applications (SIRENA) [10] and Service-Oriented Cross-layer infRAstructure for Distributed smart Embedded devices (SOCRADES) [11] have implemented SOA-based approaches by using DPWS as a framework and base technology. Moreover, the Industrie 4.0 initiative regards interoperability as an essential part of future industrial automation, which implies industrial equipment within a plant should be able to understand, share, and process information from the equipment of different manufacturers. The Industrie 4.0 initiative has also resulted in the Reference Architecture Model Industrie 4.0 (RAMI4.0), which is a three-dimensional architecture showing structurally Industrie 4.0 related approaches and participants. The RAMI4.0 is based on SOA and ensures the vertical and horizontal integration of industrial system components [12].

The OPC Foundation's vision is to provide a new standard to bridge the differences among industrial ICT. OPC UA fulfills SOA requirements of industrial automation and has already been successfully used in several projects, automation and control systems, such as Beck-hoff TwinCAT [13], Siemens SIMATIC [14], B&R Automation Studio [15], etc.

Communication interfaces provided by OPC UA make Industrie 4.0 compliant communications between the control

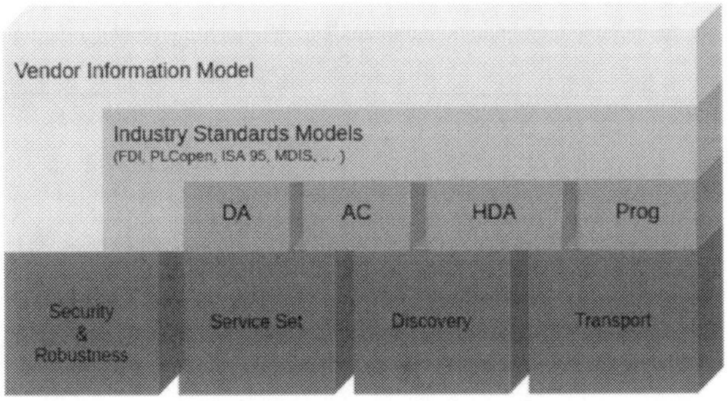

Figure 3. OPC Unified Architecture

level and MES, as well as MES and ERP possible [16] [17], as seen in Figure2. The OPC Foundation specified an object-oriented information model which can be used as a baseline to match the application's needs. The base information model is specified in OPC UA specification Part 5 (the Information Model) [18] by using instances and types defined in OPC UA specification Part 3 (the Address Space Model) [19]. OPC UA meta model uses instances and types provided by the base information model to describe other information models (e.g., Data Access, Historical Data Access, Alert and Conditions, specific industrial domain information models, etc.) and to build the OPC UA server address space. Together with OPC UA infrastructures, Service Sets, Transport, Discovery, Security and Robustness, OPC UA enables interoperability at the semantic level. The multi-layered architecture is shown in Figure 3.

Along with information model related specifications, OPC Foundation works with other organizations for providing the dedicated industrial-domain specifications, such as the OPC Unified Architecture for AutoID, the OPC Unified Architecture for MTConnect , the OPC Unified Architecture / PLCopen Information Model, etc.

For legacy COM/DCOM based OPC systems, OPC UA specification protects legacy OPC standards by using an OPC UA Wrapper software or OPC UA Proxy to enable the communication between COM/DCOM based OPC Client/Server and OPC UA based server/client [20].

2) Communication capability: Following the initial transition of industrial automation communication from dedicated automation networks (fieldbus systems) to Ethernet-based networks [21], and following industrial communication technologies with requirements, such as real-time, low-latency, etc., numerous standards and solutions have been proposed by researchers in recent decades. Industrie 4.0 poses new requirements for future manufacturing; smart factories use communication technologies to improve connectivity quality and efficiency at lower costs. These improvements can be guaranteed by two Industrie 4.0 objectives: cross-layer structural connectivity and semantic interoperability of components and systems along with open vendor-independent architecture [22]. As a result, communication takes places at every layer of the automation pyramid. It can be expected that the Internet of Things (IoT), Cyper-Physical System (CPS), Time Sensitive Network (TSN), etc., together with ICT technologies will create new opportunities for making information exchanges more efficient and comprehensive [23].

There are various industrial systems (e.g., ERP, MES, Supervisory Control And Data Acquisition [SCADA], Distributed Control System, PLCs, etc., as seen in Figure 2) that exist in industrial automation; the communication complexity among them is explicit [24]. The research in [25] presents the requirements of the Industrie 4.0 vertical and horizontal communication aspects and the author indicates communications from factory level to field level could be categorized in the following way:

- *Enterprise level and Control level.* Between the enterprise level and control level, cyclic communication with various latencies would be employed to meet the requirements of enterprise applications. The enterprise applications (e.g. the software used for tracking from materials to the final products) are usually running on PCs and providing the best-effort traffic with reliable transmission.
- *Human Machine Interface (HMI) and Control level.* HMI applications running on a PC or mobile device communicate with a control level device within latency 100ms, and provide the best effort traffic with a reliable transmission.
- *Control-to-Control (C2C).* C2C communication between high level embedded devices provides latency less than 1ms and prioritized traffic with an unreliable transmission.
- *Control and Field level.* The latency of communication between control level and field level devices is smaller than 1μs. The communication provides scheduled traffic with unreliable transmission.

According to different requirements and resources, industrial solution providers choose the Client/Server mode or the PubSub mode to implement communication between industrial devices or systems.

1) Client/Server mode
Physical industrial devices could be an OPC UA Client or an OPC UA Server or both, depending on the requirements. For example, if a field level device is used as an OPC UA Client, timely updates could be "pushed" to the OPC UA server. If a sensor is used as an OPC UA Server, physical world values can be accessed by the OPC UA Client through the server's address space. If the sensor is used as both client and server, both mechanisms mentioned above are available. However, with the connection-oriented communication, the Client/Server mode requires a great deal of resource allocation when devices are used as an OPC UA Server. This could potentially cause problems, especially for embedded devices.
2) PubSub mode
Different from the Client/Server modes connection-oriented communication and a one-to-many scenario, PubSub enables a many-to-many communication paradigm to address new, flexible, and scalable industrial application scenarios, especially for resource-constrained embedded devices.
The PubSub specification describes broker-based and brokerless-based communication between the sender (Publisher) and the receiver (Subscriber).

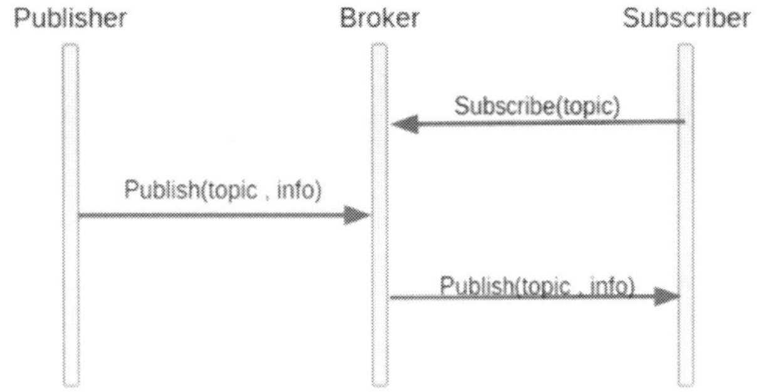

Figure 4. MQTT Publish/subscribe process

In broker-based mode, the Publisher sends a NetworkMessage to the broker. Then, the broker dispatches a NetworkMessage to subscribers according to the topic subscribed. NetworkMessages are created by using a PublishedDataSet defined DataSetMessages and topics. The broker-based mode decouples the communication between the entities in space, time, and synchronization.

In brokerless mode, the Publisher and Subscriber communication depends on the infrastructure provided by the network with less latency. Transport protocols, such as Advanced Message Queuing Protocol (AMQP), Message Queue Telemetry Transport (MQTT), OPC UA UDP, and OPC UA Ethernet can be used for message transmission.

B. *MQTT (Message Queue Telemetry Transport)*

MQTT is a topic-based Publish/Subscribe protocol. It is characterized as a simple, lightweight messaging protocol and aims at connecting resource constrained devices and low-bandwidth, high-latency or unreliable networks by using Message Oriented Middleware [26]. In Figure 4, the MQTT Subscriber sends a subscribe(topic) to inform the broker (Message Oriented Middleware) the topic which interests it, the MQTT Publisher sends a Pub(topic,data) message to the broker, if there is a match between the MQTT Publishers topic and the MQTT Subscribers topic, the broker then transfers the Pub(topic, data) message to the subscriber. The MQTT Subscriptions and publications can only be made on a specified set of topics. That means, the MQTT Publisher/Subscriber can only use the topics which are fixed during the design phase of an application.

III. OPC UA PubSub MQTT Configuration Tool

In order to facilitate the distribution of data and control commands among various industrial components, many OPC UA based projects have been taking place during recent years. The research presented in [27] uses OPC UA and MQTT for SCARA robot's control command transmissions and monitoring data collections. The control commands are sent by an OPC UA Server running on computer A to an OPC UA Client integrated gateway, then be relayed to a SCARA robot. The monitoring data collected from the SCARA robot will be sent by the gateway's MQTT Publisher to a broker running on computer B for further distribution. The MQTT messages' topic is fixed in the implementation. Another research [28] presents a solution for low-level integration of CPSs. The proposal is described as "a Plug&Play solution that allows plugging a self-describing device producing self-described data to a larger system". The solution utilizes OPC UA Server/Client mode and Semantic Web technologies to achieve integration at various levels. The devices described in the research are OPC UA Server based sensors, and the related configuration is fixed during the development phase. Though the sensor configuration is repeatable during the design and development phase, the introduction of our OPC UA PubSub and configuration tool would provide more flexibility to device manufacturers and users to set up the OPC UA PubSub enabled devices and systems according to the specific application scenario.

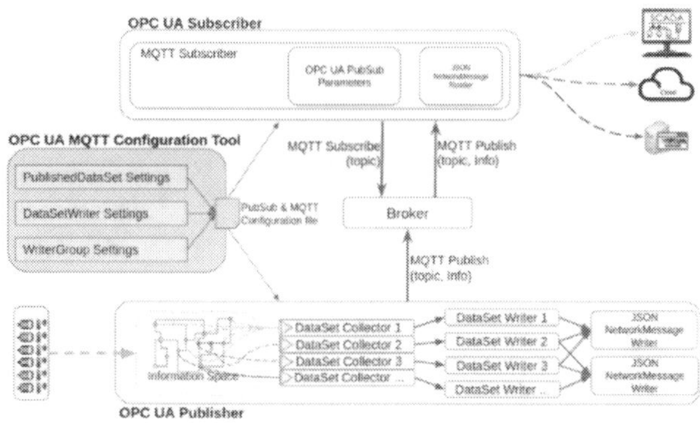

Figure 5. OPC UA Publisher&Subscriber and the configuration tool

A. *OPC UA PubSub Configuration Procedure*

In our implementation, the OPC UA Server is extended with PubSub related parameters and configuration procedures, thus the OPC UA Server is used as the Publisher. We use the subscriber of a MQTT implementation, Mosquitto [29], as our Subscriber. Correspondingly, the Subscriber is extended with PubSub related parameters and configuration procedures, too. The Publisher, the Subscriber, and the configuration tool are shown in Figure 5. The configuration tool is based on the OPC UA Client to which a pair of sockets is added for configuration transmission. Before the configuration tool launching, the OPC UA Publisher, the OPC UA Subscriber, and the Mosquitto broker are launched. After the connections between the configuration tool and OPC UA Publisher and Subscriber are successfully established, the connections between the Mosquitto broker and OPC UA Publisher and Subscriber would be established. Then, the operator launches the configuration tool, edits the configuration in the tool's GUI (see Figure 6) and sends it to the OPC UA Publisher and OPC UA Subscriber. The OPC UA Subscriber will subscribe with a specified topic and the OPC UA Publisher will start collecting data from the nodes, which are specified by the configuration, and creates DataSetMessages. DataSetMessages are packed into NetworkMessage for publishing.

After the security channel and session are established between the configuration tool and the OPC UA Publisher, the operator can browse nodes of a View by using a View service and Query Service provided by the OPC UA. The View is a subset of the AddressSpace, which includes the data source nodes. These data source nodes will be specified by the user in the configuration file for "pushing" data to other local or remote components of the industrial system. Available data

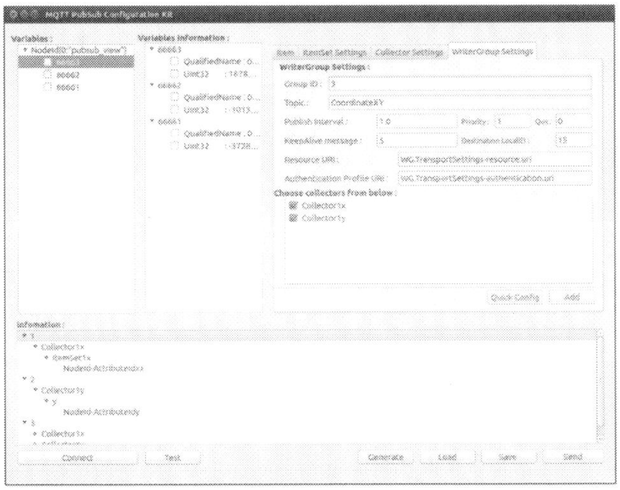

Figure 6. OPC UA PubSub MQTT Configuration Tool Graphic User Interface

sources (nodes listed in the View) are displayed in the widget "Variables" of the GUI. The configuration tool can retrieve related nodes information (e.g., NodeID, Attributes, etc.) and display them in the widget named "Variables Information" of the GUI. Configuration parameters configured by the user can be saved locally in prefixed text format, or previewed in the "Information" widget of the GUI before being sent to the Publisher and Subscriber.

The work thread pubsub_server_config of the OPC UA Publisher uses the acquired parameters to initiate and create entities of the OPC UA Publisher, such as DataSet Collectors, DataSet Writers, and WriterGroups. Another work thread pubsub_mosquitto_publisher of the OPC UA Publisher is responsible for the output collection of field devices, creation of DataSetMessages and NetworkMessages, and publishing of MQTT. Correspondingly, the Subscriber is able to subscribe topics configured by the tool, receiving a NetworkMessage and decoding a DataSet received for further usage.

B. OPC UA PubSub Components and Parameters

The OPC UA Server and Client can be extended either as an OPC UA Publisher or Subscriber depending on the scenario. Existing PubSub entities in our implementation that require configuration include: the DataSet Collector, the DataSet Writer and Writer Group at the Publisher's end, and message topic at the OPC UA Subscriber's end. Transport protocol mappings and message mappings are grouped into different data types and/or classes. Parameter values are serialized and sent in prefixed text format to the Publisher and the Subscriber. Configuration parameter data types, such as DataSetMetaDataType, PublishedDataSetDataType are used for the OPC UA Publisher and the OPC UA Subscriber. DataSetWriterDataType and WriterGroupDataType are used in the OPC UA Publisher side. DataSetReaderDataType and ReaderGroupDataType are used in the OPC UA Subscriber. The descriptions of the functionalities of each parameter are given below:

- *DataSetMetaDataType.* It describes the content and semantics of a DataSet. The data structure DataSetMetaDataType defines the field data type and data structure of a DataSet (e.g., field name, data type, unit, etc.). The parameter is edited in the widget "Item" tab of the configuration tool's GUI. The parameter is received by both the Publisher and the Subscriber who are interested in a certain DataSet. The Publisher uses it to orderly fill collected filed values in the DataSetMessage. The Subscriber uses DataSet field types and data structure descriptions for decoding the received DataSet.
- *PublishedDataSetDataType.* It is used to configure a DataSet collector and filter of the Publisher. The parameter is configured in widget "Collector Settings" tab of the configuration tool GUI. The DataSet collection uses NodeId and AttributeId of a Node in AddressSpace to continually collect values produced by the Node, and fills the individual field of the DataSet.
- *DataSetWriterDataType.* It provides necessary information to DataSetWriter of the Publisher for the creation of the DataSetMessage from the DataSet. The parameter is configured in widget "Collector Settings" tab of the configuration tool GUI. A specified number of DataSetWriters would be created by using this parameter. A DataSetMessage is created from the DataSet specified by the PublishedDataSet. The DataSet field of a DataSetMessage may exist in different forms (Variant, DataValue, or RawData) according to the DataSetMessageContentMask of the DataSetWriter.
- *WriterGroupDataType.* This parameter configures the NetworkMessage creation process. The NetworkMessage is the container of DataSetMessages. It is configured in widget "WriterGroup Settings" tab of the configuration tool GUI. A specified number of WriterGroups would be created by using this parameter. The parameter indicates also the MQTT related parameters, such as the NetworkMessage topic of a certain WriterGroup and the Quality of Service (QoS) of the connected broker.

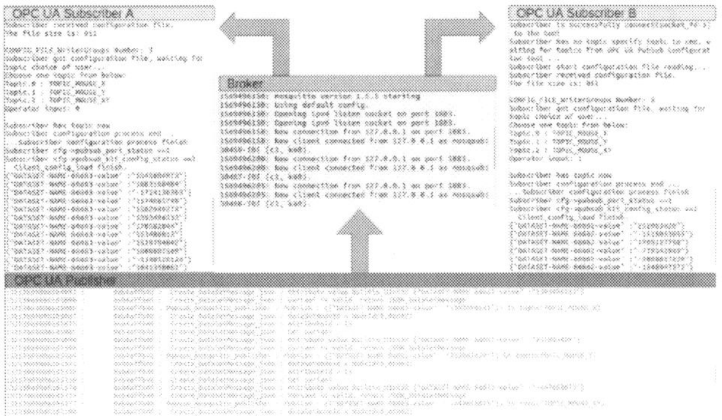

Figure 7. Configured OPC UA Publisher and OPC UA Subscriber

IV. OPC UA PUBSUB COMMUNICATION EXPERIMENT

Figure 7 shows a validation experiment of data distribution between our configured OPC UA Publisher and OPC UA Subscribers. The OPC UA Publisher is configured by the configuration tool for publishing real-time mouse coordinates. The coordinates data are produced by dynamic libraries loaded after the OPC UA Publisher is launched. Coordinates x and y are described in an XML file and mapped into the address space as Variables. Their NodeIds are 66663 and 66662, respectively. The coordinates are published in three topics: "Topic MOUSE X, "Topic MOUSE Y, and "Topic MOUSE XY. The OPC UA Subscribers A and B show that they received topics from the configuration tool and are waiting for the operators topic choice for each OPC UA Subscriber. In our experiment, we let the OPC UA Subscriber A subscribe with topic MOUSE X and OPC UA Subscriber B subscribe with Topic MOUSE Y. Then, the OPC UA Subscribers send topic-subscriptions to the broker and start receiving MQTT messages that interest them.

V. Conclusion and Future Work

Firstly, this paper provided a brief history of ICT applied in the manufacturing field, from CIM to present-day Industrie 4.0. It also introduced OPC UA and related application scenarios. Then, we introduced its new specifications, the OPC UA Part 14 PubSub, and highlighted two OPC UA's specific features, namely, the interoperability and communication capabilities. This was followed by a description of a configuration tool that we propose and its implementation is undergoing. The configuration tool can be easily added to any C/C++ OPC UA implementation. We tested it with our own implementation of an OPC UA Publisher and Subscriber. But our work is not integrated into other OPC UA implementations due to access limit to their nodes and attributes. We presented some necessary configuration parameters for applying OPC UA PubSub communication following Part 14 of the specifications. Future research and implementation are planned on the performance test of OPC UA PubSub, supporting of asynchronous message queues, and cybersecurity through Network Message encryption and decryption. When compared with manually editing the configuration for each OPC UA Server/Client and loading it locally, the configuration tool can provide flexible and modifiable configurations to an OPC UA Publisher/Subscriber.

Acknowledgment

This work is part of the project WIZARD, a FEDER-FSE, Operational Program of CORSE project.

References

[1] J.-Q. Li et al., "Industrial internet: A survey on the enabling technologies, applications, and challenges," IEEE Communications Surveys & Tutorials, vol. 19, no. 3, 2017, pp. 1504–1526.

[2] S. Terzi et al., "Product lifecycle management-from its history to its new role," International Journal of Product Lifecycle Management, vol. 4, no. 4, 2010, pp. 360–389.

[3] T. Sauter, S. Soucek, W. Kastner, and D. Dietrich, "The evolution of factory and building automation," IEEE Industrial Electronics Magazine, vol. 5, no. 3, 2011, pp. 35–48.

[4] S. Jeschke, C. Brecher, T. Meisen, D. Özdemir, and T. Eschert, "Industrial internet of things and cyber manufacturing systems," in Industrial Internet of Things. Springer, 2017, pp. 3–19.

[5] H. Xu, W. Yu, D. Griffith, and N. Golmie, "A survey on industrial internet of things: A cyber-physical systems perspective," IEEE Access, vol. 6, 2018, pp. 78 238–78 259.

[6] "Industrie 4.0," 2019, URL: https://www.plattform-i40.de/PI40/Navigation/EN/Industrie40/WhatIsIndustrie40/what-is-industrie40.html [retrieved: Sep. 2019].

[7] "Opc 10000-14 - part 14: Pubsub," 2018, URL: https://opcfoundation.org/developer-tools/specifications-unified-architecture/part-14-pubsub/ [retrieved: Sep. 2019].

[8] "Opc ua technology," 2019, URL: https://opcfoundation.org/about/opc-technologies/opc-ua/ [retrieved: Sep. 2019].

[9] F. Jammes and H. Smit, "Service-oriented paradigms in industrial automation," IEEE Transactions on industrial informatics, vol. 1, no. 1, 2005, pp. 62–70.

[10] H. Bohn, A. Bobek, and F. Golatowski, "Sirena-service infrastructure for real-time embedded networked devices: A service oriented framework for different domains," in ICN/ICONS/MCL, 2006, p. 43.

[11] D. S. et al., "Socrades: A web service based shop floor integration infrastructure," in The internet of things. Springer, 2008, pp. 50–67.

[12] "Reference architectural model industrie 4.0 (rami4.0)," 2019, URL: https://www.plattform-i40.de/PI40/Redaktion/EN/Downloads/Publikation/rami40-an-introduction.html [retrieved: Sep. 2019].

[13] "Beck-hoff twincat," 2019, URL: https://www.beckhoff.com/twincat/ [retrieved: Sep. 2019].

[14] "Siemens simatic," 2019, URL: https://w3.siemens.com/mcms/topics/en/simatic/pages/default.aspx [retrieved: Sep. 2019].

[15] "Br automation," 2019, URL: https://www.br-automation.com/en/technologies/opc-ua/opc-ua-br/ [retrieved: Sep. 2019].

[16] M. Müller, E. Wings, and L. Bergmann, "Developing open source cyber-physical systems for service-oriented architectures using opc ua," in 2017 IEEE 15th International Conference on Industrial Informatics (INDIN). IEEE, 2017, pp. 83–88.

[17] M. Melik-Merkumians et al., "Towards opc ua as portable soa middleware between control software and external added value applications," in Proceedings of 2012 IEEE 17th International Conference on Emerging Technologies & Factory Automation (ETFA 2012). IEEE, 2012, pp. 1–8.

[18] "Opc 10000-5 - part 5: Information model," 2019, URL: https://opcfoundation.org/developer-tools/specifications-unified-architecture/part-5-information-model/ [retrieved: Sep. 2019].

[19] "Opc 10000-3 - part 3: Address space model," 2019, URL: https://opcfoundation.org/developer-tools/specifications-unified-architecture/part-3-address-space-model/ [retrieved: Sep. 2019].

[20] "Upgrade your legacy opc systems to opc ua," 2019, URL: https://opcconnect.opcfoundation.org/2017/12/upgrade-your-legacy-opc-systems-to-opc-ua/ [retrieved: Sep. 2019].

[21] J.-D. Decotignie, "Ethernet-based real-time and industrial communications," Proceedings of the IEEE, vol. 93, no. 6, 2005, pp. 1102–1117.

[22] O. Givehchi, K. Landsdorf, P. Simoens, and A. W. Colombo, "Interoperability for industrial cyber-physical systems: An approach for legacy systems," IEEE Transactions on Industrial Informatics, vol. 13, no. 6, 2017, pp. 3370–3378.

[23] M. Wollschlaeger, T. Sauter, and J. Jasperneite, "The future of industrial communication: Automation networks in the era of the internet of things and industry 4.0," IEEE Industrial Electronics Magazine, vol. 11, no. 1, 2017, pp. 17–27.

[24] A. Balador, N. Ericsson, and Z. Bakhshi, "Communication middleware technologies for industrial distributed control systems: A literature review," in 2017 22nd IEEE International Conference on Emerging Technologies and Factory Automation (ETFA). IEEE, 2017, pp. 1–6.

[25] A. Eckhardt, S. Müller, and L. Leurs, "An evaluation of the applicability of opc ua publish subscribe on factory automation use cases," in 2018 IEEE 23rd International Conference on Emerging Technologies and Factory Automation (ETFA), vol. 1. IEEE, 2018, pp. 1071–1074.

[26] "Mqtt," 2019, URL: http://mqtt.org/faq [retrieved: Sep. 2019].

[27] T. Mizuya, M. Okuda, and T. Nagao, "A case study of data acquisition from field devices using opc ua and mqtt," in 2017 56th Annual Conference of the Society of Instrument and Control Engineers of Japan (SICE). IEEE, 2017, pp. 611–614.

[28] V. Jirkovský, M. Obitko, P. Kadera, and V. Mařík, "Toward plug&play cyber-physical system components," IEEE Transactions on Industrial Informatics, vol. 14, no. 6, 2018, pp. 2803–2811.

[29] "Mosquitto," 2019, URL: https://mosquitto.org/ [retrieved: Sep. 2019].